Shifting Ground

SHIFTING GROUND

Reinventing Landscape in Modern American Poetry

BONNIE COSTELLO

HARVARD UNIVERSITY PRESS

Cambridge, Massachusetts, and London, England 2003

Page 217 constitutes a continuation of the copyright page.

Library of Congress Cataloging-in-Publication Data

Costello, Bonnie.
Shifting ground : reinventing landscape in modern American poetry /
   Bonnie Costello.
      p. cm.
   Includes bibliographical references and index.
   ISBN 0-674-00894-4 (alk. paper)
   1. American poetry—20th century—History and criticism.
   2. Landscape in literature. I. Title.
PS310.L3 C67 2003
811'.50932—dc21   2002032892

Designed by Gwen Nefsky Frankfeldt

In memory of Richard Tristman, mentor and friend

Contents

Abbreviations

Poets' works are referred to in the text by the following abbreviations (for full bibliographical information, see Works Cited).

AMMONS
BR	Brink Road
CP	Collected Poems, 1951–1971
CT	A Coast of Trees
GL	Glare
SM	Set in Motion: Essays, Interviews, and Dialogues
SP	The Selected Poems: Expanded Edition
SV	Sumerian Vistas: Poems
TTOY	Tape for the Turn of the Year

ASHBERY
AG	April Galleons
AWK	As We Know
DDS	The Double Dream of Spring
FC	Flow Chart
HD	Houseboat Days
HL	Hotel Lautréamont
RM	Rivers and Mountains
RS	Reported Sightings: Art Chronicles, 1957–1987
W	A Wave

CLAMPITT
CP	The Collected Poems of Amy Clampitt

FROST

C P, P, & P   *Robert Frost: Collected Poems, Prose, & Plays*

MOORE

CP   *The Complete Poems of Marianne Moore*

STEVENS

CPP   *Collected Poetry & Prose*

WRIGHT

TWTTT   *The World of the Ten Thousand Things: Poems 1980–1990*

Shifting Ground

1

Introduction: Frame and Flux

This book is a tribute to the vitality of landscape as a figurative and representational focus in twentieth-century American poetry. I read the work of six poets who have renovated landscape by drawing new tropes from the natural world and creating new forms for imagining the earth and our relation to it. Their landscapes respond to the sense of constant change, and the disruption and acceleration of life, characteristic of modern experience. They disassemble traditional images of nature as a place of permanence and unlimited freedom. But theirs is not the rhetoric of grief or rage over a damaged ideal. Their nature is itself quick, quicker than our images, and spurs our creative ongoing. These poets respond to the conditions in which we live, to new models of perception, and to the challenge of a dynamic nature with a nomadic rather than an expansionist impulse. Imagining and moving through various landscapes, they configure spaces that feature the sense of flux. Their poetics of adjustment teaches us to dwell on shifting ground.

Recent studies of the environment—historical, ecological, and aesthetic—find us embedded in a paradox: that we are part of nature, and that nature is our construction.[1] Gertrude Stein captured this chiasm in typically gnomic terms:

> What is nature.
> Nature is what is.
> But is nature natural.
> No not as natural as that.
> (*The Geographical History of America*, 200)

She anticipates the insights of environmental historians such as Simon Schama, who, in *Landscape and Memory* (1995), recognized how deeply the nature we evoke is formed in the crucible of culture. Our occupation of the space we call "nature" is inevitable (9). The facts of our material and imaginative entanglement with the earth, and our conflicting and evolving ideas of nature, belie efforts to fix priority in our relation to nature, as demonstrated by the symposium of historians, scientists, literary critics, and ecologists in William Cronon's anthology, *Uncommon Ground* (1995).

Not only the scene, then, but also the structure of landscape has altered, as any comparison of nineteenth- and twentieth-century landscape poems reveals. For William Cullen Bryant, writing in the first third of the nineteenth century, the American landscape provided a common ground of value; here was the garden of the world, the original condition of the earth, origin itself. What is landscape for Bryant as he writes to the painter Thomas Cole upon his departure for Europe? An unoccupied wilderness,

> A living image of our own bright land,
> Such as upon thy glorious canvas lies;
> Lone lakes—savannas where the bison roves—
> Rocks rich with summer garlands—solemn streams—
> Skies, where the desert eagle wheels and screams—
> Spring bloom and autumn blaze of boundless groves.
> (*Poetical Works*, 219)

Bryant may be aware of certain subtleties of priority in applying the term "earlier" to the American landscape when he implores the British-born Cole to "keep that earlier, wilder image bright" as he departs again for the "fair scenes" of Europe, with "everywhere the trace of men." But for Bryant and Cole, nature, the great authority and source of inspiration, recorded its teachings in "the mind's eye." Yet as Barbara Novak has pointed out, the great teacher may be Claude Lorrain or Salvador Rosa rather than creation (228). The "trace of men" is everywhere in Cole's paintings. The bison and eagle of Bryant's poem give American markings to an idea of landscape embedded in the European pictorial tradition, making the poet's "bright land" a tertiary effect. Bryant's imagery does not record the seen world or the particulars of place, but presents generic, patterned elements, ringed with garlands, open to the horizon, enhanced by wheeling birds and cycling seasons. The geography of the New World, given the reach of the undeveloped continent of Bryant's day, may have deepened the features of the ideal landscape's expanse. But the temporal and historical realities of dwelling in this geography are suspended in this image of nature's "solemn streams" and "boundless groves" where the spectator seems the solitary master of all he surveys. As Stein pointed out in *The Geographical History of America,* "there being so much space in America where nobody is has nothing to do with this that if nobody had ever died that is if everybody had not died there would not be room here for anybody who is alive now" (54). In the shadow of such historicity Bryant's wilderness has come to seem a lost Eden to some; to others it is an instance of America's discredited imperial romance.

Those "alive now," in Stein's day and more recently, have been creating new modes of landscape, more fitted to the textures of their experience and to modern ideas about perception, knowledge, and the sources of art. The contemporary poet Charles Wright, as I have written elsewhere, has made landscapes the focus of his visionary project. But his insistence on the distinction between nature and landscape reveals the active, intervening quality of his vision, in contrast to Bryant's faith in nature's authority. Nature is a stimulus and force, but not the authority, behind Wright's images. "Landscape is something you determine and dominate. Nature is something that determines and dominates you." A modernist rather than a romantic, Wright insists that landscape is "design," while nature is "dis-ease" and "quicksand," the recalcitrant material of his vision. Like Bryant, Wright often associates his art with painting, but he replaces the pictorial illusions of deep space with Cézanne's built-up surface and the dynamic tension between framed design and fluent subject.

> —Mist in the trees, and soiled water and grass cuttings splotch
> The driveway,
> > afternoon starting to bulk up in the west
> A couple of hours down the road:
> Strange how the light hubs out and wheels
> > concentrically back and forth
> After a rain, as though the seen world
> Quavered inside a water bead
> > swung from a blade of grass.
>
> (TWTTT, 121)

The scene itself is a constructed world, a second nature: the poet's own back yard. Bryant's wilderness savannas have been subdivided. Wright's landscape is no less capable of producing a visionary effect, but it has more the tenor of absence than presence, of transience than stability. Whereas Bryant imagines beholding a "bright," transparent order given by nature and eternally awaiting man's return, Wright presents an image somewhat blurred, an effect of light and water on the eye, seen through the splotch and grid of human presence. Like Cézanne, Wright tries to capture a fugitive moment of perception, when the shapes of consciousness have not solidified, when the flux of the world is coming into form. Bryant's "earlier image," Cole's indelible origin, presents a unified image of enduring nature; Wright's belated "water bead," like Marvell's metaphysical drop of dew, is on the verge of evaporating.

Wright owes no apparent debt to Bryant, but he did often acknowledge Whitman's influence. The grass clippings strewn in Wright's driveway scene certainly suggest the image of a shorn American transcendentalism. "All goes onward and outward, nothing collapses," sang *Leaves of Grass* (33–34). The "hubs and wheels" of light suggest Whitman's sun in the float, and similar American negotiations of mobility and permanence. But Wright's road, his metaphoric car, the hours piling up and stretching out, remind us that while landscape involves the arrangement of space, its real theme is time. Bryant's "earlier" scene is a donor of presence because it opens onto an untrammeled, limitless wilderness, something prior to culture, a place where change has not yet happened. Whitman's "beautiful uncut hair of graves" promises an organic immortality. But Wright's landscape is drenched in unredeemed temporality and human mediation. The rhythms and forms of American landscape have obviously changed materially—cars speed where bison roamed—but more important, the structure of beholding, as captured in landscape art and poetry, has changed as well.

> —Blue jay's bound like a kangaroo's in the lawn's high grass,
> Then up in a brushstroke
>   and over the hedge in one arc.
> . . .
> Yesterday's cloud banks enfrescoed still
>   just under the sky's cornice . . .
>   (TWTTT, 122)

Bryant's semi-ecphrastic sonnet evokes a permanent, timeless design to which both poem and painting pay tribute. Wright's world is coming into being artistically, nature and art converging in the phenomenon of landscape. "I am nature," Jackson Pollock famously declared; Wright might add, completing the chiasm he inherits from Cézanne, that nature itself appears as an action painter, more involved in dynamic gestures of color and shape than in stable patterns and infinite prospects.

The visionary impulse is not the only one expressed in landscape poetry, of course. I will explore a variety of motives for landscape in the chapters that follow. But landscape continues as a vital source of spiritual and metaphysical reflection in modern poetry, developing generically to reflect changing ideas of the invisible. Wright's still-wet landscape registers a sliding, ephemeral world, not Bryant's boundless, abiding savannas but a scene where "trees dissolving against the night's job / houses melting in air" bespeak an absolute not of them, a negative metaphysics. Wright's visionary equation involves nature's and his own subtractions, a calculus of being and nothingness which art and memory record. The early nineteenth century held to a different arithmetic, one that tended to cancel the influence of time. The poem's function was to find sums greater than the parts. Emerson formed this landscape aesthetic into a philosophy in "Each and All." The poet is both part of the totality and its beholder. "The health of the eye seems to demand a horizon," he wrote (*Nature*, 16), and he invented landscapes to meet that demand. A centered, hierarchical order determines Emerson's sight lines. Because our paradigms have shifted, Emerson's transcendental identity can seem pallid and impersonal beside the dynamic subjectivity of Wright's unfinished designs.

"Each and All" addresses the reader as a Napoleonic type, "thee from the hill-top looking down," at a great distance from the "red-cloaked clown" who labors, unconscious, in the field below. The aim of the poem is to overcome that distance without relinquishing the power the viewer's perspective implies. As he shifts to first person, Emerson orders the features of nature in relation to himself, then "yields" himself to the very order his subjectivity has created, as if that order were divinely given. When landscape is accomplished, the artist-observer, the controlling presence surveying the terrain, becomes invisible. The otherness of "each" diminishes beneath the inhaling and encompassing "all"—its wreath, its unchanging repetitions and returns, its eternal sky, regulate the flux:

> The ground-pine curled its pretty wreath,
> Running over the club-moss burrs;
> I inhaled the violet's breath;
> Around me stood the oaks and firs;

Pine-cones and acorns lay on the ground;
Over me soared the eternal sky,
Full of light and deity;
Again I saw, again I heard,
The rolling river, the morning bird;—
Beauty through my senses stole;
I yielded myself to the perfect whole.
                              (*Collected Poems*, 9)

In "yielding" himself to the whole which he has earlier failed to possess piece by piece, the poet has made himself at once the center of it (the "I" and the "me" structuring object relations), and coextensive with it. Thus while the poem operates in an apparent reversal of priority, it sustains the beholder's authority. His lofty stance is reified rather than subverted, despite his gestures of relinquishment. Wallace Stevens, a century later, would reverse Emerson's visionary logic, making his artistic intervention visible by placing a jar in his poem "Anecdote of the Jar" and finally yielding the "all" to the "each" in Tennessee. A. R. Ammons would find, in "Gravelly Run," that natural entities are indifferent to the poet's desire for unity: "the sunlight has never heard of trees." The "surrendered self" is "among / unwelcoming forms." The imperial self has become something of a hobo in the landscape: "stranger, / hoist your burdens, get on down the road" (CP, 55).

But modern poets do more than negate old coherences of landscape. Jorie Graham's "The Visible World" presents a particularly striking contrast to Emerson's unifying, framing, and abstracting process, his mosaic arrangement of parts into a whole. Graham's sense of the relation of "each and all" comes from phenomenology rather than transcendentalism, from film ("frames of reference moving") rather than painting, and from Heisenberg and Einstein rather than Bacon. Instead of landscape we are given an image of vision as landscaping. The referential "plot" of ground and the "plot" of the imagination coincide on the page, and the poet, shoveling in, breaks them open:

I dig my hands into the absolute. The surface
                              breaks
into shingled, grassed clusters; lifts.
If I press, pick-in with fingers, pluck,
I can unfold the loam. It is tender. It is a tender
maneuver, hands making and unmaking promises,
Diggers, forgetters . . . A series of successive single instances . . .
Frames of reference moving . . .

The speed of light, down here, upthrown, in my hands:
bacteria, milky roots, pilgrimages of spores, deranged
                                        and rippling
mosses . . .
. . .
                Upthrown like this, I think you can
                        eventually
abstract it. Do you wish to?
Disentangled, it grows very very clear.
Even the mud, the sticky lemon-colored clay
hardens and then yields, crumbs.
I can't say what it is then, but the golden-headed
                        hallucination,
mating, forgetting, speckling, inter-
                        locking,
will begin to be gone from it and then its glamorous
                        veil of
echoes and muddy nostalgias will
be gone.
                (*The Dream of the Unified Field*, 194–195)

Graham has come down from Emerson's "hill-top"; she presents a figure
kneeling in a "black green glade" penetrated by light. Her looking is not
the lofty, bodiless activity we associate with landscapes of the nineteenth
century, but the work of hands, a manipulation of fecund reality, that
phenomenon of spores, roots, and bacteria as well as sky. At the same
time, she subjects her local perspective to the pressure of others that
might change the look of things. We separate things out as objects from
the mud, the each from the all, and desire to hold the visible world, to see
it clearly with the mind. Matter brought to light has a numinous glow,
but crumbles. Through a chiasm typical of modern landscape poetry,
Graham begins to compare her own acts of composition and erasure
with organic revolutions of generation and decay: "make your revolu-
tion in the invisible temple," she tells her digging hands as they probe the
absolute, but the temple itself is a human construct: "make your temple
in the invisible revolution." This is not Emerson's sleight-of-hand rever-
sal in which the poet "yields" to the "all" he has himself determined.
Rather, it recognizes the poet's orders as a "muddy cartoon of the pres-
ent," a tentative sketch of being. This is a verb-centered, not a noun-
centered art—not an art of landscape but one of landscaping. The poet
works to plant a seed in this temple, the seed of insight, of knowledge
perhaps, a star-seed or fixed point of vision that might be converted to
abstraction and language. The heat of poetic composting would "thaw

time" in the pursuit of presence, but the speed of light is faster than vision or representation. "I put the seed in." But "the beam moves on," stimulating the imagination to new pursuit. So the poem is a making and unmaking, frame upon frame, which attempts to keep up with (not fix) the visible world.

Can the visible world that includes the speed of light and moving frames of reference be a landscape? Or does landscape always necessarily memorialize the experience of the visible world? A frequent criticism of Graham's work is that it does not sufficiently tie thought to experience, at least for the reader. In the pursuit of presence, she forfeits the pleasures of vision in the retarded frame. But the poem may serve nevertheless as an allegory for the work of other modern poets engaged more directly in making and unmaking landscapes, in creating "frames of reference moving."

II

For the poets in this study, all we know is landscape, that second nature of human collaboration and intervention. Nature as a place of origin and authenticity, or as an essence we can comprehend, dissolves in this entanglement. The structure of landscape retains an opposition between mastering spectator and expansive scene that masks our involvement in what we view, that makes parts seem to be wholes. But modern poets have exposed this structure in order to reconfigure it. The poems I will discuss here foreground their acts of shaping and encoding nature. They heighten our sense of the frame and the boundaries and conditions of beholding. Vision remains eccentricity. While language, human anatomy, cognition, the rapacious will, and all the mediations of beholding, bring nature toward us, they also miss it. "In a field / I am the absence of field . . . Wherever I am, / I am what is missing," writes Mark Strand, as if resisting Emerson's summons to the encompassing All. Yet in missing nature as unmediated spectacle, these poets show us, we may encounter it as process. For all landscapes, like all metaphors, are superfluous, formed in a condition of fecundity and waste. Our activity in giving shape and meaning to nature puts us in touch with the fluency of the universe even as one invention becomes the casualty of another. This rhythm of our interacting, sometimes contending metaphors, which come to life, die, and are replaced by new ones, is often represented as part of the broader evolutionary course of nature. "I move," Strand concludes, "to keep things whole." Yet the imagination is not altogether comfortable in this sense of superfluity and mobility; it contends with loss and with backup, and longs for what Stevens called "the outlook that would be right / . . . the view toward which they had edged" (CPP, 435).

Recently environmental critics such as Donald Scheese, Cheryll Glotfelty, Patrick D. Murphy, Jonathan Bate, Leonard M. Scigaj, and Lawrence Buell have begun a taxonomy of nature writing, delineating a distinctly "nature-oriented" literature, an "environmental imagination" distinguishable from work that employs nature as trope or aesthetic object. William Wordsworth and other nineteenth-century poets have been reclaimed as ecologically-minded naturalists rather than transcendentalists (Kroeber, Bate). The writings of Robinson Jeffers, Wendell Berry, Gary Snyder, and W. S. Merwin have been celebrated for their "referentiality" (Scigaj) and for their practical and ethical import in the depiction of nature (Murphy). This new emphasis on literature's role in environmental advocacy has refreshed the connection of art to real-world concerns. With the exception of Ammons, however (who in *Glare* distances himself from the labels "nature poet" and "environmentalist" so often attached to him), the poets in this book are rarely considered in ecocritical studies. Yet their work can enrich and complicate our reflection on environmental themes. In calling the group I study here "landscape poets," I wish to add to the discussion of the environmental imagination a consideration of work that foregrounds our transitory manipulations and abstractions of the physical world as it is lived in and imagined. How do we know when we are really referring to nature, as opposed to plundering nature for metaphor, especially when the definition of nature is so contested? In bringing together representational and descriptive with more abstract and metaphoric work, traditional formalism with more experimental styles, I want to highlight the continuum in which landscape operates as an artistic focus, and to override the distinction between nature as reference and as trope. "Landscape" implies both. For these poets landscape is always metaphor, a conceptual more than a descriptive phenomenon, but it is not merely metaphor. The physical environment is a profound resource for the imagination as it seeks to describe and satisfy the inner life, and as it seeks to describe and order social existence. But the physical environment is also both a given and a referent, a condition of human experience and thought, and a reality we seek to structure and understand. These poems express such reciprocities without fixing priority. The given world and the built world collide, converge, coexist, and cooperate. Nature, for these poets, is not so much a state as a process, one that inevitably involves us, even as we try to imagine it as other. They may describe nature as something at the margins of cultural forms, or between the seams of civilization, or even as a force within our constructed world. But landscape is the relationship we build with nature, and it is that coevolutionary, phenomenal space that poetry occupies. These poets' landscapes are never still within the frame. The world is a moving target and the perceiver himself a part of the flux, shifting his perspective, casting all forms as provisional and partial.

What, then, is landscape? Whether the referent is art or environment, some ambiguity lingers in the term and, I want to suggest, in the figure itself. The "shaping" of the land is an indeterminate process, for while the artist shapes the scene to his composition, he is also responding to a space already composed, not only by his angle of vision, but also by the society which has preceded him, and which has divided and rationalized natural space. To "notice" wilderness, Gertrude Stein observed, is already to add the "as if it were wild" (84) which makes nature into landscape. Indeed, the word "land," unlike the word "earth," may evoke the physical world in its potential for human framing, even for real estate. The poets in my study highlight this shaping of landscape, both as meaning and as structure. On the other hand, land has its own shapes, which have variously stimulated the human imagination. Landscape even at its most abstract suggests an engagement with the material world. The effects of landscape may derive from compositional relations within the image, or may allude to experiential effects, the effects of the shaped land itself.[2] Landscape is subject, as well, to constant revision in response to the changing environment and developments in the history of perception. Thus landscape may be a potentially broader concept than any single scene or historical schema. Landscape is the world under the gaze of man. It is a mirror reflecting our fears and fantasies, but also our evolving determination and understanding of man's place in the world. I will use the term "landscape" here in reference to the shifting concept of constantly changing human arrangements of the visible environment. "Landscape," then, is a figure for our real and symbolic entanglement with the earth as we take the view of it. Landscape is something we build as well as see, inhabit as well as escape to, put meaning into and take meaning from. Landscapes can be forms of dwelling, the houses we make out of nature, which is never in itself a home. But for the poets here, landscape is often a mutating image of our restlessness.

Landscape poetry involves a further remove from nature as a kind of stepchild to landscape painting and design. But in various ways at various times, nature has been for us a book, and the literal texts we make of landscape draw upon this prior habit of mind. If we no longer read in nature the Puritans' typology or Emerson's metaphors of the human spirit, we nevertheless respond to a set of signs and even a grammar. We encode natural form, and manipulate the physical world in language-like structures.[3] Even if we maintain our sense of the complexity and distinction of landscape and language as human arrangements of meaning and experience, we may see how their interplay and analogy stimulate the literary imagination. Both involve a lexicon and a grammar; both draw from a comprehensive system of differences to produce particular manifestations. The poets in my study have explored this relationship by thinking about the landscape not only as a resource for images and signs, but also as a structure to which they might adapt their forms. Landscape, like language, evolves, and their coevolution is apparent in these poems.

In claiming the vitality of landscape in modern poetry and art, I am challenging the dominant argument in the humanities over the past forty years that landscape is an exhausted, even an insidious genre. This is part of the larger denigration of vision in contemporary thought described by Martin Jay. It derives from a critique of the Enlightenment drive toward objectification and mastery, which took the visual as its instrumental faculty. In 1950 Henry Nash Smith's *Virgin Land* described the perilous tendency of America to think of the landscape as an inexhaustible garden of the world; Annette Kolodny and Richard Slotkin followed with revelations of the violence legitimated by such concepts of American space. These critiques locate landscape within an imperialist project that uses nature as its medium but has power as its end. Landscape, it is said, naturalizes ideology, and particularly hierarchical and expansionist purposes. We find versions of this argument in Raymond Williams' class critique of pastoral in *The Country and the City*; in John Barrell's exposure of the "dark side of the picturesque" in *The Idea of Landscape and the Sense of Place*; in Alan Liu's *Wordsworth, the Sense of History*, which argues that nature does not exist except as it is mediated by social constructs which Romantic landscape makes invisible; in Myra Jehlen's critique in *American Incarnation* of nature's nation as the premise of liberal individualism; in Angela Miller's analysis in *The Empire of the Eye* of the everywhere and nowhere of imperial nationalism of the Hudson River School; and, more recently, in W. J. T Mitchell's collection of essays, *Landscape and Power*. The notion of landscape as the erasure of historical process and the reification of transcendental individualism underlies Carolyn Porter's *Seeing and Being*, David Wyatt's *The Fall into Eden*, Chris Fitter's *Poetry, Space, Landcape*, and several essays in David Miller's *American Iconology*. The astonishing persistence of this argument, which subordinates all landscape to a single praxis and ignores other impulses in landscape (aesthetic, religious, biological, psychological), may be a necessary reaction to the idealizations of nature that obscured the real violence done to the environment, not to mention human subjugation and suffering. Elisa New, in *The Line's Eye: Poetic Experience, American Sight,* has offered rich evidence of an alternative American tradition, running from Puritanism to Pragmatism, which is not possessive but experiential in its motives, which cultivates open engagement with the virtual world over mastery of a rationalized one. My argument continues New's reassessment of American nature writing, with a particular emphasis on modern preoccupations with frame and flux, and with landscape as the medium of that reflection.

Recent social critiques of landscape representation focus on painting in the European tradition, which, as we have seen, was imported and adapted to the American continent. In *Visions of America,* Martin Friedman writes: "In [such] traditional Western paintings of landscape, whether Italianate prospects of Claude Lorrain, Corot's soft-edged pastorals, or Monet's chromatic dissolutions of nature's façade, the artist-observer who surveyed the terrain through the rectangular picture plane was the invisible, controlling, but distanced presence" (26). An imperialist program underwrites this aesthetic, it is argued, and pervades American landscape art of the nineteenth century, where it became the model for the culture's thinking about nature. The attack is not simply against the illusionist function of art, but against the mythologizing function of landscape per se. The result is description without place: the triumph of idealized space and the inattention to particular locale and irreversible time. In founding a national identity on landscape, perpetuating an audacious Adamic freedom of the individual removed from local actualities, Americans indulged in a precarious myth-making for which we must now do penance.

Landscape can certainly be a theater in which we enact concerns not only or primarily of nature, but also of society and of the psyche. But as Lawrence Buell has pointed out in his reappraisal of pastoral, that theater can serve a revisionary purpose. For the modern poets in my study, landscape is not a retreat or respite from the agitation of the social condition, a reification of power, a conceit to legitimate the status quo, or even a superseding context or origin that we nostalgically valorize. It may in fact be a stimulus and source of renewal as we work to inhabit the world, freeing us from the immobilities of retentive culture. Even if we accept the association of "landscape and power," we can object to restrictions of the term "landscape" and the narrow sense of how that "and" might operate. In his "Theses on Landscape" W. J. T. Mitchell states: "5. Landscape is a medium found in all cultures" and, narrowly, "6. Landscape is a particular historical formation associated with European imperialism." When he further states that "landscape is an exhausted medium, no longer viable as a mode of artist expression" (5), he restricts the claim ("9. The landscape referred to in Thesis 8 is the same as that of Thesis 6"). But within this restriction the force of the argument is lost. All "historical formations" are by definition exhausted as history changes, though admittedly the forms may outlast the cultures of their genesis. Mitchell ignores landscape's supple and renewable tradition, a genre addressed to an abiding human interest in the earth. Modern poets and painters have put new life into this "exhausted medium," revising rather than abandoning its conventions. Long before cultural critics discovered the dark side of landscape, the genre had been reinvented, showing itself to be ideologically and epistemologically flexible. The poets in this book find landscape's relationship to what Stevens called "doctrine" a restless, elusive one. As these poets highlight flux and frame, foregrounding our agency in the formation of landscape, they loosen ideology's hold on perception.

A similar attack on landscape as a genre has come, surprisingly, from ecocriticism. Landscape, several critics have protested, forgets the otherness of nature, or it sees nature only as object, displayed for human consumption and pleasure. Neil Evernden exemplifies the link between environmentalism and cultural criticism: "If the entity we consider nature is really false nature, then we are no longer dealing with what we think we are. Nature as physical reality does not enter into this usage at all, yet is seen to validate it" (89). But where Mitchell and others would focus on the social work being done in the name of that "false nature" and its naturalized conventions, ecocriticism evokes an ontologically prior "true nature" which environmental writing can help to recover. One finds versions of this argument in John Elder's idea of "nature's refrain," in Lawrence Buell's "aesthetics of relinquishment," in Donald Scheese's "pastoral ideology," and in numerous other contributions to the discussion of environmental literature. Patrick Murphy sums up the argument of a decade when he states that "the land is more than a scape" (12) and critiques the approach to nature as view, a picture to which we can escape, one that projects nature as something separate from ourselves.

But if nature is not a "scape," if we cannot escape into a "view," viewing remains one of the primary modes of our relation to the physical world, as much from the inherent structure of our awareness as from our will to power. The changing technologies of viewing have come to the foreground of poetic contemplation of nature. We always do want to hold it to the light, to see it framed and assembled in a pattern that discloses physical reality, not just ourselves. But landscape need not imply a static formula of seeing or shaping environment. As Daniel Botkin has written in *Our Natural History*, "The nature that is best is not a simple, idyllic scene from a Hudson River School of painting, but a moving picture show, mosaics on a video screen, many different conditions in complex patterns across the landscape" (quoted in Postrel, 154). The poets in this study create and respond to landscapes, to the places we live in, to changing social and environmental patterns, and even to the places we have blighted and which we try to ignore. Their landscapes are entangled with human presence and purpose, but they are also transformed by natural events.

It is that very foregrounding of its acts of mediation that makes poetry a particularly rich medium for considering how we construct our ideas of nature and our relation to it. And here the ecocritical preference for referentiality over textuality, for real world over rhetorical and aesthetic concerns, seems misguided. Whether they are interested in "subject matter" (as Stevens said of Frost) or "bric-a-brac" (as Frost said of Stevens), poets draw us into the drama of their configurations and make us aware of the workings and limits of metaphor and symbol. Poetry manifests the difference words and images can make in how we apprehend the world. Certainly a rhetorically oriented criticism is aware of the text (and indeed all mediating forms) less as a statement about reality than as a series of motivated strategies and structures, which communicates something to an audience or makes something happen imaginatively. But such a criticism can involve real-world concerns in that it reveals the entanglement of nature and culture, the interplay between our desires, our concepts, and our perceptions, and possibilities for renewal and vitality within that entanglement. Poetry, for these poets, is not designed to establish epistemological or ethical truths, but neither is it indifferent to epistemological inquiry or immune from ethical motivation or scrutiny. The vitality of poetry is of the imagination and necessarily abstract. But abstraction does not necessarily imply hostility, evasion, or alienation; more often, it involves an engagement with substance, both aesthetic and intellectual. Abstraction can be nourished and influenced, made flexible and dynamic, by that which it abstracts, and can draw us toward the natural world rather than away from it. Abstraction cannot renew itself; it needs a stimulus, a fluent resource. Here the role of poetry is not to forward an agenda but to encourage this love of abstraction for its source and object, a love which inevitably has some violence in it, but which may nevertheless, in other arenas of human purpose, lead to acts that materially support the wildness and abundance of what is loved. This kind of indirect ethics may sound like humanist evasion, and will certainly not displace the legitimate urgencies of the environmentalist, but it engages the distinct role of art in society without reducing art's role to aesthetics alone.

III

The modern era's preoccupation with time (existential flux, deep memory, evolutionary process) had a profound effect on its conception of space. Temporality intrudes itself into the descriptive, visionary, and emblematic landscapes of the early twentieth century, forcing imaginative adjustments. In representing these adjustments I have organized the next three chapters into two parts, shifting from an emphasis on the poets' scenic tropes and patterns, their frames, to their concern with entropy, flux, and historical change as these impact landscape. I begin with Robert Frost, a poet drawn to older, pastoral and Romantic, patterns of nature writing, but also engaged with evolutionary theory and physics, historical transformation of the rural landscape, and various pragmatist and skeptical philosophies of his day. As Frost constructs landscapes, he draws consistently on the trope of chiasmus, which allows for boundaries, but also reciprocity, between him and the world he beholds. Frost refused modernist displacement of nature with art, asserting, "Earth's the right place for love" (C P, P, & P, 118). Yet he recognized how greatly the "love" was involved in the selective construction of its object. Chiasmus also functions to negotiate Frost's sense of flux in the landscape, indicating his lyric desire for cyclical structures, for repetition and retention, while allowing for the metamorphoses of evolutionary time.

In Stevens' work, as in Frost's, the desire for the real, and for nature, must reckon always with the fact of the frame, with landscape. At the same time, even Stevens' most abstract images often derive from objects in the visible world. Frequently in his poems the transcendental reach of the Romantic landscape encounters the human and material sources of its illusions. This is particularly true in *Parts of a World*, which many critics read as transitional, but which I find central to Stevens' canon. While Stevens longs for a godlike view from the center, in which reality is revealed in its wholeness, he acknowledges man's "fated eccentricities," his landscapes. These eccentric landscapes are nevertheless enabling structures, making vision possible; and they become a part of the real. In "Auroras of Autumn" Stevens gathers up the fragments of his eccentric landscapes, not to produce the "amassing harmony" of earlier aspiration, but to address in spatial terms the radical temporality of vision. He submits the transcendental fictions sustained in "Notes" to a modern agony of spatial transformation through time.

For Marianne Moore the "trace of men" is everywhere, but nature is never fully seen through the succession of frames. Moore critiques the impulse to plunder the world for quick images and postcard landscapes, which obscure "the genuine" and obstruct access to experience. But her sense of the genuine is subtle, and distinct from the American obsession with the primitive and with originality, with Bryant's "earlier image" or what Stevens called "the first idea." The poet paradoxically makes a "place for the genuine" by getting us lost in our labyrinth of maps and simulations. Like Frost and Stevens, Moore examines the formation of American identity in relation to place. But Moore is far more engaged than either Frost or Stevens in specific cultural interventions and constructions of place. As she turns her attention from wilderness parks and pastoral resorts to historical places, Moore works to distinguish these sites from the touristic sights we make of them. In each case she sets facile heroic rhetoric against recalcitrant material and cultural realities. In doing so she reinstates a feeling for time and history as process, and discovers an evolving entanglement of man and the land, which belies the fictions of manifest destiny.

The modern generation, then, disassembled the expansive, unified natural scene with its invisible, controlling spectator, typified by Bryant and Emerson. The Moderns complicated the image of nature as a space of origin, an unveiled truth where man might ground and authenticate his ideas. Their landscapes are mediated and continually changing, spaces to act in or dream in, but never quite possess. A later generation, to which I turn in the second half of the book, fully embraces this dynamism as a source of poetic identity, a fluent subjectivity. If nature is flux rather than stability, shifting form rather than infinite expanse or ground of origin, the imagination must respond with ultimate mobility, resisting all that is stagnant in culture and in the psyche. These poets identify with the protean, adaptive, transgressive, and generative impulses in nature—its tendency to invent and dissolve forms, to relocate, move in, fill space, and adapt to or disrupt what has been erected. Amy Clampitt, for instance, transforms her alienation from the immobilities of prairie culture into an active nomadism. Clampitt's sense of the frame comes in literal window scenes (sometimes from buses and planes), as well as in inventive formalism and metaphoric flourish. But while she elaborately domesticates the natural world through art, she also refuses to stay at home. Against an ethos that stresses the value of deep roots and origins, she presents the virtues of rhizomatic connections, ad hoc maneuvers, and entrepreneurial actions. Her geographic restlessness becomes a model for the pulsive energy she finds in herself and nature.

Ammons' early work expresses a longing for Emersonian transparence and the unity of landscape with being. He tries repeatedly to throw away consciousness of the mediating self, until that gathering and dispersing of the image becomes its own structure of identity. By widening his scope he would match his consciousness to nature's flow. But Ammons' late work largely abandons the visionary stance, except in the postmodern-sublime of *Garbage,* where it arises in response to the awesome landscape of our discarded forms, and nature's own expenditure and waste. He turns for the most part to an ordinary nature, one close by, which cannot be embraced by the imperial imagination, but might be known in adjustment and transition of limited frames.

In John Ashbery's work landscape provides the image, but also the dimension, of consciousness; and consciousness is a space of time. Where Clampitt's landscapes have a descriptive and emblematic function, where Ammons' landscapes are analogical and parabolic, Ashbery's landscapes may seem to typify a postmodern, horizontal allegory. Meaning is mobile but detached from experience. Distinctions of map and territory or mind and scene slide into a single fictive surface. The structure of correspondence yields to a sense of constantly mutating image. But while the temporality of Ashbery's poetry is disconnected from particular experience, it is not without a sense of the real. His mapping of cognition onto landscape recalls our desire to ground knowledge and reveals the permeability of inside and outside. The fundamental metaphor of thought as landscape yields in Ashbery to the truth of an unsteady and unknowable but nevertheless inescapable "ground" of reality, which no perspective can fix. Knowledge is not a stable landscape or a home because "time and the land are one" (AWK, 81).

Modern poetry has demonstrated that landscape, as mimesis or metaphor, is a productive, flexible focus for presenting the mind's engagement with the world. All of these poets, however, and especially poets of the postmodern era, express an anxiety that landscape might become mere image, disengaged simulacra to which we become passive spectators of our own creations, rather than channeling experience. Stevens wards off "the vast ventriloquism / Of sleep's faded papier-mâché" (CPP, 452). Moore warns against mistaking the reality of the wilderness for a "dime-novel exterior" (CP, 55). Ammons predicts that we will "replace our mountains with trash" (*Garbage*, 71). This anxiety has long been with us. More than twenty years before Jean Baudrillard announced the "precession of simulacra," Daniel Boorstin in *The Image* was lamenting the way that media and technology had displaced experience, giving us pseudo-events, travel without exposure, invention over discovery, maps supplanting territories: "The life in America which I have described is a spectator sport in which we ourselves make the props and are the sole performers" (182). The rigorous project these poets undertake within the genre of landscape is to keep the image supple by an active connection to flux and frame. Ashbery comes closest to expressing the postmodern extreme in which the real disappears into its image, but his work never relinquishes the aspiration for the real. Rather, temporality itself becomes a vital form of extension, offsetting the shallow space of the mutating image. If the modernist tension between subject and object, image and reality, is slackening, we need not assume that landscape leads only into the thin atmosphere of the image. Precisely because landscape is so susceptible to iconographic detachment, it has been the genre in which poets have launched their most intense quest for the genuine. For these writers, the function of art is to find new ways into the vital dimension of experience.

2

Frost's Crossings

Language and Landscape

"The highway dust is over all," says the Oven Bird. Modernity and mortality have entered the landscape, and that fall we call "The Fall" has left our garden of the world a "diminished thing." In "framing" the "question" of "what to make of a diminished thing," Frost reveals his part in making a landscape. Frost's poems operate in the complexities of a late second nature where priority cannot be recovered, not Emerson's "original nature" but his mid-world. Frost's landscapes, and the language that shapes them, convey a strong sense of frame and flux. The American Eden, either lost or found, had little interest for him, except as an inherited notion to be scrutinized within the labyrinth of language and cognition. From "For Once, Then, Something" to "All Revelation" we see Frost presenting human perception as something mediated and transitory, yet meaningful within these conditions. Frost's negotiations of the frame and the flux produce a poetry of crossing: discourse across a boundary, nature affected by and affecting human presence, life both entropic and retentive, man moving on and thinking back. The mind seeks and creates patterns in time, which struggle against the anti-landscapes of undifferentiated wilderness, the frozen swamps and desert places we cannot inhabit.

A compass set in an urban culture points to Frost's pastoral scenes in *North of Boston*. So "Mending Wall" (C P, P, & P, 39), the first poem in the volume, *begins* with human divisions and boundaries, and with a sense of the frame. Nature's presence is hard to locate, spatially, in the poem. It is not on either side of the wall, since these areas define entirely husbanded, contained spaces, identified with their owners ("he is all pine

and I am apple orchard"). Nature here is best identified with movement
and energy, and in particular energy that dissolves form. Nature is
"something that doesn't love a wall," and so knocks it down, a force
rather than a space, more verb, as it "sends the frozen ground-swell" and
"spills the upper boulders," than noun. But even here we have negative
definition. Spatially nature is known in the "gaps" it makes in walls, gra-
tuitous rather than utilitarian gaps, the poet reminds us. To use the word
"nature" is in itself to fill the gap as Frost refuses to do. This "something"
is not a knowable, therefore not a nameable essence or common ground.
The imagery of magic and elves, and the implicit pun on the poet's own
name in the subversive frost that upheaves the wall, stand in for this in-
effability. But like a reverse of the machine in the garden, the incursive
presence of this "something" is clearly felt, not as wilderness but as wild-
ness (which does not, like wilderness, require an illusion of originary na-
ture or a distinction from the world of man). Indeed, the wall is what
allows this "something" to express itself. And here is where Frost is ahead
of his self-quoting speaker, the elf of the self, who would impose his ver-
sion of reality on another, would project a landscape in the name of na-
ture. The erosion of boundary does not, for Frost, suggest Romantic
continuity—the unity of man and nature under a metaphysical light. The
modern principle of discontinuity rather than holism is alive precisely in
the word "gaps." If there is a primal condition invoked in the poem, it is
not nature but the apparently primordial human order that works to
sustain itself "like an old-stone savage armed." He is the conservationist,
the one who would preserve an original "state." And in a sense the
speaker is just like him, digging in his heels, even building a wall. Nature
is not a state but a process, gratuitously subversive, a secondary energy or
wildness that asserts itself within and against static forms, especially
forms of ownership and exclusion. This, too, is one of the "figure[s] a
poem makes." And the wall itself is a participial, not a stationary thing—
a mending wall. The speaker of the poem clearly sees these "gaps" as an
expression of an impulse within himself, a violence in him that resists
boundaries. "Spring is the mischief in me." But Frost's imagination oper-
ates between the speaker and his neighbor, recognizing that the "game"
requires two players—running between them, between the first, arbi-
trary erection of a wall ("there where it is we do not need a wall")—and
the gratuitous dismantling that brings them annually together to restore
it. The erasure of human boundaries, to uncover some primal, undi-
vided space to which we might "return" or "retreat," is not an attainable
or desirable goal. Instead, boundaries with holes in them, permeable

walls, give us the sense of the wild. The sense of the wild is discovered, that is, within the sense of the frame.

If nature is a force of mobility against static forms, for Frost, the beholder is also often in flux, "turning to fresh tasks" (C P, P, & P, 101), and this equally affects Frost's sense of landscape. "A Passing Glimpse" (227) may be a rather mixed response to Ridgely Torrence, whose *Hesperides,* the dedication tells us, provoked these lines. (Does Frost give Torrence no more than a passing glimpse? Does he suggest that Torrence's idealized vision of nature depends upon not looking too closely?) But the poem also names the way modernity affects what is seen and how it is seen. The anapestic couplets hurry the poem along the tracks of the train, although the mind goes back, wanting to recollect in tranquillity. Frost's backward look does not produce the Wordsworthian completion of vision in afterimage, but rather a *via negativa* of quickly canceled frames. He creates a series of unromantic, fragmentary landscapes, places where beauty arises within the impoverishments of that "diminished thing." Frost finds nature at the margins of man's world, growing alongside the railroad track, not in the garden of Hesperides. While he tells us these are not the flowers he is trying to recall, they were glimpsed and have a reality that delights even as the ideal eludes him, or remains a thing of the mind only:

> Not fireweed loving where woods have burnt—
>
> Not bluebells gracing a tunnel mouth—
> Not lupine living on sand and drouth.

We may give these images merely a glimpse, considering them without visionary potential. Yet Frost clearly admires the ad hoc resilience and opportunism of this uninflated nature. He suggests that these tentative, mixed landscapes that form along the track of man's hurry may have more value than the questionable brushing of the mind with the eternal garden of the gods "that no one on earth will ever find."

Counter-Love

Frost's liking for walls sets him apart from Emerson, who imagined ever-extending horizons and dissolving boundaries where "each" is absorbed into an infinite all in all. Frost resisted even dialectical syntheses. "Hegel saw two people marry and produce a third person. That was enough for Hegel—and for Marx too it seems. They jumped at the conclusion that so all truth is born." Frost preferred the kinetic energy of opposition to any dialectically produced "monomania or monometaphor." "Life sways perilously at the confluence of opposing forces. Poetry in general plays perilously in the same wild place. In particular it plays perilously between truth and make believe. It might be extravagant poetry to call it true make believe—or making believe what is so" (*Selected Letters of Robert Frost*, 467). I am interested in the structure—called antimetabole or chiasmus—as well as the content of this statement because the pattern of reversal is so typical of Frost, and can be seen not only in his phrasing and in local moments of paradox or irony, but in the structural and conceptual levels of whole poems, in their visual as well as their verbal arrangements. Chiasmus is central to the phenomenology of perception, as it was described by Merleau-Ponty in the 1960s.[1] His resistance to Cartesian dualism and Kantian transcendentalism, and his suggestion of reciprocal subject/object relations, have been carried forward in the work of cognitive science (see Varela, Thompson, and Rosch, *The Embodied Mind*). A few contemporary critics of lyric—deconstructive, psychoanalytic, formalist, and ecocritical (de Man, Irigaray, Bahti, Spiegelman, Stewart, Scigaj)—have drawn attention to the trope of chiasmus, the rhetorical structure that produces this effect of reciprocity. But its role in Frost's poetry has been noticed only in passing.

We hear chiasmus in early poems such as "Mowing" (C P, P, & P, 26), where inversion appears to function merely as verbal enhancement ("perhaps it was something about the heat of the sun— / Something, perhaps, about the lack of sound"), but then leads up to the paradoxical "fact is the sweetest dream that labor knows." In "The Mountain" (45) chiasmus serves to bind together human and natural places, mountain and town giving their name to each other ("Hor is the township and the township's Hor"), while in "Spring Pools" (224) the trope aligns the poet's metaphors with nature's own reflective powers ("These flowery waters and these watery flowers"). In "Meeting and Passing" (115) structure marks a disappointing exchange: "Afterward I went past what you had passed / Before we met and you what I had passed." Chiasmus in Frost is the non-idealist figure that admits "our being less than two but more than one as yet." "The Gift Outright" (316) turns chiasmus to an ideological principle: "the land was ours before we were the land's." But the priorities are so criss-crossed in this poem as to dissolve complacent concepts of nature's nation. We can recognize a similar motion in Frost's treatment of the seasons, as abrupt reversals and inversions (in "The Onset") rather than inevitable cycles. In "To Earthward" (209) the human life cycle is given this pivotal, inverted shape; the many criss-crossings (rhythmic, dramatic, spatial, syntactic) lead to an overall inverse ratio between sensory pressure and feeling. While the poet in youth felt lifted and "lived on air that crossed me from sweet things" in their downward flow, he now longs to press back, to stretch his body's length into the earth. In this way the logic of diminishment becomes the logic of fulfillment, and the odd, redundant title ("To Earthward") suggests both a lover's address and a mortal's destination. "Two Look at Two" (211), a poem about a man and woman on a mountain path who encounter a doe and buck across a barbed-wire boundary, doubles the crossing to a perpendicular. "Two had seen two whichever side you spoke from," and the poem speaks from all four. James Wright imitated this poem in "A Blessing" but left out all the chiastic structure, producing a much less interesting, more neo-Romantic poem. Frost's poem uses syntactic ambiguity to sustain a threshold experience, culminating in a richly ambiguous, but affirming reciprocity: "as if the earth in one unlooked for favor, / Had made them certain earth returned their love." (Of course, it may be through death that earth returns our love.) The "as if," as I will show, is crucial to this exchange. Chiasmus structures a more combative but still reciprocal narrative of "The White-Tailed Hornet" (253), where the speaker struggles in a mock-heroic manner with the encroachments of Darwin's "downward comparisons." Animal defeats man when the poet invades nature, but entering the human world, nature can provide a fable. Midway in the narrative Frost highlights his chiastic structure: "That's when I went as visitor to his house. / As visitor to my house he is better." These inversions, these movements of "both going and coming back" (118), of "backwards motion toward the source" (238), these chiastic sentence sounds and sounds of sense are so pervasive as to form a master trope.

Chiasmus organizes not only the line, but also relationships, spaces, sensory and temporal experience. It forms the grammar of Frost's landscapes and the structure through which he imagines the effects of frame and flux. It emphasizes relations of parts rather than the sum, so that it seldom offers wide prospects, preferring narratives of encounter to descriptions of integrated scenes. One could argue that these are not really landscapes. If American landscape tradition reflects the Enlightenment episteme in which nature is an object of contemplative or material possession, Frost's landscapes revert to an older model, in which our relation to nature is one of resemblance rather than mastery. Yet it emerges in a post-Enlightenment context and cannot simply return to old ways of knowing. The poet does not stand outside or above a vista, but finds himself in the midst of things, occupying a part as he discourses on or with another part, or at most imagining the correspondences between elements in a landscape. Crossing (as mirroring, circling, reversing, exchanging) becomes Frost's way of imagining the dynamic of parts (rather than the prospect of the whole), and of countering the tendency of wholes to fall apart.

While Frost's concern with frame and flux is a sign of his modernity, the scene of these reflections need not depict contemporary life. As with Marvell, Frost's pastoral medium allowed him to play out modern preoccupations in the stylized simplicity of the garden. But as with Marvell, we know this garden as a place in time. "Fireflies in the Garden" (C P, P, & P, 225), for instance, shows how Frost uses the mirror image (echoed in the two triple rhymes) to reflect on the transience and belatedness of images.

> Here come real stars to fill the upper skies,
> And here on earth come emulating flies,
> That though they never equal stars in size,
> (And they were never really stars at heart)
> Achieve at times a very star-like start.
> Only, of course, they can't sustain the part.

The "emulating flies" embody a bitterness the poem will suppress, about the subjection of the speaker's ambition to frame and flux. These flies do not soar; they hint at the body's decay and the mind's derivative nature. But they capture the sense of correspondence for the modern poet, and the transitory delight he takes in the making of images. And as "part" of nature, even the part that plays a part (and Frost is, like many modern poets, interested in nature's mimicry), they complete the landscape. Chiasmus is the figure of landscape as a mirror. Man's transitory representations are included in the nature of things.

The reference to master tropes may recall Harold Bloom (borrowing from Kenneth Burke). The critic of poetic crossings draws on the American Romantic tradition of Emerson, Whitman, Crane, and Wallace Stevens. For Bloom, the crossings of strong poets are dialectical and ultimately progressive, one-way psychological successes, at least within individual poems. The poet's crisis, his aporia, is overcome or gotten over, through sublime, transumptive will, whether it be a crisis of vocation, of otherness, or death. Bloom's crossings are like Emerson's, from each to all, from nature to mind, from individual beholder to expansive vision. I'm not sure this model fits Wallace Stevens. I'm sure it doesn't fit Frost, though the crises (of vocation, love, mortality) are all central to his work.

Frost's crossings retain the sense of gap and polarity, and of wholes as re-lations between parts. They are reciprocal and kinetic rather than dialec-tical; they are non-transcendent and engage cognition and will together rather than subsuming one to the other. Frost deals with crisis through a crossing back and forth that creates a sense of completeness rather than a sense of triumph. "Reality is the cold feeling on the end of the trout's nose from the stream that runs away," Frost wrote (quoted in Faggen, 30). But the imagination craves "completeness" as well as reality. In an interview, Frost listed "incompleteness" as one of his major dislikes. In poetry he found a form of completeness that admitted the fragmentary and incomplete state of knowledge and of reality itself.

Frost's logic of inversion and reciprocity particularly informs his ap-proach to the doctrine of correspondence, what Frost called "the metaphor" of man's relation to the non-human world. As George Bagby has pointed out, Frost's correspondence has ties, through Emerson and Thoreau, to the seventeenth-century emblem tradition, the "book of na-ture." But Frost's skepticism defines the reading of nature as "a text, albeit done in plant" (C P, P, & P, 323). Like other modern poets, he reads in a book of nature for which the great code is lost. ("Whatever the landscape had of meaning appears to have been abandoned," writes Elizabeth Bishop, as she observes "forests standing in gray scratches / like the ad-mirable scriptures made on stones by stones" [*Complete Poems*, 67]). Frost is more evolutionist than transcendentalist in reading the vegetable text; he may borrow a poetics from the past, but he does not share its epistemology. The "albeit" of "albeit done in plant" admits a problem of translation; it admits even that the text derives from our nature as read-ers as much as from some spiritual code to which all creation is keyed. He clearly did not subscribe to typological or Romantic modes of reve-lation, but neither did he eschew correspondence. Pressing Frost's claim that he is a "synecdochist," critics overlook the evidence everywhere in Frost that undermines the epistemology of this part/whole trope with its implication of governing design. His epiphanies are often dispiphanies. ("What but design of darkness to appall?— / If design govern in a thing so small" [C P, P, & P, 275]). The modernist penchant for setting metonymy against metaphor recognizes the dominant experience of fragmented knowledge; Frost found a way to continue a practice of correspondence without a confidence in the epistemological grounds of synecdoche. He could have parts correspond to parts without a vision of the whole. Frost's "correspondence" may derive from the emblematic tradition, but it suggests an indirect, mediated relation between mind and world in which origin and hierarchy disappear. Frost places correspondence in a figurative structure that retains difference—not A : B but AB : BA. (He employs it as rhyme scheme as well as syntactic structure.) For Frost, correspondence does not get beyond this relational structure to an ultimate unity, for the unity lies below the relational structure, in the undifferentiated flux of life that subsumes rather than fulfills purposive order.

Chiasmus in Frost allows for the will to go out, for the human mind to seek its reflection in nature. But it also allows the image of nature to suggest to us our own creaturely natures, our biological, rather than nature's spiritual, origins. Much of the time Frost's correspondences lead back to cognition of nature, not beyond it, to a revelation of universal mind. Behind the chiasm, too, is Darwin's separation of the species. Nature and man are different not in absolute terms, but in historical terms—they are not created separately, but they evolve in separation. The analogy that constitutes a correspondence between mind and nature may derive less from some transcendental truth than from the homology of embodied mind. Behind a great many of Frost's reversals and inversions, then, lies a central chiasmus with which modern thought struggles: that man emerges from and is subject to nature, and that "nature" is a human construct, something arising from the frame.

Apostrophe is the trope most often associated with the Romantic crossing of correspondence, in its address to nonhuman entities. Like Whitman's spider, it casts filament, filament, filament out of itself, hoping to catch somewhere past the void. The poet addresses inanimate or inhuman nature in order to link human feeling to some universal spiritual principle. But apostrophe has a tragic aspect. Since the apostrophized object cannot answer back, the ecstasy of lyric projection often turns back to pathos, and to a narrative of failure and isolation exposing the pathetic fallacy. One of Frost's earliest poems, "My Butterfly" (C P, P, & P, 36), is an elegy from the outset, mourning the loss of nature's companionable presence and memorializing the lyric flight beyond time and death which it inspired with its "dye-dusty wing." As a first poem it is clearly also a statement of poetic disposition, and, strangely, an elegy to a certain kind of lyric ambition. It suggests the belated Romantic posture from which Frost will redirect his representational ambitions. "To a Moth Seen in Winter" (C P, P, & P, 323), published in 1941 in *A Witness Tree*, but written about 1900, just a few years after "My Butterfly," tells a similar story of hindered flight.[2] But it points the way out of the dead-end of apostrophe. Although not a landscape poem, it suggests a set of problems that Frost's landscapes will address. Again, apostrophe evokes an unsustainable lyric aspiration to escape isolation and temporal limits. As Jonathan Culler has shown in *The Pursuit of Signs*, narrative is apostrophe's repressed other, the sequential structure that ecstasy seeks to transcend but to which it inevitably succumbs. No trope has an essence—apostrophe or chiasmus—but Culler's theory is borne out at least in the practice of many post-Romantic poems, including Frost's early ones. The poem begins this way:

> Here's first a gloveless hand warm from my pocket,
> A perch and resting place 'twixt wood and wood,
> Bright-black-eyed silvery creature, brushed with brown,
> The wings not folded in repose, but spread.
> (Who would you be, I wonder, by those marks
> If I had moths to friend as I have flowers?)
> And now pray tell what lured you with false hope
> To make the venture of eternity
> And seek the love of kind in wintertime?

Ironically, after asking a question of the moth, he immediately begs it to listen, disrupting all fiction of conversation. The poet answers his own question.

> But stay and hear me out. I surely think
> You make a labor of flight for one so airy,
> Spending yourself too much in self-support.
> Nor will you find love either nor love you.

Halfway through the poem, he admits the artifice of his sympathetic narrative. His feeling is "something human," not a real connection to nature. He "cannot touch [the] fate" of the moth, and turns back to his own inevitable desire and belatedness.

Frost's gloveless hand might signify an initiating desire to reach beyond the figurative to a moment of presence, a "perch and resting place" between fictions (between the make-believe of "would and would"). But from the beginning the hand recedes back into its rhetorical pocket. The poet has no name for this marked creature (it is only on such "terms," he admits, that he maintains his friendship with flowers). We hardly need to be told that "what I pity in you is something human," for after the initial non-identifying details, there is little more moth in this exchange than there is moon in Sidney's "with how sad steps." It is the poet's own figurative wings that cannot launch him out of solipsism. His hyperbole cleaves from the remnants of metonymy. He is "spending himself too much in [rhetorical] self-support." The "old incurable untimeliness" may provide a pretext for the poet's effort of connection with the moth, but the "untimeliness" of poetic representation itself, the temporality of rhetoric behind this rhetoric of temporality, prevents it. If what he pities in the moth is "something human," it relegates the moth to an allegorical status. Apostrophe is too ambitious; it aims "across the gulf of well nigh everything," and inevitably reifies the gulf.

We can find a latent alternative even here in the abjection of "To a Moth." If the gloveless hand cannot touch the moth and must relinquish its presence, the language hints at reciprocity even though the representation denies it. "Nor will you find love either nor love you." The poet may be empty-handed at the end, and resigned to the isolation of the lyric position, unable to locate kind-ness in the world; but the crossing in this line, even with the negatives, suggests a congruence which the poem does not pursue but which establishes completeness. As the poet turns back from "your fate" to "my own" at the end of the poem, one feels the completion of a correspondence, respective and analogical rather than mutual and symbolic, even in the relinquishment of an ambition. The close of the poem almost forms another chiasmus as "your fate . . . save" reverts to "save . . . my own." There he will make this formal crossing conceptually active. Much of Frost's later poetry presents an effort to get beyond this elegiac structure of apostrophe.

Apostrophe is a figure of the will that lies against time and materiality. But poetry, Frost said in "The Constant Symbol," is a "figure of the will braving alien entanglements" (C P, P, & P, 787). Critics attracted to pragmatist philosophy have had a lot to say about this notion, but it is fundamentally a poetic, not a philosophical, idea. Poetry is entangled with what is alien; it is a figure of the will and cognition of its limits, both at once. In this way, I think, chiasmus is central to Frost's work and especially to his landscapes. In it the will crosses over and is crossed over; it does not overcome, in sublimity, nor merely succumb, in pathos. (This may be the instinct that led Keats to end his apostrophic poem "Ode to a Nightingale" with a chiasm: "was it a vision or a waking dream / fled is that music, do I wake or sleep?" which provides a criss-cross completion to reverse the terminus of the poem's narrative of transport.)

A quarter-century after composing "To a Moth Seen in Winter" Frost is still making overtures to nature, but the rhetorical gloves are acknowledged. Frost's apostrophe in "Tree at My Window" (C P, P, & P, 230) is openly framed. Indeed, the frame is the beginning of correspondence.

> Tree at my window, window tree,
> My sash is lowered when night comes on;

But let there never be curtain drawn
Between you and me.

While many modernists drew the curtain on nature, Frost addressed himself to a nature arranged for human connection through trope. Indeed, the tree's iconographic history stands quietly behind this image. As the other vertical in the landscape, the tree is available as a medium of self-reflection and for focused association with the physical world. Rhetoric (window tree) follows from observational fact (tree at my window). Nature exists for us not in itself but in its relation to us. If our relationship to this tree of knowledge involves us in a hermeneutic circle, that circle does not define an arc of ambition and failure such as apostrophe alone might do. The poem elides linear narrative and instead moves through a series of transpositions that reiterate and sustain correspondence. After the initial horizontal axis of window correspondence, the poem shifts in the second stanza to a vertical axis of matter ("ground") and mind ("profound").

Vague dream-head lifted out of the ground,
And thing next most diffuse to cloud,
Not all your light tongues talking aloud
Could be profound.

But just as the first stanza used chiasmus to cross the gulf between poet and tree, here the up/down, high/low opposition is kinetic. Mind and nature slide and invert through personification and pun, maintaining the *abba* logic that the rhyme scheme underscores, but also undermines as the phonemes begin to mesh. The tree, while grounded, is a dreamer-poet; the poet, while uprooted, is by inference "profound" but pragmatic. The stanza, with its encircling rhyme of ground and profound (echoed in the internal cloud/aloud), describes a complete movement up and down the vertical axis, a departure and return analogous to the out-and-back movement of the first stanza. The stanza pivots on a "not" (not all your light tongues . . . could be profound) that marks a sharp anti-Romantic boundary between human and natural things. There's no pretense in this poem, as there is in "To a Moth," of a dialogue; trees do not talk back. Similarly, Frost is fully cognizant of the fiction that reassures him of his existence, that tells him he is there when he sleeps. But the figural inversions and reciprocities form a bridge, which leads to the "but" and to stanza 3, allowing the swerve away from the narrative of failure. If the window creates a frame around the landscape, the movement of the tree reminds the beholder of the flux:

> But, tree, I have seen you taken and tossed,
> And if you have seen me when I slept,
> You have seen me when I was taken and swept
> And all but lost.

Chiasmus is again working in the syntax: "I have seen you" and "you have seen me" goes beyond the mere detached parallelism to which the speaker of "To a Moth" is resigned. This reciprocity is qualified, of course, like everything else in Frost. He never forgets the window, for like the net in tennis, it occasions the game. You need a separation to have a relation. (In this sense Frost's chiasmus works differently from what Luce Irigaray and others argue is a trope of blurring boundaries. Chiasmus in Frost stresses an intertwining of parts, not a holism.) The "if" in "if you have seen me" works not only to register variations in the weather, but also to recall us to the figural nature of the exchange in which a tree becomes a "you" in the first place. In "To a Moth Seen in Winter" this acknowledgment breaks the bond. Here, by contrast, the "if" is enabling. We move from this relational fact—the speaker's observation of the tree, "I have seen you"—to fiction: "if you have seen me." We can move next to a fiction believed, the fact of imagination where the "if" is now dropped: "you have seen me," that "true make believe" that is generated from "making believe what is so" (what is so being here the tree at his window which is now part of a system of correspondence). It is just this perilous confluence that we find in the last stanza:

> That day she put our heads together,
> Fate had her imagination about her,
> Your head so much concerned with outer,
> Mine with inner, weather.

The poet's rhetorical agency gives way to a third party called "fate." Yet this fate has an imagination. A hierarchical relation (imagination crossing over fate) is thus reversed and re-crossed. The single rhyme of the four lines (imperfect, keeping difference in play with the first vowel sound) sonically fuses the two parties, while the syntax yokes outer and inner under "weather." The closing zeugma and pulled-in last line of each stanza mark the move toward connection, but the poem resists total closure. The Romantic model of unity subordinates weather (change) to transcendental permanence. But "weather," for Frost, is the principle underlying man's unity with nature, his word for the flux, the evolutionary dynamism, the chance, working against purposive development. Weather is what modern cognition exposes under all its metaphors, the law which all structures, inner or outer, must obey. Imagination then becomes a superstructure for articulating natural connection, not a vehicle for attaining supernatural connection. But it does not follow from Frost's acknowledgment of metaphor and language as the enablers of correspondence that this correspondence is, as Paul de Man has said of Rilke, a rhetoric of figuration rather than a rhetoric of signification (*Allegories of Reading*, 49). (This might be true of Rilke; it is not true of Frost.) Why can't we see the duck and the rabbit? Language is a window, not a curtain. Here I am inclined to invoke Kenneth Burke's distinction between a merely symbolic action, which has no praxis, and a genuine symbolic action, which becomes equipment for living. This tree may be a forebear of Frost's witness tree, which he impressed, by violence, into service as a reciprocal sign of his own state of bondage, his proof of being not unbounded.

In comparing "To a Moth Seen in Winter" with "Tree at My Window" I have tried to show that chiasmus is Frost's defense (however tentative or qualified) against the failure and fragmentation latent in the trope of apostrophe, a trope he almost never uses after "Tree at My Window." The elegiac mood of apostrophe is displaced by the reciprocal completeness of chiasmus. Where apostrophe calls out to the absent other, projecting a union, but falls back into solitude and repetition, chiasmus forms a relation in difference and reverse mimesis. Chiasmus foregrounds the fictional aspect of correspondence, the "as if." It does so not in order to subvert correspondence, but in order to sustain its relational structure.

Later poems, such as those in *A Witness Tree*, incline to make "the most of it." The volume opens with the witness tree itself, "Beech," which marks out a property boundary and as such defines the contours of a landscape.

> Where my imaginary line
> Bends square in woods, an iron spine
> And pile of real rocks have been founded.
> And off this corner in the wild,
> Where these are driven in and piled,
> One tree, by being deeply wounded,
> Has been impressed as Witness Tree
> And made commit to memory

My proof of being not unbounded.
Thus truth's established and borne out,
Though circumstanced with dark and doubt—
Though by a world of doubt surrounded.
           THE MOODIE FORESTER
                  (C P, P, & P, 301)

His imaginary line is not the expanding horizon of Emerson's "Circles," but something disciplined in poetic form, a practical, immediate limit that for Frost instantiates the "alien entanglements" of life. The odd rhyme scheme of the poem is itself circumstanced, but not squared. The geometry of space creates perspective but not the illusion of infinite space. In the second line it "bends square in woods" marked out by the "iron spine" of immovable fact. That place itself becomes a figure, however, in the form of the "witness tree," and a certain poetic authority gets reaffirmed within limits, even through limits. The terms of correspondence are richly figured here. The poet wounds the tree with his signature (as Marvell wounds his in "The Garden"). This becomes a sign of his own vulnerability and suffering; he impresses the tree into service and makes an impression upon it (literally, but in effect figuratively too) as a sign of his own bondage. "Truth" forms itself, is "circumstanced," in the awakening to this boundary. At the same time truth locates itself within the poet's "imaginary line," and is continuous with his limited domain, "though by a world of doubt surrounded." Once again human truth and imagination find themselves on the same side of the line, an "imaginary line" established and borne out in "proof." We begin with a square, but the "circumstance" of truth suggests a circle and a sense of completeness. By finding the limits of metaphor, this poem seems to say, we also find its truth, the area within which it has authority. Conversely, without extending the imaginary line, without the extravagance of metaphor, truth is never discovered. This prefatory poem of *A Witness Tree* frames the volume in a demonstration of how duality can be crossed without becoming mere repetition, how poetry might become "true make believe" or "making believe what is so."

Frost's animal-encounter poems are very often landscape poems as well, with the animals moving between identity within the inanimate world of unconscious being (animals are like the cliffs, boulders, and so on that surround them) and the human world of cognition (animals have opinions, attitudes, feelings, like the people who look at them)— between rocks and hard-headed places. They provide, therefore, another form of crossing between mind and matter, perceiver and perceived. In his various and vicarious crossings the Adam figure in "Never Again Would Birds' Song Be the Same," recounting Eve's effect on nature, who "would declare and could himself believe," despite all his perhaps's and admittedly's, is more successful than the stubborn male figure in "The Most of It." For him, nature remains transfigured. The two poems from *A Witness Tree* present contrasting models of correspondence. The post-lapsarian Adam, through Eve, can enjoy the lyrical round "in all the garden round," the tone of meaning (the "sentence sounds") that evolves in the crossings between words and birds. "Her voice upon their voices crossed." The ambiguous agency of this double crossing (why not "her voice crossed over theirs"?) suggests a kind of gardener's grafting in which reality is changed, made hybrid; also a two-way crossing, a cross-fertilization in which origins recede. However she got there, "she was in their song" and had become part of the external reality. In "Never Again" Eve is already present in the garden, not just as muse figure, but also as speaker, mediating Adam's vocative power. Adam by himself might be caught in the crossing's self-echoing solipsism ("He would declare and could himself believe"). But Eve's remembered presence gets him beyond this narcissistic circle. The correspondence with the birds is preceded by human connection and discourse. (Notably, this poem about lyric's origins leaves out not only Adam's priority, but his Fall as well. There's no nostalgia for a prior condition. We start in the middle, in the condition of language.)

The man in "The Most of It" (C P, P, & P, 307), by contrast, seeks a primal, inter-subjective relation to the natural world outside the social context, and outside human discourse. Some readers find the figure heroic in his refusal of brute reality, but he is surely also blind in his all-or-nothing approach to correspondence. His apostrophes to nature have resulted in nothing but a "mocking echo." He seeks "counter-love, original response" and recognizes nothing less. He differs from Frost's Adam also in his solitude:

> He thought he kept the universe alone;
> For all the voice in answer he could wake
> Was but the mocking echo of his own
> From some tree-hidden cliff across the lake.

But the poet, whose sharply alternating rhymes put difference into echo, offers the reader an alternative to this failure, colloquial and scaled down by comparison to the bombastic poet-figure at the beginning. Acknowledging the failure to turn make-believe to truth, figure to revelation,

Frost, unlike his subject, moves to making believe what is so, to putting what is so, physical nature, into a figurative structure even though what is figured is nature itself, not mind or voice.

The cliff may be behind the trees, but there is nothing behind the cliff except more nature. But animate nature is to inanimate as mind is to matter; the first correspondence answers in place of the second. Hence the cliff's "talus" as he calls it in line 10 is not just a pile of rocks, but also, figuratively, the ankle of a foot—something that can move and soon does. Real animal nature breaks the speaker's solipsism. The buck appears in line 15 "as" a buck without any presumption of spiritual identity behind it (evoking perhaps but passing over classical or Christian symbology). The buck is the embodiment not of the answering voice the speaker longs for, but of the cliff, of cold, inhuman nature; he is a liminal figure, like so many animals in literature. We put him in relation to ourselves by making him a sign, even if, like the tree at the window, all he signifies is himself and the physical environment from which he comes rather than a transcendental principle or companionable consciousness. This "tone of meaning" continues in the metonymic treatment (as opposed to the symbolic treatment desired by the figure), as the buck becomes associated with the landscape ("pouring like a waterfall") rather than "someone else additional to" the human figure. An inversion has occurred in the figurative language: on the one hand the cliff becomes animated, its "talus" or ankle leaping forward in the form of the buck; on the other hand, the buck becomes associated with inanimate nature—he is "like" the waterfall.

The correspondence the human subject seeks is hierarchical: natural fact must be converted, he thinks, to revelation of something human. But the poem defines a different correspondence in which natural fact becomes sign (so that it can become part of knowledge) but refers back to itself. The poem's shift in style corresponds to the shift in figurative values. The highly subordinated thought of the first half of the poem (for, from, that, but) gives way to a list of observations (and, and, and) after the "unless." Ungraceful as this presence is (crumpled, stumbled, crashed), it has movement and power, a masculine power unreceptive to the male figure's domineering terms of love. But this is not an impasse; a crossing does occur. The buck crosses the reflective surface of the lake and the poet/reader "makes the most of it," finding a satisfying completeness if also a diminishment of expectation (and that was "all") in this unlooked-for response. Another poem, "All Revelation," articulates the idea: "Eyes seeking the response of eyes / Bring out the stars, bring out the flowers [. . .] / All revelation has been ours" (C P, P, & P, 302).

("All" has for Frost all the complexity that Empson gave it in *The Structure of Complex Words*.) The "all" in "The Most of It" does not totalize; it may be a diminishment, but it can also be a "boundless moment," a moment of expansion and mystery, and in this sense more than the sum of parts. We are finally part of nature through our physical being, and that is awesome. We do not, this poem implies, keep the universe alone. We share it with other creatures. And in accepting this we must relinquish the frame we project from a static position; we must look into the flux.

Frost's distance from the man in "The Most of It" is established in the successful encounters of earlier poems. The pair in "Two Look at Two" (C P, P, & P, 211), who experience the full emotional success of the poem's chiasmus, stand in direct contrast to him. But Frost is no deep ecologist. Insofar as that sharing is to be part of our consciousness, and in that sense "kept," it must be drawn into a system of representation, where "as" is the relational term. It is in the "as if" that we formulate, and earth returns, our love. As so often with the poets of this study, the landscape is known at its edges, where the frame breaks down spatially and temporally. A journey through landscape discovers disintegration, not apotheosis. For Frost this tends to be also the place where an alternative frame arises, taking its coherence from another angle of vision. This poem brings together two configurations of landscape: one in which the humans are subjects of the beholding, another in which they are the objects.

The couple pursue a mountain path at dusk and encounter a doe and buck across a barbed-wire boundary. "Love and forgetting," the first words of the poem, are just what the human figure in "The Most of It" does not have, and what the poet, for Frost, must have in his extravagance. If their "onward impulse" suggests the reach of the will, it quickly finds its range. ("If a stone / Or earthslide moved at night, it moved itself.") Here apostrophe, the figure of the will, might end, yielding to elegy. The "failing path" suggests just such a narrative, but Frost swerves from it. Indeed, the initial extravagance seems to meet defeat in a dispirited "this is all" that Frost echoes at the end of "The Most of It." But the terminus becomes a turning point, a place where the poem pivots. The boundary is permeable; the something that doesn't love a wall has been at work, inviting a crossing even as another impulse asserts a division. The couple encounters a "tumbled wall / With barbed wire binding." Such a boundary can be seen through if not transgressed. It is a threshold, and this is a threshold moment. With his healthy respect for difference and distrust of monometaphors and holistic illusions, Frost nevertheless accomplishes a criss-crossing in the pronouns that the narrative evokes only at the end. "She saw them in their field, they her in hers." The stuttering them/their, her/hers emphasizes difference, but the shift of object to subject and subject to object (she/them; they/her) marks an exchange.[3] This will be a narrative of reciprocity, a love in the form of chiasmus. The next line momentarily suspends all pronoun reference. Frost makes maximum use of lineation in order to sustain the ambiguities of his crossings. We struggle through the syntax, slowing the encounter. "The difficulty of seeing what stood still" is shared by human and animal observers, though evenually located in the doe: "the difficulty of seeing . . . was in her clouded eyes." We do not really see from the doe's point of view, but we can imagine that perspective by seeing her seeing, and in this sense the gazes cross. "They saw no fear there" again suggests a crossing in which they are both subject and object, but without mere repetition. (The couple do not see themselves mirrored in the doe; they see her seeing them.) It remains a human seeing, but while they remain subjects in this exchange, and the doe an object of perception, a reverse arrangement has entered the configuration. They have projected their fear onto the doe and seen it transformed to assurance, sent back as love. This ambiguity carries on throughout the passage that follows the couple's conjecture of the doe's perception. "She seemed to think that two thus they were safe." Does safe here mean harmless? Is the doe concerned with her own safety, assured that they do not present a threat? Or is she concerned with the humans' safety, in her role as a nurturing nature to wanderers in dark woods? All these conjectures about the doe are located within the human perspective, and are, in a sense, figurative. The narrative itself reaches this place where correspondence breaks down. That limit is given figurative representation in the doe's behavior: "Then, as if they were something that, though strange, / She could not trouble her mind with too long, / She sighed and passed unscared along the wall." The correspondence lapses because it lacks a kinetic force of opposition, but another soon emerges.

The two-to-one ratio of couple to nature may be a kind of metaphor for the familiar paradox of love's equation. The sense of connection to the natural world becomes an expression of the lovers' own connection to each other. And this reminds us that what happens in the poem happens between humans in a social context, as much as between animal and man. Again, this may be why they succeed in the vision where the figure in "The Most of It" does not. But the couple is one as "some upended boulder split in two." Here the poem shifts ground. If this image suggests primordial unity and carries over to describe the duality between man and nature, it does not evoke a spiritual or Platonic but a material unity. It is also an image of unconscious nature, a reversal in which nature is now mind and the human world reduced to insentient matter. There's a sort of zoomorphism going on here, in place of the expected anthropomorphism of apostrophe. As the exchange with the doe reaches its limit and strangeness reenters the poem, the correspondence breaks down. "This, then, is all . . . / But no, not yet." Frost swerves from failure once again. With the entrance of the buck, twoness reasserts itself, not as the end of correspondence but as its motor. While the poem does not explore the sexual difference between the couple, the emergence of the buck becomes a figure for it, which makes the crossing now a perpendicular one. The correspondence begins again, echoing the earlier "across the wall as near the wall as they." But, as the narrator insists, this is not mere repetition ("not the same doe come back"). This time the comma has been removed. Is the exchange less hesitant? Difference allows the narrative of exchange to continue, and the confrontational male presence marks difference just as the female invites sympathy. He does not merely look and sigh, he snorts and jerks his head, suggesting (with another "as if") not just sensibility but language. Indeed, the buck, like the doe, mirrors human attitudes toward the physical world, projecting them now back onto the human. The linguistic dare cannot be realized. "Why don't you give some . . . sign of life? Because you can't." We have come to think of nature as insignificant; it now returns the insult. The couple withholds the "proffering hand" that the speaker of "To a Moth" extends, because to reach thus is to break the spell imagination has cast. Yet a transaction has occurred—"two had seen two whichever side you spoke from" (and the chiastic poem speaks from both).

The closing words of the poem seem designed to warm the hearts of environmentalists: "earth returned their love." Now the split boulder of the Cartesian world can be made whole again, beyond confusion. Our love for the earth is validated in a universal principle. But that principle may be death. As with so many closing moments in Frost, the risk of extravagant sentiment is hedged here by linguistic ambiguities.

> A great wave from it going over them,
> As if the earth in one unlooked-for favor
> Had made them certain earth returned their love.

The passage raises more questions than it answers, and it suggests several possible crossings. What is the antecedent of "it"? Does it refer back to the experience just narrated? Forward to "earth"? Does "it" evoke the act of imagination the poem records, or even the poem itself? What is the substance of this "great wave"? Does it refresh and unite? Does it drown? Is it perhaps a sign rather than a force, a gesture of recognition and well-wishing like the one the woman recognizes as an annunciation in "West-Running Brook"? Has the earth in fact returned their love, or does the "as if" make the moment merely fictional? Who is not looking for a favor? The couple, presumably, but perhaps also the unconscious earth that has no desire for the love we bestow on it. All these possibilities are held in tension at the end of the poem. The penultimate line begins with an "as if," but the final line contains a subjective certainty. Earth stands in both lines, in a way that is not necessary for syntactic clarity. Frost could have written "as if the earth in one unlooked-for favor / had made them certain it returned their love." But Frost may want the doubling to remind us that the earth we love is necessarily an earth we have brought into relation with ourselves through language and imagination. It is this "window earth" that returns our love, corresponding as it may to the thing itself.

I have been emphasizing how Frost treats correspondence under the figure of chiasmus and how it differs from the figure of apostrophe in terms of direction and priority. Discovery in the wrong direction, the art of being lost, is a central theme throughout Frost's poetry, and the cross-purposes of chiasmus, unlike the directives of apostrophe, are one way he achieves it. Whereas the totalizing prospect of the picturesque landscape allows the imagination to wander along various eddies without terminus or constriction, Frost's landscapes are full of choices, boundaries encountered and roads not taken. My emphasis has been on spatial subject/object relations and the forming of landscape as a mirror. The figures of apostrophe and chiasmus also function differently in relation to lyric time. "This must be all. It was all. Still they stood," we read near the end of "Two Look at Two." Poetry thwarts plot and evades terminus; it ends in non-ends. Chiasmus works to suggest but also to resist direction and consequence. That is a topic for the next section. But I will note here that while fear and a sense of failure have haunted these poems, the work of chiasmus has been to resist the drawing of the curtain.

Pastoral Time, Evolutionary Time, Lyric Time

Frost's encounters, we have seen, involve a structure of reciprocity across real and rhetorical boundaries. His poems are often made of changing but congruent frames of reference. These spatial reciprocities complicate the sight lines and directional structures of Frost's landscapes. Frost's temporality is similarly ambiguous and shifting in direction, with moments that are neither fully boundless, nor fixed in sequence. Both nature and man are on the move, and the poet in the landscape both conveys and redirects this flow.

On the surface, Frost seems not to have adapted himself much to modernity's timespace. Time in Frost's poems is rural time, tied to the seasons and agricultural cycles, without a strong sense of consequential change. The grass that Frost's mower turns nurtures a pasture rather than splotching a driveway. "A Passing Glimpse" may give us some inkling of modern technology's impact on perception, but such examples are rare. For the most part Frost's beholder is a pastoral figure, whose observations are tied to the regenerative patterns of nature. At the same time, his poems bear witness to the near-disappearance of the way of life they depict—the inevitable exposure of the rural life to the forces of history. Many readers have also recognized a less than solacing emphasis on entropy. If pastoral time ties human life to turns of the harvest, the principle of entropy shifts attention to nature's and culture's creative and degenerative processes. Although Frost concerned himself only occasionally with the technologies of perception and changes in the physical environment brought on by technology, he was interested in modern conceptions of time and change emerging in science and philosophy, especially in the work of Charles Darwin, Niels Bohr, Henri Bergson, and William James.[4] While the pastoral orientation to time absorbs entropy and generation into stable, cyclical rhythms, the modern emphasis on change, flux, and evolution follows a dynamic, one-directional rhythm of retention and expenditure that can sometimes seem abrupt and discontinuous. Proponents of pastoral ideology, such as Wendell Berry, emphasize cooperative ecological cycles, and the value of attachment to agricultural rhythms for a sense of location and community. But ecology is gradually being reconceived in relation to dynamist theories of environmental change. While poetry traditionally draws on pastoral time to establish mythic patterns of eternal return, the identification of nature with what I will call evolutionary time provoked changes in poetic response, especially from Frost. Nature is a space where evolution and entropy preside, and within which the poet must fabricate his lyric structures of abidance. Frost's landscapes arise in the crossing of these models of time, framing scenes charged with transition and yet ballasted with the figures of return, scenes constructed of knowledge and desire. In this sense too we can see that Frost's poems integrate realist landscapes (imagining nature as a series of dissolving forms, and rural life as a losing struggle against the forces of entropy and modernity) with pastoral landscapes (imagining nature as a space of eternal return, and rural life as a harmonious relation between man and nature).

While Frost spoke of Darwinism as his day's prevailing metaphor, it was clearly more than a passing metaphor for him, as Robert Faggen has thoroughly demonstrated. It was a description of the world borne out again and again in observation and experience. Nature (and human history, as part of evolutionary nature) flows on in a process of creation and destruction; it does not retain individual forms. "Waste was of the essence of the scheme," he wrote in "Pod of the Milkweed" (C P, P, & P, 425). Poetry too, he remarked to John Coffin, is a wasteful keeping. Its grief and joy make nothing happen. But poetry is also a way of entering the flow. Creativity is not just futile retentiveness but strong expenditure. Man's metaphors (his knowledge) are ceaselessly changing toward no end but refreshment. As Frost wrote to Louis Untermeyer, he was "not going to let the shift from one metaphor to another worry him" even though paradigm shifts might seem like the jarring of tectonic plates. "The shift has to be made abruptly. There are no logical steps from one to the other. There is no logical connection." Poetry becomes a model for an active relationship to this historicity of knowledge through changing frames.

But if the enterprise of poetry embraces an evolutionary sense of time, the structure of the genre is retentive. Lyric engages sequence but defies terminus. It works more by repetition than by transformation, denying time and calling us back to beginnings. The work of lyric is to contain, to keep, and to dwell. From its beginnings poetry has drawn on pastoral cycles to convey this sense of stability and to suggest a mythic pattern. Diverse critics of lyric (Bloom, Cameron, Vendler, and Bahti, for instance) tend to agree that lyric time involves a resistance to, suspension of, or transcendence of experiential and historical time. It aims to gather temporal flow and consequence into a dynamic circulation in form.[5] Frost's poems, then, convey a tension, at many levels, between two rather different temporal orientations, arising from two different concepts of nature. The tension is resolved or represented variously in the relation of frame to flux, but few poems merely capitulate to one orientation or another. Often, as evolutionary time encroaches on pastoral time, Frost employs chiasmus as a defense, to reestablish motions of return within lyric time. Thus he creates landscapes in which the imagination both moves on and looks back.

We can get an idea of how Frost integrates the pastoral and the evolutionary, the stable and dynamic senses of time, from his essay "The Future of Man."

All growth is limited—the tree of life is limited like a maple tree or an oak tree—they all have certain height, and they all have certain life-length . . . our tree . . . has reached its growth . . . It doesn't have to fall down because it's stopped growing. It will go on blossoming and having its seasons . . . Then I want to say another thing about the god who provides the great issues. He's a god of waste, magnificent waste. And waste is another name for generosity of not always being intent on our own advantage, nor too importunate even for a better world. We pour out libation to him as a symbol of the waste we share in—participate in. (C P, P, & P, 868)

The blossoming tree suggests pastoral time and its appropriation by lyric into myth's eternal order, as in the chestnut tree of Yeats's "Among School Children," for instance. But Frost's attention to life-length and waste places this cyclical idea within an evolutionary frame that Yeats does not address.

Pastoral time, evolutionary time, and lyric time converge and collide in a variety of ways within Frost's landscapes. The result is an imaginative timespace built on crossings, producing effects of complexity, paradox, irony, or aesthetic transfiguration. "Spring Pools" (C P, P, & P, 224) offers an introduction to these converging time structures in a poem that draws attention to its framing impulse even as it bears witness to the mutability of all it would enclose. Pastoral time is clearly suggested in the reference to seasonal cycles (winter, spring, and summer are each evoked), and the continuities among natural forms, especially water and plant forms, suggest a stable ecological system. (Precipitation in the form of snow leads to pools that nurture the growth of wildflowers and later of trees.) But evolutionary time enters the poem in its emphasis on the ephemeral quality of these forms (the flowers and pools "will soon be gone"), and on the competitive relations among forms of the same order. (The trees will overshadow the flowers in their competition for light, just as the pools develop at the expense of winter snows.) In this poem the evolutionary implications are mild and do not really threaten the stability of seasonal renewal, but until the last line the emphasis in the description is on a linear rather than a cyclical transformation.

It is mainly through anti-mimetic, lyric strategies that the images are rescued, imaginatively, from that serial and linear momentum. The speaker brings the seasons to mind synchronically, describing spring by anticipating summer and recalling winter. In lyric time, all seasons exist at once. The play on Keats, Shelley, and Villon in the last line (the pools derive "from snows that melted only yesterday") turns the reassurances of pastoral time into nostalgia. But the sudden move backwards rather than forwards draws the poem into imaginary, lyric time. Through his shift from a metonymic description, with its contiguous and contingent relation between objects in the scene (the flowers are "beside" the pools), to a metaphoric structure, in which the objects relate in an abstract pattern of resemblance (the flowers are "like" the pools), Frost resists the linear flow and consequence. The mirroring in lines 3 and 4 ("And like the flowers beside them . . . / Will like the flowers beside them . . ."), and the chiasm in the penultimate line ("flowery waters . . . watery flowers"), remove the objects from the transience of representational space. The result is a lyric of rich temporal dimensions, in which the solaces of pastoral time and the anxieties of evolutionary time meet in the completeness of lyric time.

One can identify a shifting orientation in Frost's poetry from the pastoral and mythic quality of *A Boy's Will* to the evolutionary and historical concerns of *A Further Range*. Accompanying the imagination of change in literary tradition and in popular imagination is the mood of elegy. Landscape has been a site of mourning and, in modern times, an object of mourning. Frost recognizes that what we mourn is a particular framing of landscape, an ordering of nature and man according to a specific, historical perspective. But in all his work Frost mediates between the pastoral and evolutionary ways of representing time. *New Hampshire* is preoccupied with themes of environmental transition, especially the decline of the rural way of life. "The Census-Taker" and "A Brook in the City" are only the most explicit examinations of this theme. But many of the poems also find value in the human desire to seek stability, and solace against loss, in pastoral constructions of time. This is particularly clear in "The Need of Being Versed in Country Things" (C P, P, & P, 223). The landscape Frost creates in this poem is built on a series of crossings, both vertical (house, chimney, pistil, pump, lilac, elm) and horizontal (sunset, will of the wind, stony road, scurrying hoofs, birds "out and in," and, most emblematically, barn "across the way" from the house). To be "versed" in country things is also to see things as traversed and reversed, to see a landscape in transition, a design in flux.

The poem mourns the destruction of a house by fire and the consequent abandonment of a farm. While the poem focuses on the demise of a particular house, it is clear that the house will not be rebuilt, and indeed that the way of life around it has come to an end. The absent "teams" coming from the stony road may not be heard from again, we suspect, in this age of engine-driven machinery. The house burning marks the end of the cyclical patterns of agrarian harvest. Nature's reclamations are not so much a return to origins as an example of the transfiguration of all forms, however retentive in their structures. But the poem refuses this view and turns instead to the traditional elegiac solaces of pastoral time. The lilac will renew its leaf, the bird will build its nest again. Life doesn't just go on, it comes back. But this structure of natural recurrence at the end of the poem emerges to displace a more strained and disturbing rhetorical recurrence in the opening of the poem. And the first, rhetorical recurrence makes us aware of just how rhetorical the solaces at the end of the poem are as well.

The poem's title seems to promote a tough-minded, unsentimental "seasoned" perspective of the farmer who knows loss as part of life. To mourn is human, the poem acknowledges; not to, natural. To be "versed in country things" is to resist the pathetic fallacy. Readers have agreed about this central theme in the poem. But if country verse is anti-romantic, it is still poetic. The poem moves toward a re-versing of its fictions and a re-inscribing of nature. Although the poem's discursive argument relies on a distinction between human feeling and nature's ways, the poem's rhetoric reveals that these are not so easily disentangled. And while the poem's narrative suggests relinquishment of the past and delight in new order, the poem's structure suggests recurrence and return. Frost thus attempts a poetic framing of the flux.

The first stanza in particular demonstrates the way this lyric rebels against the terminus it describes. Here the recurrence arising at the level of metaphor is disturbing; it represents a violation of the natural rhythms of pastoral time that are evoked at the metonymic level.

> The house had gone to bring again
> To the midnight sky a sunset glow.
> Now the chimney was all of the house that stood,
> Like a pistil after the petals go.

The opening semi-chiasm suggests abrupt, even ironic reversal rather than continuity of return ("gone"/"bring again.") Similarly, the second line converts grief to aesthetic pleasure, loss to beauty. The euphemism of a blaze as a sunset appropriates the natural cycle, but locates it on an aesthetic plane. Irony arises here in the tension between an experiential disorder and an aesthetic order. The house burning suggests an apocalyptic collapse of order into chaos, making the backward, rather than forward, sequential cycling of nature all the more disjunctive and disturbing. The sunset gets a reprise against the midnight, but this only enhances the disruption of reassuring pastoral rhythms. There may be a second sunset, but there will be no sunrise for this house. The last line of the first stanza further registers the complex temporality going on in the poem between its metaphoric and descriptive levels. The "now" of representational time is put in relation to a natural, gradual occurrence (with its evocation of nature's generative cycles), and to an abrupt, violent, unnatural occurrence. The simile exposes the strain between the two levels, for a chimney is not like a flower's pistil. It will not bloom again. The burning of the house, for humans, is a violent, abrupt, chaotic occurrence, evoked by a smoking gun (reminding us that the chimney's smoke here does not come from the hearth). Surely Frost must have considered the more specific and poetic "petals blow" to rhyme with "sunset glow." The reader still hears it, in the speaker's resistance to the violent implication of the scene, the evidence of the pistol hiding in the pistil. The imaging of catastrophe with natural processes (house burnings as sunsets, bare chimneys as defloriations) is consoling only in its establishment of an aesthetic pattern, not in its implications. Its evocation of a natural pattern is dissonant. The poem will go on to seek a realignment of this poetic impulse toward recurrence and a natural, sequential rhythm.

But before the poet can again move forward in time, he must dwell on the past. If the first stanza registers loss and recurrence in a tension between discontinuous (human) and continuous (natural) figures of temporality, the second stanza introduces a lost correspondence between human and natural orders. The barn embodies the old sympathetic trope of man's harmonious relation to nature within the structures of the rural life. The barn corresponds to the house in a chiasmic relation, "opposed across." In his characteristic play of literal against figurative meanings Frost places checks on that trope of correspondence. The barn "would have joined" the house not of its own will but rather of the "will-of-the-wind," which is not a will-of-the-wisp, but a name for weather, the medium of unpredictable change (the bane of the farmer). The stanza's last line, which pairs weight and absence in the oxymoronic phrase "to bear forsaken," recalls the opening paradox of absence and return ("gone to bring again"), further establishing the figure of chiasmus as the poem's defense against consequence.

In stanza 3 Frost exercises poetry's power to resurrect what is lost in lyric time. We hear the "scurrying hoofs" of the teams from the road, not only through reference, but also through onomatopoeia. They make a low sound antiphonal to the higher-sounding birds of the next stanza. The shift from hoofs to wings parallels the play of weight and lift. The poem crosses between ground and sky and between poetry and nature. But this obsessive, lyric grieving ("the sigh we sigh") must be broken by a turn away from human concerns. The poem has indulged redundantly in "too much dwelling on what has been" and needs to abandon house and barn for some new order emerging in the yard. Stanza 5 promises a turn, a throwing off of old tropes. The previous stanza has suggested impatience with lyric's static circulating around absence. Certainly the poem's narrative suggests that mourning—and in particular lament for a lost agrarian way of life—has its limits. The phoebes sing not in mourning but because it is morning—the midnight of the conflagration has passed and the imagination must move forward with nature, not backward against it.

But Frost does not abandon elegy in making this move. In fact, he follows its characteristic turn toward cyclical renewal. The argument of the poem may call for distinguishing nature's ways from human feeling, but rhetorically nature is once again appropriated to represent human feeling. Exhausting its grief, elegy turns to what it evokes from the outset, through its pastoral frame—the promise of renewal in nature's cycles. The lilac that renews its leaf has of course taken a page from Whitman. The poem has not surrendered correspondence in its play of literal against figurative. The elm and the poet are both, though differently, "touched by fire." The inanimate world participates in the redemptive process through active verbs: "the dry pump flung up an awkward arm," both as a gesture of renewal and a protest against the end of its human use; "the fence post carried a strand of wire," as a sacramental gesture and a perch for new life. The paratactic "ands" modify the hint of cooperative agency, but do not eliminate it.

We cannot really dwell in a world of country things. "For them there was really nothing sad," nor glad. But we must build a house for our longing, and the birds' nests, which replace the burnt house, are as much figures of poetic as of natural making. The mourning song gives way to a mating song, but all "rejoicing" has been ours. Ours is the need, and ours the verse. The not believing is made possible because of new belief. The return to the title in the penultimate line, as well as the metaphor of construction in the last stanza, swerves the poem away from a terminus. The poem thus remains "open with all one end," though it begins with an ending. Evolutionary, pastoral, and lyric time converge here.

Each of Frost's poems rebels against its terminus, and turns back from the dismal swamp. "The Census-Taker" (C P, P, & P, 164) multiplies zeros, confounded by the image of extinction. "It must be I want life to go on living." In "The Oven Bird" (116) the count-down ("Mid-summer is to spring as one to ten") is also a count-up. In "Desert Places" (269) the speaker resists the void by "filling" it with his loneliness. But if the mind resists absolute zero, it rebels as well against the incompleteness of ongoing transformation. Lyric reversals and recurrences create a sense of completeness without a terminus. As he represents the seasons Frost is impatient with the slow turn-around of pastoral time, and converts cycles to chiasms, subverting direction and consequence.

"The Onset" (C P, P, & P, 209) beautifully illustrates this pull of the mind toward extinction, then reversal. Landscape becomes a visual pattern embattled by the encroachment of oblivion, but never quite erased, covered and uncovered each year. Here lyric time, by short-circuiting the cycles of pastoral time, evokes the tension between creation and destruction, retention and expenditure, in evolutionary time. The title marks a beginning, but the beginning of "being overtaken by the end." The poet braces himself, but his opening phrase, "Always the same," clues us to the recursive structure that will rescue the poem from its melancholy. The fated night is not doom but the first snow of winter. Going, going, gone turns into going and coming back. Pastoral time is restored. But again, the seasonal cycle is not a gradual, repetitive coming round, but a pivot (marked by a triple rhyme) and chiasmic inversion, making the recovery seem anything but inevitable. Rather, a battle is won against oblivion and marks a poetic more than a natural achievement.

The scene is merely the first snowfall, but this melodramatic speaker compares himself to the figure defeated by fate, stumbling toward oblivion with life's business still incomplete—"nothing done to evil, no important triumph won, more than if life had never been begun." But the rhyme ("end/descend" leading to "won/begun") tolls him back to "precedent," which is on the side of returns rather than ends. The poem pivots on the negatives, which in the second stanza are all on the speaker's side. "Yet all the precedent is on my side," he boasts. In fact, he skips winter death altogether—or leaves it as the disjunctive force of the poem's white space between stanzas. Siding with the earth (which of course winter death is neither for nor against), he defeats his defeatism, and the "nothing" of his own imagined failure becomes the shrugged-off "nothing" of snow.

> the snow may heap
> In long storms an undrifted four feet deep
> As measured against maple, birch, and oak,
> It cannot check the peeper's silver croak;

The reversal (marked by the parallel stanza structure) is not quite a victory, of course. As in "Design," white and black are not just reversed but complicit in the work of oblivion, until a chiaroscuro creates the visible scene. If the will is not defeated, neither is it triumphant. The "evil" of the first stanza (where the snow is "hissing on the yet uncovered ground") turns up as the simile, the too-lyrical "slender April rill" slinking off in the second stanza "like a disappearing snake." Life's business is not complete; evil is still unvanquished. And evil in this poem is another word for temporality. The closing couplet confidently asserts: "Nothing will be left white but here a birch, / And there a clump of houses with a church." But in "nothing will be left white" we hear both relief and a loss of innocence. The church stands as a symbol of hope and faith in an imperfect world. Meanwhile, the poem's form has, through chiasmus, established a formal perfection.

In each of the poems I have explored so far the various tensions and convergences of evolutionary time, pastoral time, and lyric time find expression in a vocabulary of direction. In this way again Frost deviates from his nineteenth-century precursors, British and American, whose wandering is confident of a transcendental reality, beyond time and space. When the road leads to the teleological vision of an infinitely traversable All, the beholder abstracts the framed space into a map. But in Frost direction becomes a medium for reflecting fate and choice, and for the experience of time and history. He is always *in* the landscape, not the master of the maze, and the landscape obeys the law of flux. But he is not bound by a sequence of stations. If flux subverts frame, cross-currents of imagination remain. Frost engages the lyric's freedom to suggest but also to subvert direction, to resist linear and teleological structures. This freedom in lyric lies behind Frost's interest in wrong or uncertain directions. His speakers are often "wrong to the light"; they follow "roads not taken," and find their way through digression. From fairly early on Frost was interested in disoriented speakers. He is "just far from home" in "The Wood-Pile." He lives in a "strange world" in "A Boundless Moment." Frost, the regional poet, is greatly interested in social and geographic dislocation. But creative habitation counters the lostness inevitable in the dynamist, evolutionary view of reality. The poet makes a home through imaginative configuration, in lyric time.

This fascination with misdirection (which is not the same as wandering) culminates in the poem "Directive" (C P, P, & P, 341–342). The speaker reaches us from lyric time. He is no longer a figure in the landscape, but he invites us to become that figure, to get lost as his previous speakers have done. The landscape is never organized as a prospect because we are moving through it. And the traces of others, and their arrangements of space, are everywhere, crossing our sight lines. In "Directive" evolutionary and geologic time on the one hand, and pastoral or mythic time on the other, converge and collide. One can hear the tension even in the title, which functions in both the relative world of the adjective and the absolute world of the noun. By getting us lost in these convergences, the poet projects the poem as a place where we might indeed "be whole again beyond confusion."

There is surprisingly little agreement about just what the poem's directive really is. For Reuben Brower "directive" is a noun, and the poem reaches a unique height of poetic and numinous wholeness. Richard Poirier despises the rhetorical posturing and obfuscation in the poem, finding it not wholesome but fragmentary. "The poem is not sure what it wants to say. . . . There is little in it strongly felt except the landscape"; he objects to the "pretentiously large rhetorical sweeps and presumptuous ironies" (*Robert Frost: The Work of Knowing,* 100). "Directive" for Poirier is a tendentious adjective. John Elder has celebrated Frost as the exemplary poet of "return to nature," his "directive" leading "back out of all this now too much for us, / Back in a time made simple by the loss / Of detail," but Elder ignores the residual layers of cultural myth and iconography that structure that "intimacy with the earth" and the poem's distinction between memory and experience in terms of the "loss of detail" ("Nature's Refrain," 707–708).[6] Detail is for Frost one of those saving obstacles that prevent us from submitting passively to static idealities. For Elder the opening lines represent the refrain of nature and its simpler, unifying presence. But for Robert Faggen, Frost's "Directive" shows him again a "pied piper of the diabolical" (276). For some readers the poem's convergence of "source" and "destination" points to an eternal return of mythic time (drawn from the pastoral time of life's cycles). For others this convergence proves a "destiny" of endless, material destruction and creation, of "forms in time, and in the horror of historical duration, not beyond them" (*Robert Frost and the Challenge of Darwin,* 275). These readings emphasize the poem's ending, and its developing rhetoric of quest. The speaker may "only have at heart [our] getting lost," but lostness, most seem to agree, is a Dantean preparation for finding The Way. What we find, so Roger Gilbert (49–74) and Robert Faggen argue, is not a spiritual connection (to mythic time through pastoral time) but an evolutionary absolute, the cold stream of mortality, "beyond confusion" because outside human orientation and self-preservation, "too lofty and original to rage" because past the anger and mourning of human attachment. This conclusion, such readings suggest, is not the fulfillment of synecdoche, the whole to which the parts aspire, but the collapse of meaning into a nonrelational state, a hollow wholeness. The stay against confusion is nothing but the stasis of death, the end of think-ing, a return to matter—this "beyond" leads nowhere but the void.

But such a grim reading of the poem can't explain the sense of plea-sure and rightness that the last lines of "Directive" convey. If at the level of signification and referential time the lines point more toward material than spiritual transformation, they nevertheless carry a rhetorical and aesthetic satisfaction. This grows from the development of a lyric time in the poem, which runs counter to the sequential, narrative progress. Per-haps we have put too much emphasis on this ending, and on the teleo-logical movement of the poem, since Frost as much as admits that his Grail is arrived at by obsolete metaphors. The formal, even high-blown idiom of the closing draws attention to its rhetorical, rather than repre-sentational, role. It plays to our desire for a romance plot. We must inevitably come down off this rhetorical mountain, back into the frag-mented world and its multiple directions, into the complexities of lan-guage, thought, location, and identity, where Frost's poetry lives. In particular, we can find a bidirectional pull throughout the poem be-tween creation and entropy, which directs us to the conclusion's meeting of origin and end. In this way Frost transforms evolutionary time into a satisfying lyric time.

Richard Poirier may be right that Frost doesn't really know where he's going. But that is precisely the point. Critics have not taken seriously enough Frost's confession about getting us lost. The directives of the poem—temporal and spatial, literal and figurative, representational and textual—work at cross-purposes, undermining the conventional coordi-nates by which we map experience. We get our signals crossed in a series of structural chiasms. In this way Frost, whom we think of as the most conventional of twentieth-century poets, anticipates John Ashbery. Frost challenges not only the procedures of language and logic, but also our accustomed beliefs about the nature of time and space. In "Directive" we see that lostness is not a matter of having no compass, no sense of direc-tion. A sense of direction is inevitable, a requirement of consciousness it-self. Rather, lostness comes from a sense of directions constantly crossed. Lyric time is not a new location but a potent lostness of direction through conflicting signs.

Spatial orientation claims our attention first in the poem. We are given a road map of the journey, in reverse: house, farm, town will ap-pear in the poem: town, farm, house. We adjust easily enough to this rear-view mirror since we are told we are going "back." But the backward logic has many dimensions that make for a difficult transfer from spatial to temporal coordinates. We don't go, that is, from a modern town to an old-fashioned town, but from a town to a farm to a house. Pastoral time is superimposed on historical time. It's hard to get a footing as the compass points several ways at once. The horizontal road becomes a vertical quarry (evoking geologic time) whose ledges show "lines ruled southeast northwest." We find direction again in the vertical, setting foot on a mountain path, but the adjustment skips any transition. The perspective, too, keeps shifting, in inconsistent scales of size and time span. We move from local cemetery and farm to mountain, to glacier, and then back to cellar holes. Frost knows we deal with non-human scale through personification, and he makes mischief with this habit. Susan Stewart writes that "we move through the landscape, it does not move through us; this relation to the landscape is expressed most often through an abstract projection of the body upon the natural world" (71). But Frost derails this logic of projection. The "ordeal of being watched from forty cellar holes" may be serial, but its collective reference makes it simultaneous and intimidating. Halfway through the poem we learn that we are not only gazing up but climbing, and soon the road disappears altogether; space contracts and we are left to "make ourselves at home" near "a field . . . no bigger than a harness gall." Space contracts, that is, just where we expect it to expand. Time is strongly spatialized, but not spacious. This poem may suggest nostalgia in its invitation to go back in time, but in fact it is radically anti-nostalgic, refusing all opportunity to dwell in the past. The speaker invites us to a "house that is no more a house" and refuses to describe what we cannot see. As Gertrude Stein said of Oakland, "when you go there, there is no there there." What "height of . . . adventure" can be found in the transition between cultures when "both of them are lost"? We may be on an archaeological and geological expedition, but the findings are lean and there is little reconstruction in the works.

The poem's temporal orientation is mapped onto this spatial plane, but according to more than one key. We see the past approaching, so that what is behind us seems up ahead. But the "now" does not recede; it stays with us as temporal duration, both at the representational and at the textual level. This "now" of representational time can be found in the young trees in the woods, the images of new growth, but also in the deteriorated condition of older structures, natural and human. If we were really going back into the past the apple trees would not be pecker-fretted; the cellar holes would be covered with houses. For Wordsworth, recalling his childhood on the banks of the Wye, "the picture of the mind revives again" (*Poetical Works*, 92). This stroll down memory lane encounters only ghosts. A person from the past may be, paradoxically, "just ahead of you on foot," but he is never fully embodied. We can't, unfortunately, back out of all this now; it comes with us. The "height" of the adventure might be where two village cultures fade into each other—a height, then, not only of excitement, but of perspective (we are outside or above both cultures). But just at that point the poem withdraws altogether from history and geography, into personal or inward location. But here, too, temporal sequence is disturbed. Why do we encounter the child's house before the "house in earnest," if we are going backward in time? The logic of narrative (unlike the logic of lyric) can only accommodate one direction. Presumably the "house in earnest" is a place of womb-like preconsciousness, with child-play to follow, in a Wordsworthian decline toward adult alienation. But by now it is also clear to the reader that the movement backward has also been a movement forward, that the return to origins can only be experienced in human time as a forward march toward death. The "house in earnest" is, then, both womb and tomb. The simile for a simpler time at the beginning of the poem, "like graveyard marble sculpture in the weather," foreshadows this revelation. The "belilaced cellar hole" suggests elegy as well as home. The hole slowly closing "like a dent in dough" suggests nature's womb-like expansion swallowing up human identity. It is only in this sense that Frost can, like Emerson, "yield himself to the perfect whole." (In the circular logic of the poem's personifications, death is like a disappearing navel—the erasure of identity, not its reification.) In its bidirectional momentum, all ruins from the past are signs of ruin in the future.

The poem matches directional confusion with figurative confusion, moving between a metonymic/descriptive level and a symbolic/mythic level. Inside keeps posing as outside. The anagogic logic of this "ladder road" is again bidirectional. Which metaphors are "in earnest" and which are "playthings"? How can we seriously drink from the child's "make believe" cup when we have so condescendingly gazed on the ruins of their imaginative constructions? The quasi-religious imperative in the last line must be set beside the earlier, sardonic imperative to "weep for what little things could make them glad." A bidirectional pull informs the tone, then, as well as the figurative scheme of the poem. The speaker compares his parabolic method to that of St. Mark, but in a tone that undermines the authority of such a method ("so the wrong ones can't find it, / So can't get saved, as Saint Mark says they musn't"). Presumably this ambiguity of tone is part of modernity's gaiety, its sense of play as serious and seriousness as play. But that attitude itself leaves us homeless since the instruments of our understanding are borrowed, not believed.

Such truthful lies, however, are the essence of poetry. The textuality of the journey surfaces throughout—not to cancel the signification but to locate the adventure in lyric time. The poem is all about brokenness until its end, the competing coordinates adding to this sense of competing coherences. The "destination" of wholeness, the "essay" of the poem, relinquishes synecdoche, however. The whole at the end absorbs the parts into flux. As if to reinforce this point, Frost follows "Directive" with "Too Anxious for Rivers" (C P, P, & P, 342), an acknowledgment that points of origin and destination remain outside human cognition. The poem's dactyls suggest Frost's imagination: swimming in the flux but against its current. "The river flows into the canyon / Of Ceasing to Question what Doesn't Concern Us, / As sooner or later we have to cease somewhere." The achievement of Frost's lyric is to make this lostness in duration seem like a place in which we can dwell.

In Frost's poetry, we have seen, frame and flux are in tension. The poet would frame nature in pastoral time, but his experience maps an evolutionary time of constant metamorphoses. Lyric time transforms this tension between frame and flux into a formal and emotional satisfaction. Frost invents landscapes that sustain a double vision, in which truth and make-believe unite in making believe what is so.

3

Stevens' Eccentricity

Beholding the World in Parts

The imperial fictions of traditional landscape depend upon the principle of a center, a single vanishing point that organizes space in relation to a viewer outside the scene. But Stevens' landscapes are eccentric. Stevens would like to submit his imagination to the fiction of the comprehensive frame. Like Emerson, he often implies a desire to "yield himself to the perfect whole" while becoming a visionary "master of the maze." But Stevens lives in his "fated eccentricities." As he writes in "The Ultimate Poem Is Abstract," he lives in

> Writhings in wrong obliques and distances,
> Not an intellect in which we are fleet: present
> Everywhere in space at once, cloud pole
>
> Of communication. It would be enough
> If we were ever, just once, at the middle, fixed
> In This Beautiful World Of Ours and not as now,
>
> Helplessly at the edge.
>
> (CPP, 370)

The ultimate poem may be abstract, but the poems we are "fated" to write are eccentric landscapes, temporally and spatially contingent. Our ideas are never completely coextensive with the world; frame and perspective define our distance from the center of "This Beautiful World Of Ours." Stevens' language of space, then, remains one of edges and obliques, in constant adjustment and erosion, aspiring toward a perspectiveless ideal. Edges and obliques imply a center—Stevens is not postmodern. But that center and its "central poem" are nothing less than the turning world itself, "the composition of blue sea and of green, / Of blue light and of green" (379). This "primitive" is only "like an orb" (377–380) in the sense that the poet can name the turning world only in metaphor; his imagination turns with it. Yet in creating eccentric landscapes rather than total images, he projects a "giant ever changing, living in change," and a "central" view, of which his landscapes are at once "a part" and "apart." But Stevens enjoys his eccentricity, which allows him to turn with the "orb," relishing its kaleidoscopic landscapes, yet at the same time never to forget the "giant of nothingness" at the center. While Frost depicts himself scenically, as a worker in the landscape, discovering fact as the dream of labor, Stevens' figures are either contemplative or "striding." But they are "makers" and unmakers of the world they see and walk in, and in this process they join in the primitive turnings of the orb, by participating in its transformations.

The Adequacy of Landscape

> We never arrive intellectually. But emotionally we arrive constantly (as in poetry, happiness, high mountains, vistas). (CPP, 911)

From the time of *Harmonium*, Stevens is as much a landscaper and a planter in an allegorical sense, as Frost is in a mimetic sense. His Crispin pursues a reciprocal logic similar to Frost's in the complex interdependence of identity between man and "the land." "The land was ours before we were the land's," remarked Frost in "The Gift Outright," his poem of American emergence. To become ours required an exercise of our superfluity, to use Emerson's term from "Experience," in deeds of human blood, but also of story, art, and other enhancements. We became "the land's" by excess, not by a relinquishment of ourselves before the primacy of nature. Frost's possessives make a counterintuitive assertion that dislodges notions of primacy. Stevens writes a similar plot of landscape's history in "The Comedian as the Letter C" (CPP, 22–37), his epic poem of aesthetic colonization. "Man is the intelligence of his soil," Crispin proposes at the start of his journey. But he forms a colony with the reverse proposition: "Nota: his soil is man's intelligence. / That's better. That's worth crossing seas to find." Critics have found an imperialist implication in these poems, in particular an inattention to the native people whose "land" this was before it was "ours." Stevens' double aphorism, like Frost's, seems to suggest an American incarnation in which culture becomes naturalized and thus removed from historical contingency.[1] But the crossed possessives of Frost's poem, and the neutrality of "such as we were, such as we would become," resist imperialist logic, suggesting, rather, a pragmatist logic of experience and process over prospect and power. While the chiasmus is given a narrative plot in both poems, it is more consistently, in each, an unfinished dialectic necessary to landscape. Again, efforts to define ontological priority come up against a condition of the middle. Stevens writes in "Comedian" of the longing for "The liaison, the blissful liaison, / Between himself and his environment." Such may be "chief motive, first delight, / For him, and nor for him alone," but "relentless contact" remains an ideal consummation rather than an achievement. And Crispin does not colonize "his polar planterdom" of the pure north, the first idea. Rather, he relinquishes the sublime of unmediated nature for the local and provisional "day by day" arrangements of landscape. Thus the "first idea" must submit to the "late plural," the "chits" produced from his intercourse with nature. The economic metaphor mingles with the generational one to suggest how Crispin's quest for the frameless real has succumbed to the system of figurative exchange. Death subverts the incarnational model of imagination, which would establish the continuity of all landscapes with original nature. Like Whitman, Stevens' Crispin is "stopped / in the dooryard of his own capacious bloom." The fecundity of his landscapes betrays his own mortality and his subjection to the flux.

Stevens would be pleased by the changing critical climate around his work, for "it must change" (CPP, 336). The poet of supreme fiction has been replaced in our criticism by the poet of contingencies. Psychosocial, political, economic, and linguistic contingencies have held our attention most; toward these Stevens is variously described as evasive or engaged.[2] What we have not addressed as much are the physical conditions of consciousness and the perceptual base of its activity, which Stevens so often invokes as both limit and need. Stevens' Romantic resistance to materialist views of reality has blocked this line of relatedness. We have tended to follow his lead in addressing the Cartesian split as a problem to be solved by the preeminence of mind. But the body in the mind remains a part of his poetics even at its most abstract. Stevens' profound association between "idea" and visual arrangement, and in particular landscape, may be tied to the fact that visual experiences sometimes triggered ideas.

In a letter to Ronald Lane Latimer (November 15, 1935), Stevens describes his need to believe in both a subjective order and the contingency of all human orders:

> In 'The Idea of Order at Key West' life has ceased to be a matter of
> chance. It may be that every man introduces his own order into the life
> about him . . . But then, . . . These are tentative ideas for the purposes
> of poetry . . . everyone is busy insistently adjusting. Possibly the unity
> between any man's poems is the unity of his nature. A most attractive
> idea to me is the idea that we are all the merest biological mechanisms.
> If so, the relationship of origin is what I have just referred to as unity
> of nature. (*Letters*, 293–294)

This is a long way from the unity of Nature imbued with Mind as
Wordsworth, Coleridge, or even Whitman understood it; Stevens' nature
is conspicuously lowercase. Rather than reflecting Romantic psychology,
Stevens' remarks anticipate our latest advances in cognitive science. The
poet also referred frequently to the dependence of the mind and culture
on the outer world for its forms: "All our ideas come from the natural
world: Trees = umbrellas" (CPP, 903). This is rather different from Emer-
son's claim that nature is a metaphor of the human spirit. It asserts, in-
stead, the material base of our ideas. It is generally argued that while
Stevens insisted on "an alliance . . . between naturalism and a visionary
faculty," the visionary faculty came to dominate his poetics.[3] But Stevens
stressed the contingency of that visionary faculty throughout his career,
and critical serendipity is just beginning to uncover the particular stim-
uli of his most elusive images.[4] To Ronald Lane Latimer's query about
the sources of poetry, Stevens replied: "While, of course, my imagination
is a most important factor, nevertheless I wonder whether, if you were to
suggest any particular poem, I could not find an actual background for
you . . . The real world seen by an imaginative man may very well seem
like an imaginative construction" (*Letters,* 289). This "actual back-
ground," this "soil" of "man's intelligence" defines not only an opportu-
nity for the imagination but the limits of its independence as well.

At the same time, Stevens would come to affirm the "adequacy of
landscape" and the need for its mediations. If our desire for the trans-
parently real persists, many satisfactions are won from our provisional
arrangements. The "inescapable choice of dreams" that is our apprehen-
sion of reality may serve rather than hinder our engagement, if it is a
choice constantly renewed, in "the never-ending meditation" (CPP, 397).
Hence while dream is inescapable, creative choice is involved in each
particular landscape. The idea of Nature with its lure of metaphysical
presence, its promised totality, is something else, a term Stevens almost
never uses. Stevens' landscapes are pragmatic and provisional, affording
aesthetic and emotional if not intellectual arrival. Frequently Stevens'
poems propose landscape as an alternative to confusion, as the only way

of seeing an otherwise chaotic world. But increasingly he would limit the claims of landscape, valuing its affective power rather than its epistemological purposes. Frost's sense of the frame led him to create landscapes marked out by boundaries, crossings, and transitory mirror images. For Stevens, the sense of the frame is felt when we come to know the edges of perspective, when we know our images as trash. Landscape is not a single act but a work in progress, constantly adjusting in relation to the fluency of thought and world. The sense of the frame, in a broader sense, keeps vision from becoming ideology. It knows it is not the whole of the real even as it delights in the mingling of the given and the made. Landscape in Stevens, as in Frost, is a figure of the will going out into the environment, but landscape also reveals perspective and the beholder's part in shaping what he sees.

While landscape remains a prominent subject in Stevens' poetry, his approach to it changed considerably in the course of his career. He began with a series of discrete experiments in perspective: "Thirteen Ways of Looking at a Blackbird," "Six Significant Landscapes," and so on. He moved to a circumscribing vision, of parts amassing to a whole: "The Idea of Order at Key West." The consequence of such ideas of order was less teleological revelation than local observation and insight, achieved by establishing point of view. Later in his career the observer's angle of vision and role in creating the prospect become important and the landscapes more provisional. The work of creating landscape becomes embedded in the representation, foregrounding the frame and its transitory authority. In making this argument for the adequacy of landscape as a negotiation of the mental and the environmental, I want to shift the accents given to certain points in Stevens' career. Instead of highlighting "Notes Toward a Supreme Fiction" and "Description without Place," those moments where vision seems to free itself from the locality of landscape, I give greater import to *Parts of a World* as a transitional volume leading to late poems such as "The Plain Sense of Things." In these works the ideal of the "first idea," of original vision, is replaced by the necessity of proliferating frames. We behold the world in parts.

The ambitions of landscape poetry have been bold, not merely decorative. Romantic poetry often imagines an intentional, subjective universe where the physical serves as grounds for, not a condition of, the mental. A location becomes a site of transcendental fade-out. So Stevens' beloved Coleridge, from the confinement in "This Lime-tree Bower, My Prison," can transcend his dissonant feeling of isolation and follow the "black wing / (Now a dim speck, now vanishing in light)" as it crosses "the Mighty Orb's dilated glory." In the modern period the taste is less for vanishings than opacities: the tactile real held in the objectivist fixed gaze; the substantiality of "no ideas about the thing but the thing itself." The autonomous fictive space of High Modernism, Eliot's "still point in the turning world" (*Collected Poems,* 177) or "the poem of the mind," is not qualitatively different from these investments; all are concerned with closing the gap between the material and the mental, establishing a unified vision. Stevens experimented with all these stances. But often for Stevens a disjunction seems truer to experience: "the mind is smaller than the eye" (CPP, 130). The "thing itself" is a sound more than an object to be seen—a "scrawny cry" reverberating the "letter c," as he suggests in his closing work of *Collected Poems.* He seeks "a new knowledge of reality" (452). In his emphasis on landscapes (the genealogy and rich variety of which are not my subject here), Stevens suggests an alternative to the unified vision. Without abandoning the habitual split of mind and world or promising utopian reconciliation, he seeks a creative liaison in provisional forms of arrival that acknowledge contingency and avoid the sense of crisis in object relations. "To live in the world but outside of existing conceptions of it" (904) is his goal. Landscape is a temporary dwelling, an alternative to both skepticism and idealism.[5] To say that this is more an emotional and aesthetic than an epistemological project for Stevens is not to suggest that he views the aesthetic as a discrete realm; quite the opposite is true. But it is nevertheless a distinct realm.

I don't mean to suggest that landscape description—mental picturing—is a primary aspect of Stevens' poetry. Even the early scenic landscapes are propositional, and the movement early on is obviously toward an abstract geographic mapping of aesthetic sensibilities.[6] In contrast to Frost, Stevens' poems do not invite us to picture landscapes; the mind's eye is more a referent than an agent in the working out of the poem. Stevens' visual language often seems to block rather than create illusion. But landscape—as a way of imagining the world and representing ourselves—remains a prominent trope and should not be taken for granted. We need to ask not only what kinds of landscapes Stevens imagined, but how he imagined them, how he understood their function.

"The exquisite environment of fact" (CPP, 904) is for Stevens primarily visual, and the eye reveals an aesthetic environment, to be probed less for its objective actuality than for its poetic "source of supply" (*Letters,* 247). The root of "exquisite," as Stevens well knew, means to search out; the mind, unsatisfied with what it owns, seeks out what is "not realized before" (CPP, 904). "The world must be measured by eye," not by abstract ideas of "the truth." Yet the eye is also, at times, "the inexquisite eye" (399), not searching out but apprehending, seizing reality for the mind, forming it to a landscape. He does not imagine the eye as an objective measure, a transparent conveyor of material truth. We have come (largely by way of feminist and ideological criticism) to critique the visual as a faculty of objectification and specular mastery which evades contact with real lives and real time. Stevens certainly participates in the scopic tendency of traditional landscape in which the visual becomes a non-contingent faculty leading to the visionary. But for Stevens, at least, this reach for manifest destiny forms only half the story. He counters the non-contingency of the visual with language emphasizing the "force" (26) of the physical world, which "smacks" the eye, repudiating old conceptions of reality. His landscapes are formed in the "inexquisite eye" from "the exquisite environment of fact." Abstraction's engagement with the actual marks more than an afterthought or mere consequence of its power to usurp the actual.

In his essay "Painting a Landscape," John Berger suggests a kind of interrelationship that might serve as a paradigm for Stevens' own dynamics of imagination and reality. "As I work I am faithful to what I see in front of me, because only by being faithful, by constantly checking, correcting, analyzing what I can see and how it changes as the day progresses can I discover forms and structures too complex and varied to be invented out of my head or reconstructed from vague memories. The messages are not the kind that can be sent to oneself" (*The Look of Things*, 173). Berger's chief example is, incidentally, Stevens' as well—Cézanne.[7] Despite his penchant for abstraction Stevens was a *plein air* poet, often composing on walks in the Hudson Palisades or Elizabeth Park. Many critics contend that in Stevens the imagination usurps the authority and priority of this stimulus world, drawing it into autotelic space. But the logic of Stevens' poems often goes the other way. (From "Of the Surface of Things": "In my room, the world is beyond my understanding; / But when I walk I see that it consists of three or four hills and a cloud" [CPP, 45].) The poems, I believe, carry their contingency with them and seldom claim to surmount it completely. If nature is, as he wrote, a "source of supply," it is also a condition of the imagination.

I will grant, for now, that in retaining landscape as the site of imaginative action Stevens withdraws from direct encounter with social and historical contingencies. But social and historical process, our constantly changing arrangements of reality, is what the transformation of landscape in Stevens is often about. "Life is an affair of people not of places. But for me it is an affair of places" (CPP, 901), Stevens wrote, "and this is the problem." He did not embrace the standard Romantic apologies for this preference for place over people. He reminds us that places are created *by* people. Landscape is not a sufficient partner in our self-location; it is not the only dimension in which we live. Certainly Stevens was well aware of what obsesses us since the Columbian quincentenary: that the national landscape on which we founded American identity involved more signifier than soil and required a critical erasure. To Latimer he writes of Crispin's colonizing venture in "Comedian": "I infer that, for you, environment means men and women; but for me, it means surroundings. . . . It is hard for me to say what would have happened to Crispin in contact with men and women, not to speak of the present day unemployed. I think it would have been a catastrophe for him" (*Letters*, 295). Post-colonial and feminist criticism will inevitably find fault with Stevens' representation of Southern regions, especially Florida, the Caribbean, and Mexico, as the subjugated other. The politics of Stevensian pastoral is not my subject here, however. Stevens was aware of the limits of the myth of the American Adam and does not merely repeat it. Even within the idealized image of America as landscape, as open, unpopulated spatial field, Stevens treats the desire for specular totalities and "relentless contact" (CPP, 27) as elusive and aesthetically inadequate. Certainly Crispin's ideal of a "blissful liaison" (28) between soil and intelligence requires "driving away / the shadow of his fellows / from the skies" (30)—depends, that is, on perpetuating the idea of an uncolonized wilderness, a primordial space which the mind can lay claim to. But Crispin's arrival in North America is not an instance of the Old Dominion reenacted, nor an immersion in natural plenitude. If the turn from Bordeaux to Yucatan is from cultural excess to natural plenitude, the turn from Yucatan to Carolina is from the blank plenitude of nature to landscape.

The transformation of geographical place to metaphorical site, from local particulars to landscape, does not imply an evasion of reality but a means of approaching it. Stevens' landscapes express the pragmatic and provisional nature of imaginative acts, tied to our position in time and place. They display the need constantly to return to a perceptual base in order to keep abstraction "blooded" (CPP, 333), and the reciprocal need to arrange reality as landscape. Later Stevens would emphasize the inevitability of landscape, its priority over our independent acts of consciousness. In "A Postcard from the Volcano" (128) the children, unaware, see nature not with relentless contact but with the mediations of history, with "what still is the look of things" left over from their landscaping parents. Stevens shifts accordingly, from the New World of *Harmonium* to Old World (Pompeian, Genevan, Swedish) scenes, and from agrarian to urban and suburban landscapes.

Stevens' lifelong habit of composing on walks is certainly not sufficient evidence against the notion of his poetic world as a purely fictive, autotelic space. But it is worth considering how extended experiences in parks and rural scenes, where landscapes constantly adjust in relation to the beholder's changing position, might have shaped his imagination. (For an interesting discussion of the walk as "occasion" for meditation see Roger Gilbert, *Walks in the World,* 75–106.) Stevens' early journals portray a rather unconvinced transcendentalist, retreating to nature's purer text, but suspicious of his allegorical readings of nature.[8] His journal of December 27, 1898, describes a walk through woods "avoiding paths as much as possible" and wondering, with his back to the "smoky noisy city," "why people took books into the woods to read in summertime when there was so much else to read there that one could not find in books" (*Letters,* 22). *What* can be read there he neglects to tell us. Instead, turning back toward the city, he hints at allegory, but with self-conscious irony. "Coming home I saw the sun go down behind a veil of grime. It was rather terrifying I confess from an allegorical point of view. But that is usually the case with allegory" (22).

Yet Stevens remains interested in the aesthetic, if not the epistemological satisfactions obtained there, particularly as broad vistas give way to particulars. In his journal he writes: "In a short time . . . these vast and broad effects lose their novelty and one tires of the surroundings. This feeling of having exhausted the subject is in turn succeeded by the true and lasting source of country pleasure: the growth of small, specific observation" (*Letters,* 30). This is the opposite of the Romantic logic of vision, in which daffodils become continous with the stars. The movement from broad vista and general proposition to close observation and attention to "the lyrics of song-sparrows" (30) *is* a logic, however, not a choice of one over the other. Often in Stevens' poetry we find this logic, which implies that a landscape must be established before any seeing can take place, even while that seeing may reveal particulars that call the authority of the landscape schema into question.

On business trips Stevens continued his youthful habit of walking in the countryside. The letters to his wife that record the observations on these walks portray a man uneasy away from home, struggling to find a perspective, to arrive, to see a landscape in his new surroundings. On extended business in Tennessee, Stevens wrote to Elsie describing a scene in which he cannot get his bearings: cool and damp, but it feels like summer; the roses are out though at home in Connecticut they could not be; the streets are shadowy from the foliage. He concludes: "I have always been of two minds about Tennessee. Sometimes I like it and sometimes I loathe it . . . this midway South is an uncertainty" (*Letters*, 206). But after a long walk in the Knoxville countryside he is able to describe a landscape with a broad prospect, and his tone is more positive. "From Knoxville to the South East, one can see the Appalachian Mountains. Out near the golf club, at the Western end of the city, there is a really swank view. The Tennessee River makes a great bend through woods and cliffs and hills and on the horizon run the blue ranges of the mountains" (207). From this broad prospect he moves on to enumerate the particular splendors of Knoxville, the "peonies, tulip-trees, locust trees . . . the motherly old hens guiding their broods of ber-bers through the grass, already deep," and so on. By deliberately placing himself in an elevated, spectatorial position, Stevens is able to direct his attention to details where before his environment was a blur. The pastoral selection of the details typifies Stevens' early idealizing impulse in landscape, which would give way in later work to a vision of "poverty" not less dependent on landscape for the revelation of particulars.

This movement from uncertain space to broad prospect to particular pleasures recalls the structure of "Anecdote of the Jar" (CPP, 60) and can help us read the poem as a pragmatic alternative to and not just a dialogue between imperial and objectivist impulses. In the poem more than in the letter Stevens reveals his awareness of the part he plays in constructing the vision he beholds, and at the same time the limits of his control over that vision. Even its title, "Anecdote of the Jar" over against "Ode on a Grecian Urn," marks it as provisional. The strategy of nineteenth-century representational painting was to make the jar invisible or all-encompassing, to present the order it defined as "natural" and absolute, to make the artist and observer feel one with the creator in his creation. Eliot's Chinese jar in *Four Quartets* provides another contrast, suspended in fictive space, a still point in a turning world. Unlike these, Stevens' jar and gesture are located in time and space, yielding to local particulars. At the same time, the previously unyielding, slovenly wilderness, converted to "surroundings" by the positioning of the jar, now "gives" of bird and bush as perhaps it could not before. The jar and the landscape it creates also bring those particulars into focus, just as in his experience of Tennessee Stevens needed a landscape in order to see the flowering trees. The giving of bird and bush mark both the limits of the jar and the landscape it defines, as well as a tribute paid to its qualified dominion. Stevens' imagination, in creating landscape, takes on an imperial air and defines an empire for the eye. Landscape is intoxicating in the power it lends to the beholder, but the placed jar may carry moonshine in an age of prohibition, and the intoxication wears off. No longer "of a port in air" (port wine? portent?), no longer a modernist aesthetic still point, the jar is still a portal, estabishing a point of view by which the world can begin to reveal itself for the beholder even as it qualifies his authority. This is not a poem of lost or regained presence but of affects, "The way when we climb a mountain / Vermont throws itself together" (CPP, 476). "Anecdote of the Jar" anticipates this language from "July Mountain" (1955) and implies Stevens' early awareness of the part he plays in the formation of landscape.[9] Furthermore, the jar is not an entirely alien object, but most likely a native product—not quite the essential image of a mythological age "out of the fields / Or from under his mountain" (476), but regional nonetheless and close at hand. Stevens' is not an organic but a contingency theory of poetry.

"Anecdote of the Jar," in combination with the letters Stevens wrote from Tennessee, reveals a process by which landscape enables the poet to respond to his world affectively. Landscape involves the exclusion of certain realities and the transfiguration of others, but it also has the effect of disclosing what is otherwise unobservable. A similar process is more elaborately revealed in "The Idea of Order at Key West."

The letters from Key West show Stevens in an environment full of disturbances—not a slovenly wilderness, certainly, but a disordered and forbidding place, no locus amoenus. James Longenbach, in his commentary on the pastoral impulses in the poem, notes how the warships at bay in Key West had disturbed the ease of the poet and are transformed to fishing boats in the poem (155–165). But if the poem is a version of pastoral, it is not a static pastoral or simple utopian escape. It disengages from political troubles (not only the Cuban political disorders but the Depression at home), but it stages an encounter with disturbances in the physical world and works out a temporary peace with them. Landscape becomes, that is, a theater in which the poet can confront troubles that may be more recalcitrant in the social world. But the poem turns toward the town. This is the pastoral of retreat and renewal, not an escape or a defense of the status quo. Stevens' emerging idea of order is by no means static or complacent. It helps to establish, not to delimit, an apprehension of the world.

This transposition of trouble from human to natural scene is already at work in the letters Stevens writes from Florida. The wind itself seemed, by a pathetic fallacy, determined to destroy his holiday composure: "While the sky is as blue and the sun as hot as ever, the wind cries in the eaves in a most melancholy manner, as if one were hearing the cry of the people who are tired of Winter and are whimpering about it" (*Let-*

ters, 258). The task of the imaginative man is to establish a landscape in this disturbed environment. "The Idea of Order at Key West" (CPP, 105) certainly does not open in a landscape. We begin with nature red in tooth and claw. Indeed, the wind he complains about in the letter finds its way into the poem, gasping against the sea's grinding force. The first response is to turn away from the alienating landscape to the solitary singer, as if the poet's task were simply to determine who she is, what her higher origin and destiny might be, indifferent to the background that is "merely a place." But Stevens will abandon this question and turn to the task of landscape, converting place to site in the second half of the poem. For Stevens, the idea of order turns out not to be thematic or nominative but spatial, not aural but visual first, a shaping of reality into landscape, not a theory of creation. In the second half of the poem, problems of expression and authority drop away and the poem turns to spectacle. Stevens redefines his project. Unable to establish questions of authority or metaphysics, he begins to construct a landscape.

The first landscape in "The Idea of Order at Key West," with its mountainous atmospheres and bronze shadows, its theatrical distances and high horizons, is certainly reminiscent of nineteenth-century American sublime painting. This spatial arrangement comes, the poet says, as a direct consequence of the song, just as the jar placed in Tennessee turns the wilderness to a surrounding. But the images become more technological, revealing (without diminishing) the constructedness and hence the contingency of the vision. Surveyor's or navigator's instruments mark "acutest" angles and "measured" distances. These distances are also "measured to the hour," subject to time. Their angle is subject to the angle of the sun, which is declining in the west; it will soon be night in the poem and the sublime bronze landscape will be erased. The vanishing point in this landscape (her song made the sky "acutest at its vanishing") is demystified while its effects are still admired. It no longer sustains a notion of the beholder as a bodiless, metaphysical mind. The nightscape that replaces these "mountainous atmospheres" has no single vanishing point but many "fragrant portals." It cannot be centered or totalized. The navigational imagery suggests the pragmatic side of these landscapes. They help us make our way across the "veritable ocean" which we cannot face unaided. The connection between the boat lights and the stars, then, is not an absolute but a pragmatic, navigational one.

But landscape is not the end of the poem. The poem has been moving through time and the sunset vista vanishes, giving way to a nightscape in which the human charting reveals itself. The lights of the fishing boats, like Frost's fireflies, gather in a transitory ordering of the stars. Finally the poem withdraws from its visual idea, becoming interiorized as "ghostlier demarcations" pivot into "keener sounds."

There is plenty of evidence that Stevens considered abandoning landscape during the 1930s, and certainly after "The Idea of Order at Key West" landscape, with its exalting vanishing points and theatrical distances, wanes as a scene of description. Gone too is the charting impulse that sought to place landscape and imagination on the same indeterminate map. But as Helen Vendler points out, the meditations themselves become more localized—prompted and propelled by the contours of actual place. As Stevens launched a critique of the composed, unified space of ideal and Romantic landscape, he began a new approach to the genre, in which landscapes become parts of a world rather than ways of summarily ordering a world of parts. Hence fragments of landscape enter meditations through the space of memory and allusion in poems such as "Like Decorations in a Nigger Cemetery," "Auroras of Autumn," and "An Ordinary Evening in New Haven."

As Stevens moved away from the scenic structures of the Romantic lyric, which inform "Sunday Morning" and "The Idea of Order at Key West," he also called into question the European painterly traditions of spatial mastery which had helped to support the Romantic vision of nature and which had been transposed onto the American scene. The names of Poussin, Claude, Constable, Corot arise in the poems, but it is the impact of these visions on American sensibility, through the art of Asher Durand, Thomas Moran, and Albert Bierstadt right up to George Inness and Albert Pinkham Ryder, that is his primary concern.[10] The imagery of Stevens' poems makes it clear how engaged he was with this landscape tradition in American painting. The exotic Caribbean, Mexican, and Floridian landscapes of these artists appear throughout *Harmonium*. Stevens' moon-lustered fields, sun-dazzled snow, and deer-studded wilderness all have their painterly analogues. These images had helped to shape how America imagined itself, grounding American vision in what was for Europeans an evasion of historical change. In Stevens' early poems, especially "Sunday Morning" and "The Idea of Order at Key West," he was certainly ready to conjure such sublime images of mountains and mountainous atmospheres as scenic symbols of individual freedom and self-determination. But at the same time he was developing a sense of the inadequacy of such images for a contemporary American aesthetic. "Constable they could never quite transplant / And our streams rejected the dim Academy" (CPP, 125). This is at once a call for an indigenous art, one that would draw its images from the soil rather than from tradition, and an acknowledgment that the whole representational model of the landscape prospect needed revision.

Stevens writes "Botanist on Alp (No. 1)" (CPP, 109) for an American audience, because he wants to suggest the inadequacy of the Claudean ideal (which so held the imaginations of American artists of the eighteenth and nineteenth century) to the modern American world. This ideal depended upon one-point perspective, making the beholder metaphysically powerful. It projected a vision of Nature as a unified, timeless realm against the vicissitudes of human history and appealed to the American wish to ground identity in a national landscape against the rotten institutions of Europe. Here the individual's yearning for expansion could be realized in the broad prospect. But American artists have always had trouble reconciling empiricist and idealist impulses. In proposing that Claude's Nature was itself "resting on pillars" of rhetoric that would crumble like the ruins it portrayed, Stevens abandons ideals of transcendent identity. As "botanist," he is drawn to the changing organic foreground, not the timeless geological background. He "lives by leaves," by transient things, rather than by final causes which remain for him in a cloud of unknowing: "corridors of clouds' / Corridors of cloudy thoughts / Seem pretty much one. / I don't know what." If "Marx has ruined Nature, / For the moment" by depriving "the peacocks and the doves" (Letters, 295) of their machinery of flight, their apostrophes and panoramas, he has not ruined it permanently for the botanist or the artist, who team up. The botanist, who insists on nature's variety rather than its grand design, has still the sense of "ecstatic air" for which he seeks a new landscape vision.

In surrendering the centered prospect of Claude (the world seen through arches) and the placid organic harmonies of Constable, Stevens resisted the alternative rhetoric of immersion that could grant natural authority to the poet's vision, the rhetoric that began to evolve in the nineteenth century with Martin Johnson Heade and emerged in the work of John Marin and Georgia O'Keeffe. In turning from Miltonic and Wordsworthian patterns he did not take the route of William Carlos Williams, aiming for "contact with the thing and nothing but the thing." For Stevens such sinking into place usually leads to a sense of panic in which signification and aesthetic order break down, in which he is washed away by magnitude. We need landscape to approach the world. The scope of consciousness cannot be grounded in the material field it seeks to embrace, even while it is dependent upon it.

"Notes Toward a Supreme Fiction" offers landscape as an alternative to both dreams of plenitude and dreams of dominion. The often quoted but misread line, "We live in a place that is not our own," suggests more than an assumption of alienation; it voices a qualified return to place. Stevens rejects dominion (we can't "own" the world), but makes a gesture of habitation which he began with Crispin but which remains incomplete. "Notes Toward a Supreme Fiction" is not a pastoral or aesthetic retreat from the dimension in which we live. Deconstructing Romantic correspondences as well as empiricism, we have tended to read poetic habitation as indifferent to place, as the writing of human value on the blank of nature, the substitution of poems for mountains. But Stevens never believed in that substitution, or even that blankness, for long. The physical world is neither intransigent glyph nor animate space. "The world is a force not a presence" (CPP, 911). Aesthetic landscape is for him a form of engagement with that force, a way of living in a world we do not own. Stevens' self-consciousness in the 1930s about the lack of social import to his work is clearly one reason for his shift away from the scenic use of landscape. But the poems also suggest the natural atrophy of a style (parallel to shifts in American cultural identity away from landscape). As he writes in "The American Sublime" (CPP, 106), "One grows used to the weather, the landscape and that" and turns to "the empty spirit in vacant space." These are the assertions of an un-endowed selfhood in an abysmal universe: certainly a recipe for modernist fictive spaces.[11] Critics have eagerly leaped from this cue to claim in Stevens what Joseph Carroll calls the "ontological supremacy of poetic figuration" (171). But this version of Stevens tells an incomplete story which largely bypasses *Parts of a World* in order to read "Notes Toward a Supreme Fiction" as the triumph of trope over matter.

Parts of a World serves as a crucial transition between the scenic idealizations of early Stevens and the later iconic idealizations that critics overemphasize. It is no accident, I think, that landscape is an important, repeated term in this volume, largely replacing the oppositional terms "reality" and "imagination" and now opposed to claims of priority and teleological truths, whether transcendent or immanentist. In arguing for what he calls "the adequacy of landscape" (CPP, 221) against the fruitless search for "the the" (186), Stevens' poetry sometimes sounds like simple perspectivism: "We were two figures in the woods. / We said we stood alone" (187). But he is more the pragmatist who knows that perception requires a gestalt, an investment in a landscape. The grapes grow fatter on the road home after the seeker turns from The Way to accept contingencies of time and place. Stevens' world of parts consists of more than the plurality of fictive worlds of fictive selves. These parts are situated in palpable places; they fail when they are not so situated.

Certainly the "anti-master man" of "Landscape with Boat" (CPP, 220–221), refusing to be situated, searching for the "neutral center" of the "single-colored, colorless primitive," is a painter in spite of himself (one in the objectivist mode which Stevens viewed as misguided). In "brushing away" he makes a gesture equivalent to a brushing on; his "phantom, uncreating night" is a scene among others ("floribund" even as it is moribund), but a fantasy escape rather than a landscape. More important to Stevens, in attempting to reach unmediated reality the anti-master man fails as an artist. His "supposed" space is not habitable. In his preoccupation with intellectually "arriving" (his journey at sea supported by a boat he will not acknowledge), he refuses to "live" and refuses the emotional arrivals available to him. Stevens' critique of the anti-master man argues rather laconically that "the world itself was the truth," including without hierarchy or center all its parts: the self, the illusions of color, the physical world as it plays upon our perceptions. But of course this "peddler's pie" (227), this assortment of parts, is not very satisfying either. We crave a landscape in which the ingredients will set. At the end of "Landscape with Boat" Stevens gives us an alternative figure of capable imagination, a latter-day Hoon who sits on a balcony above the Mediterranean, admiring the empire of his eye in which description becomes revelation; adjective, noun; singular, plural: "emerald / Becoming emeralds" (221). Appearances alone (not nature or metaphysics) declare the legitimacy of his reign. If the ascetic was the anti-master man, this latter figure is no Old Master but a different kind of Modernist. His empire of the eye has an ironic element as the personified "palms flap green ears in the heat." But he is imaginatively engaged with his surroundings. The boat (perhaps carrying the baseless anti-master man) enters the landscape of this beholder to break his solipsism. It reminds us of another perspective, another form of engagement, its wake another impression of reality. The two figures in "Landscape with Boat," then, represent a choice not between objectivism and solipsism, but between a deluded quest for transparence that leaves us at sea and a creative involvement with environment that affords aesthetic satisfaction but owns up to its limits and acknowledges the frame.

Perhaps a more defining position for *Parts of a World* is the edge of the bed in "The Latest Freed Man" (CPP, 187). The latest freed man, upon waking, acknowledges that there must be "a doctrine to this landscape" to replace the "old descriptions of the world," but the investment of doctrine in landscape allows "the moment's rain and sea, / The moment's sun" to come into his window. If the speaker of that poem forgets the window, pretentiously calling it "being without description," he is just another doctor. The speaker is more the object of Stevens' irony than the figure beholding the landscape, the freed man as the speaker calls him, who never claims to know reality, only vivid landscape. Stevens' later arguments for "description without place" and the opposite "freedom" entailed should be held to a similar skepticism about freedom (that is, the freedom of the metamorphosing imagination against the bindings of the material world). "Crude Foyer" (CPP, 271) is a kind of critic's Rorschach test with its equivocal argument "that the mind / Is the eye, and that this landscape of the mind / Is a landscape only of the eye," and with its ambiguous referents of "there" and "here." But if the "foyer of the spirit" is like the balcony in "Landscape with Boat," it is not a place in itself, not a detached space, but a perspective. We would expect a foyer to lead us into a chamber, a bronze decor, a private room for a rendezvous with the interior paramour. But if Stevens eventually hypothesizes the spirit as a final space, thought and imagination end here in the contingent space of the foyer in a landscape, a space without closure.

Despite its celebration of the "gaiety of language," "Esthétique du Mal" (CPP, 278–286) offers one of Stevens' clearest cautions against aesthetic autonomy. For if the world is poor, its poverty must be cured rather than abandoned because "the greatest poverty is not to live in the physical world." In order to make this assertion palatable Stevens must retreat, in this poem, from the volcano as object of the sublime (so popular with nineteenth-century Americans, who flocked to the base of Etna and Vesuvius). The aestheticizing of European disaster was too distasteful during World War II. He closes, instead, on an image of fertile North America with its "green corn gleaming" as the appeal against metaphysical flight. This may indeed seem like one more version of pastoral (to which Stevens has tended all along), the idealized image of America evoked in our anthems. But the assertion that hope must be based on "living as and where we live" will outlast these idealizations and confirm the importance of landscape as a perennial genre. Sight remains Stevens' line of contingency, to what exceeds the capacities of the will. ("One might have thought of sight but who could think of what it sees" [281].) If the seen world represents the spatial expansion of the imagination, it also represents a challenge of renewal to the poet. "The imagination loses vitality as it ceases to adhere to what is real" (645). The poet seeks connectedness in his aesthetic. Stevens suggests not only that creation overwhelms human capability, that the physical absorbs the metaphysical, but that our "supreme fictions," our metaphysical inventions, learn their changes less from autonomous compositional laws than from physical surroundings:

So many selves, so many sensuous worlds,
As if the air, the mid-day air, was swarming
With the metaphysical changes that occur,
Merely in living as and where we live.

(CPP, 287)

It may seem that I have made Stevens sound too much like Thoreau. That would be a healthy antidote to the obsession for linking Stevens with Emerson, that despiser of contingencies. One can certainly hear Thoreau in the outspoken "inchling" in "Bantams in Pine-Woods" (CPP, 60) who "bristles in these pines" of Georgia and scolds the "portly Az-can" (of Emersonian descent) for his inflations. Stevens' winter landscape in "The Snow Man" (8) is much more than Frost's faded paper sheet of "Hyla Brook," inscribed with the speaker's nostalgia. The Snow Man loves "the things [he] love[s] for what they are" in terms of the "first idea," after our sentimental attachments have been cleared away. But the later Stevens, having seen so many creative seasons come and go, addresses himself more directly to the superfluity that drives such seasonal changes, and the accumulation of the sloughed-off forms of the past. The grand idea of Nature has grown shabby ("the green house never so badly needed paint"), and "the great pond" of "The Plain Sense of Things" (428) hardly resembles Thoreau's Walden (although it does describe contemporary Walden pretty well). Stevens' pond is a trope of mind more explicitly than Thoreau's or even his own earlier "teeming millpond or furious mind" in "Like Decorations in a Nigger Cemetery" (121–128), where perceptual and symbolic landscapes ebb and flow. The reflective surface is dulled by the patina of so many who have looked before. Frost's "emulating flies" pointed upward, at least, but the "repetitiousness of men and flies" bespeaks the redundant mortality of all human forms.

But "The Plain Sense of Things" is also a landscape of the eye—even our idea of plainness toward the world is borrowed from perceptions of the world's own changes. I have already discussed this poem in connection with the theme of waste and superfluity, but it is also central to our understanding of the need for nature and the adequacy of landscape. We need nature to figure our own habits toward nature; the pond of the mind begins in Elizabeth Park. In "The Plain Sense of Things" the imagination turns to surroundings to school itself in its own necessities. The idea of necessity is itself contingent. Thoreau went to Walden in a less exhausted mood to "know life." His pond is not a dirty glass but a transparency and a shimmering mirror. Stevens' pond with its surroundings in "The Plain Sense of Things" is always a landscape, not a revelation of nature. When he claims "the lack of imagination had itself to be imagined" I hear less the resurgence of pride in the triumph of the imagination over fate (as Harold Bloom has suggested) than an acknowledgment that landscape is inevitable, whether our gaze is outward or inward. How far we are from the perspectiveless ideal of the Snow Man and the imperial gaze of Hoon. Stevens' imperious Romantic "walks across the lessened floors," the lessons of modern existence having reduced his Palaz, and even its Thoreauvian antithesis, to a "minor house." Nature must be reimagined since "the greenhouse never so badly needed paint." "Need" is a misleading term here, however, since it is the superfluity of human and natural creativity that stimulates change. Thoreau would strip down all superfluity and discover only the truth of necessity. Stevens recognizes in Thoreau's impulse to reduction a last nostalgia. Lyric superfluity is already bubbling up in the first stanza of the poem, through the superfluous language and negative intensification ("in . . . in . . . in") with which Stevens describes the imagination, "inanimate in an inert savoir." Stevens turns from the elegiac mood as an outlet for his lyric energy. Loss and longing are not the only roles for the imagination, and the "waste" of the lilies suggests the opposite of barrenness. Here landscape is neither transparent nor opaque; it is littered with the waste of human imagining, a mutable nature strewn with deteriorating urban forms. The poet of "The Plain Sense of Things" chooses adjective, not noun. The "rat [that] comes out to see" is no transparent eyeball and wears no turban. He is a scavenger. His angle of vision does not allow the wide prospect of the elevated Romantic beholder, but a nearly horizontal perspective, in which imagination and reality become so close as to be indistinguishable. This is evidently not the rat that appears in Eliot's *The Waste Land*, a leftover from the trenches ("a rat crept softly through the vegetation / dragging its slimy belly on the bank" [*Collected Poems*, 60]). Eliot's poem suggests an anti-pastoral withdrawal from nature. "The river's tent is broken" and the pastoral world has departed with its nymphs. But Paul Alpers has read Stevens' rat as a latter-day pastoral figure, the sign of renewal entering the poem of waste (307). There is a new kind of harmony in this muddy reality where nature and culture slide together, a repetitiousness of men and flies. This nature includes the "waste of lilies" and the waste of words as part of what it is. The imagination finds a role for itself and identifies with nature (necessity) in its production of waste. "Necessity" in this poem is a floating signifier, calling us back to the "need" of the house for paint, and conversely to the reduction of imagination to the "blank cold" of things as they are, without the ornaments of metaphor, but also calling us forward to the poem's logical turn toward imagination again. An unimagined nature is by definition (and logical 'necessity') an imagined one.

In eliminating deity from vision in the poems after "Sunday Morning" and "The Idea of Order at Key West," in coming down from the hilltop to take this horizontal perspective, the rat's-eye view, too low to see the reflections of heaven, Stevens positions himself close to contingencies (leaves, mud, the waste of lilies). This is the "near and dear" without the erotic drive toward nature. In this way I think "The Plain Sense of Things" represents a base landscape to which the poet can "return" (who cannot "return" to a pristine condition of presence) when "the total grandeur of its total edifice" and even the consoling fictions of the leaves and the rock collapse.[12]

Critics have seized on the several architectural forms in Stevens' late poetry as evidence of a shifting idea of sublimity. They are fine for Rome, but Stevens continued to prefer American landscape even as he surrendered any sublime aspirations and any sensuous hedonism in it. Stevens also gave up his treasured pastoral images of America, whether the feminized tropics of imaginative renewal, the "berries ripening in the wilderness" (CPP, 56), the open cattle ranges of Oklahoma, or the more agrarian "green corn gleaming" (286). In the late poetry place becomes important again, particularly unidealized places near home in industrial Connecticut. Such places, if they are taken up into the meditating mind, are borrowed rather than appropriated.

"In Connecticut, we never lived in a time / When mythology was possible," Stevens writes at the end of his career (CPP, 476). To live as and where we are may mean to live without essential images, to live with a series of landscapes only. If this relationship to the physical world was not the erotic consummation, the "blissful liaison" sought by Crispin and his Romantic forebears, it was still a liaison, not a submission, conquest, or evasion. Stevens' paramour may be, by the end, entirely interior, but he still looks outside himself for an aesthetic habitation in a world he knows he cannot own, something besides mere simulation, "sleep's faded papier-mâché," something glimpsed through the window as "part of the colossal sun" (452).

Timespace and Tragedy

Stevens concerned himself very little with the impact of technological change on the landscape. The "funicular" of "Botanist on Alp" figures the machinery of transport, not of transportation. Yet like Frost, he is responsive to the sense of an accelerated pace of movement and change in modern life and the challenge these present to lyric's quest for permanence. Landscape, which has been at the center of that quest, becomes in Stevens a picture of temporality. His reading of James, Bergson, Vico, and others had instilled in him an idea of the evolutionary, processional nature of mind and world, in contrast to the discrete, discontinuous frames that our understanding and representation impose. Like Frost, Stevens confronts his emotional struggle with knowledge of the flux, and expresses lyric's longing to evade time's force. But if Frost makes a compromise between evolutionary time and lyric time, Stevens expresses a tragic tension. In "Auroras of Autumn," Stevens' meditation on the ephemeral landscapes of his life, he attempts to create an image that would embody the reality of endlessly emerging and dissolving form, a landscape of time, a fluctuating frame.

I have been arguing that landscape in Stevens is not only an inevitable, but also an enabling structure for human cognition, and a metaphor for human arrangements. It involves a paradox, however. We cannot see until we have landscape, but then we have only landscape, and the sense of a world exceeding our arrangements of it persists. Landscape presumes the interaction of human structures and non-human environment, an interaction kept vital through constant reconfiguration. The mind is not a mirror of nature, nor is nature merely a trope of human mind or spirit. Stevens' emphasis on provisional landscapes aligns him with the philosophical pragmatism of his time, but it also anticipates cognitive science's recent emphasis on enactive thought and embodied mind.

Stevens' emphasis on landscape continues to suggest a visual model of cognition, however, and a spatial model of reality, in which the subject is spectator. This emphasis links him to the Romantic landscape tradition. But whereas the Romantic natural landscape involves a spatial unification of time and thus a liberation from its force, and the modernist mythic landscape absorbs time into autotelic pattern, Stevens' visionary project in the late poetry is to infuse the experience of space with the sense of time, to make space dynamic and plural, not fixed and unified.[13] Nowhere is this clearer than in "The Auroras of Autumn" (CPP, 355–363). Stevens learned from Bergson that metaphysics and the spiritual involve the intuition of time, and "Auroras" is an attempt to represent that intuition in a way that goes well beyond Bergson.[14] On the other hand, "Auroras" is a tragic poem, for it sets a recognition of the fundamentally temporal and uncentered nature of reality against an unattainable desire for centered wholeness conceived in spatial terms. "Auroras" discovers that nature is not an expression of malevolent design, that it is "innocent" in the sense that its being is without purpose or intention. The "serpent" as "master of the maze" is a human projection. But this leaves the human perceiver without a fixed point of reference, since that "innocence" is not containable as knowledge. Stevens' poem is moving both because of its exhilarating representation of landscape riven by time, and its tragic feeling toward this vision. The metaphor of theater provides an integration of spatial and temporal thinking. Tragic theater in particular is central to the entire poem, not just a phase of it, as many have argued. Even the pure principle of innocence arises within the theatrical model.

In "Auroras" Stevens dismantles the rationalized space that Erwin Panofsky so brilliantly described in 1924 in *Perspective as Symbolic Form*. The invention of the vanishing point, Panofsky argued, removed given, psychophysiological space, which is defined by an unhomogeneous, ephemeral sense of experience, to a constructed, homogeneous, unchanging and boundless plane of reference, thereby extending the realm of the self. Romantic, visionary space was, he said, a spiritualizing of rational space and an internalization of it as power. Modernism shattered the illusion of representational space, highlighting the ephemerality and disjunctiveness of the world of perception, though it reconstituted spatial order and the idea of the eternal on an abstract plane. But Stevens' auroras are not the icon of modernist eternal presence. They begin as part of nature and return to figure it in its ephemeral and variable aspect of reality. They figure, as well, the perspectivism and relativism of human knowledge and the perceiving mind.

Stevens' other poems in *The Auroras of Autumn* are typically modern in their longing for an eternal, infinite point of reference, but his supreme fiction remains a figure of the unfulfilled will rather than a triumph of the aesthetic. Since perception is embodied, it is part of the world of change it perceives. In "This Solitude of Cataracts" (CPP, 366), for instance, Stevens offers a version of transcendence, yet the conditional mood and third-person narration suggest a certain distance from the ideal. The figure in the poem has a radically internalized experience of Heraclitean truth: "he never felt twice the same about the flecked river," a reverse of the Romantic. Daniel Peck, in *Thoreau's Morning Work*, argues that in describing his trip down the Merrimack River the writer unifies time in terms of this horizontal, spatial metaphor. In this way Thoreau overcomes all sense of loss and discontinuity. But Stevens' river of time will not settle into a single spatial plane.

There is no cataract in "This Solitude of Cataracts," no stationary blast of waterfalls, no rainbow, and no firm mountain under the flow to anchor the soul to the eternal. Nor can the mind extricate itself from the temporality of its position. The only mountains are reflected, illusionary ones on the surface, "thought-like Monadnocks," ruffled by the skeptical ducks. "There seemed to be an apostrophe that was not spoken" because the transcendental object has been removed even though a place for it remains. The meditative "he" would like to identify with his principle of permanence, literally *casting* his imagination in the mold of the fixed ideal. He would be a "bronze man breathing under archaic lapis . . . / Breathing his bronzen breath at the azury center of time" with the woods buttoned down and the "moon nailed fast." But he has no Yeatsian sage to carry him away from the flux. Indeed, the central icon of this volume (as not before) is the river itself, Swatara, a literal river in Pennsylvania but also a symbol (echoed in its very name, "swarthy water") of fluent and obscure being. This is not Wordsworth's friendly Sylvan Wye that promises continuity, or even Eliot's anagogic river in the unreal city of the mind, but something fundamentally involved with change, generation and degeneration, without apotheosis. Stevens' posited "countryman" for Swatara has a mind of river, but is no more human than the snowman. Stevens' central man is increasingly evolutionary: a "giant of nothingness, . . . the giant ever changing, living in change" (380). The poet cannot place himself at the center through this figure on the horizon, cannot identify with this figure. What he represents in *The Auroras of Autumn* is not "being without history," but rather the loss of this fiction, less nostalgic than tragic. As Stevens writes in "The Beginning" (368), which ironically opens with "so summer comes in the end to . . . rust and rot," the present has the tragic dimension of time: "Now, the first tutoyers of tragedy / Speak softly, to begin with, in the eaves."

Of course I am not surprising anybody by arguing that the poem "The Auroras of Autumn" is about change and the fear of death as these are recognized in terms of embodied perception. Critics have connected this preoccupation with Stevens' own aging process or the death of his friend Henry Church (Patke), and even the threat of the atomic bomb (Berger). But I want to resist a tendency to read the poem as a victory over these through imaginative power (Bloom), mythic resolution (Carroll), or Dasein (Voros). This condition of knowledge and perception is tragic for us. Critical discussions of landscape are especially entrenched, of late, in the Heideggerian reading that emphasizes the permanence of Being over the transitoriness of Becoming. But images of homelessness and spatial instability haunt "The Auroras of Autumn" from the beginning. "These lights represent a tragic and desolate background," he tells us. I want to take Stevens at his word and understand the poem's tragic insight, its homelessness, and its bold engagement with (rather than escape from) the temporal "drama that we live."

Henri Bergson inveighed against our tendency to speak of time in spatial terms; he highlighted fluency in his own spatial metaphors. The rational construction of time, he said, has led to an image of a straight line with a series of beads on it—discrete, measurable units of time. In its place he would put something like the auroras, "flux of fleeting shades merging into one another." Bergson maintains, with Darwin and Freud, an evolutionary scheme in which the past is erased or carried into the present in an accumulative fashion, unguided by any eternal principle or teleology. This is not unlike Stevens' idea of the ultimate poem or giant on the horizon, a dynamic totality made up of the accumulative efforts of all imaginative human activity, and evolving with it. While Bergson's sense of time has much to do with consciousness, it has little to do with the body or with ideologies and institutions. It is these latter things that Stevens exposes to time in "Auroras." The longing for "being without history" is tested against a condition of being impacted with history. In this context Marx, although he was Stevens' nemesis in many ways (a materialist, different in "nature" from the idealist poet, Stevens said), anticipates the poem. Marx writes of the modern condition:

> All fixed, fast-frozen relations, with their train of ancient and venerable prejudices and opinions, are swept away. All new-formed ones become antiquated before they can ossify. All that is solid melts into air, all that is holy is profaned, and men at last are forced to face . . . the real conditions of their lives and their relations with their fellow men. (*The Communist Manifesto*, 25)

Ancestral themes and codes of brotherhood do indeed melt into air in Stevens' poem. Again, Stevens would not accept Marx's materialist analysis of the "real conditions of [our] lives" or our society, but he would certainly agree that these are exposed in modernity. For Stevens, the negations, the cancellations, are never final. Not only human institutions, but the idea of nature itself is part of this flux—not, as Thoreau would have it, "a solid bottom everywhere." The poet himself, like Marx, is an "irrepressible revolutionist," though he may long for being without history.

Stevens opens "The Auroras of Autumn" (CPP, 355–363) on sky, and the boreal light seems to dissolve surface.

This is where the serpent lives, the bodiless.
His head is air. Beneath his tip at night
Eyes open and fix on us in every sky.

Or is this another wriggling out of the egg,
Another image at the end of the cave,
Another bodiless for the body's slough?

This is where the serpent lives. This is his nest,
These fields, these hills, these tinted distances,
And the pines above and along and beside the sea.

This is form gulping after formlessness,
Skin flashing to wished-for disappearances
And the serpent body flashing without the skin.

This is the height emerging and its base
These lights may finally attain a pole
In the midmost midnight and find the serpent there,

In another nest, the master of the maze
Of body and air and forms and images,
Relentlessly in possession of happiness.

This is his poison: that we should disbelieve
Even that. His meditations in the ferns,
When he moved so slightly to make sure of the sun,

Made us no less as sure. We saw in his head,
Black beaded on the rock, the flecked animal,
The moving grass, the Indian in his glade.

We are on our way to a Romantic scheme in which human consciousness expands to become a vessel of the divine. But the ethereality of the auroras is of a different order from the fog and glow of Romanticism, which dissolve material surface to disclose metaphysical depth and height. In Stevens' poem the physical keeps reasserting itself to frustrate this transfer without anchoring us elsewhere. The auroras can't be penetrated, nor can they be framed. Much has been said and repeated about the ambiguity and instability of the "this," in the opening canto; it is at once multiply epideictic and self-referential. I would simply add that the instability of the referent is a consequence not only of the uncertain ontological status of the object, but also of its nature as motion. "This" becomes "that" as another "this" comes into focus. They form parts of a whole only if the whole is referred back to the heterogeneous and ephemeral nature of the phenomenal world. Such an uncertain "this" also suggests

that the beholder's body is involved; the eye is not the foreman perform-
ing the mind's desire, dissociated from, but master of, the flux.

The Heideggerian reading of Stevens' birthing and sloughing serpent
suggests that we free ourselves of interpretive structures and the rational
divisions of space, but never have to leave home.[15] Home just gets bigger,
until the interval between self and world dissolves. But the thinking in
"Auroras" does not lead to dwelling; Stevens is never at home in his
houses, or in the world, because the center is a moving target. The ser-
pent's tip and head are loosed from a unified spatial referent. He can't be
caught. In a reversal of Romantic gazing, the beholder becomes bound
in perspective. He is not the disembodied eye projecting the self into the
zodiac but the embodied "object" of starry "eyes [that] open and fix on
us in every sky." However, this personification of nature as Fate does not
coalesce. There is no vanishing point but our own ultimate vanishing.
Hierarchies of body and spirit reverse throughout, and bodiless spatial
images turn back into bodily temporal ones. This serpent's source may
be associated with Plato's "egg" of unity between spirit and matter, but it
is also a figure of generational process. Physical forms dissolve as well as
celestial ones. The poet struggles for location in a string of deictics
"above and along and beside" that lead nowhere. The "base" is no more
secure than the apex as the mind slides along the vertical axis of the
scene. Images of consumption (form gulping after formlessness) displace
those of generation in a struggle of body and form, the body "flashing
without skin," less a figure of divine spirit than one of the body in time.

It is with this framework of compressed temporality and spatial insta-
bility that Stevens enters, in the third person, the realm of memory,
launch pad of Romantic transcendence. But absence rules here, and for-
getting. The "we" of canto I has given way to an impersonal mode, and
the past, as it arises in the mind, remains past. Memory works with land-
scape rather differently than in Frost's reverse-reel vision of "Directive."
We cannot find our way back to this place.

Farewell to an idea . . . A cabin stands,
Deserted, on a beach. It is white,
As by a custom or according to

An ancestral theme or as a consequence
Of an infinite course. The flowers against the wall
Are white, a little dried, a kind of mark

Reminding, trying to remind, of a white
That was different . . .

If the cabin stands deserted, the memorial flowers remind us, or try to remind us, of its former vividness. The "was" of "a white that was different," an all-color white, briefly becomes a "here" of presence ("here being visible is being white"), but the ellipses relinquish the project and the duller white of the bleaching, degenerative sands of time overcomes the scene. We have a kind of reversal of the Shelleyan sublime here, for the "dome" of eternity becomes a many-colored pageantry, while the shattered glass of mutable things is white with the pallor of age. The next canto relinquishes presence in a similar way. The figure recollecting the warmth of maternal presence is left out in the cold and turns from the cabin lights to the "frigid brilliances" of the auroras. The mother's transparence inhabits a present tense of remembered image—"she gives transparence"—but her present is discontinuous with the present of the figure on the beach, whose time ultimately subsumes her own: "she too is dissolved, she is destroyed." The rifle butt raps violently in the breach of these two presents. We are made to feel the transience of an idea rather than a continuous present of flux.

As the mother's womby presence is ravished, the father's creative powers come under scrutiny. "The father sits / in space, wherever he sits, of bleak regard, / As one that is strong in the bushes of his eyes." He can say "yes to no" and transcend this destructive force because he turns to "supernatural preludes" that he hears within, to which the pageantry of change might be disciplined and tuned. Defying the rules of time and space that have defeated the mother, this figure of capable imagination would seem to be the ideal defender of the mother's house. But instead, he brings the riot in. Where the maternal peace is subject to time, the paternal riot becomes its enactment. Stevens exercises his flamboyance in this superman image, outdoing Milton's satanic extravagance in his subversion of spatiotemporal categories. But with the father's theater we are also tuned to the majesty of Nietzsche's *The Birth of Tragedy out of the Spirit of Music*.[16] Throughout the poem Stevens wavers about the identity of this father—is he Fate or Imaginative Power? Bloom of course sees Stevens settling, finally, on the latter. But in his many aliases this father weakens as a centering figure, and his incarnational appearance at the end of the poem is less a promise of redemption from time than a return to it.

The father has the dignity of a Yeatsian sage or ecstatic dancer in canto IV, a figure in the world but not of it. But if the "Master" represents the universal lyric ideal of transcendental wholeness, his "present throne"— the condition of modernity—calls into question the Logos itself. The only prelude the poet hears is the naked wind, a challenge to lyric ambition: he must give up the motionless center and find identity in motion. The so-called master of the maze is shown in canto V to be something less than masterful and more like the head of one of Shakespeare's inept theatrical troupes, or, as Vendler has suggested, a Prospero reduced to the antics of a Caliban. And this is, as we shall see, a play within a play, for the next canto describes the landscape itself as a theater. The theatrical scenes of canto V are the portrait of a culture as conjured by the father of canto IV: the mother as the principle of community, of men coming together in common need and fellowship; the father as the forming of that community into institutions and traditions. Yet it is clear at the end of the stanza that nothing authorizes these forms, that the changes are improvisatory, that the father is an illusionist fetching props rather than a transcendental master—and indeed, their theatricality, their function as illusionary props, is sharply exposed. Nature itself is a prop, something built within the communal house, not outside it, a mere construction ("vistas and blocks of wood") to give background to the improvisatory comi-tragic drama emerging as the unwritten contract of the community, "musicians dubbing at a tragedy." To dub is not only to accompany with voice or sound, but to invest with a name or title. To mooch is to steal, making the father's fetching an even less authorized appropriation. The poet's voice again stands outside the family scene, outside the social contract, skeptical and ready for change.

Yet the next canto (VI) is not a transparent picture of reality over against the constructions of culture. "It is a theater floating through the clouds." Having undermined the supernatural authority of the father, Stevens has not disposed of theater. The poet has returned to the auroras, and these too are now viewed as a theater. The theater is no longer within the mother's house but something more panoramic. The pageants are not only out of the air but in it, and reality is a theater without a proscenium. Like the "this" of canto I, the "it" of this canto ("it is a theater") hangs unassigned, pointing back implicitly to the auroras but not specifying what they represent in the poet's mind—nature, presumably, given the landscape imagery, but also human structures: "corridors," "porticos." Rather than identify geological and architectural forms as marks of stability, Stevens represents landscape as a houseless, floating world: mountains running like water, "cloud transformed to cloud transformed again," a theater that gives no shelter.

The convergence of theater imagery and landscape imagery is worth a further look here because it has been treated in the criticism of the poem as a transition—we move, it is said, out of the father's theater and into the discovery of an innocent (that is, untheatrical) earth embodied in the mother. But I tend to read the passage as foundational rather than transitional. The presiding trope of the poem is, of course, landscape, but landscape in Stevens is not transparence—it is an ordering of the natural world according to a particular perspective, a part partaking of the whole of reality but not identical with it. Theater, on the other hand, has the power to suspend our disbelief, to engage us collectively in an idiom that speaks of the world even as it is not the world. So if landscape is less than nature, theater is more than artifice. They do not represent opposites so much as versions of each other.[17] If landscape is the extension of an individual into environment through perception, theater gives that image a communal component. As Stevens hints at the end of his poem, where he invites us into a circular theology—invites us to "contrive" a specter to "contrive" a whole—there is no getting beyond theater. Innocence as an idiom goes on within the drama, and nature, for us, is known only as landscape. Both involve an endless sequence of scene changes.

Nature as "pure principle" and not as something in time or space may give a horizon to theater. But while Stevens posits this innocent, Adamic transparence, his interest is entirely in the "drama that we live," and that drama is constituted of the desire for that unattainable ideal—a tragic drama, one played in a theater. Indeed, the idea of innocence as pure principle is itself a theatrical idea and one that emerges dramatically.

For a time Stevens exults in the mere spectacle of nature. He has certainly exorcised the serpent's demonic aspect. Theatricality recedes as the poet delights in the auroras' motion "running like water, wave on wave, / Through waves of light," directed "to no end, / Except the lavishing of itself in change." This filling of space with motion rather than fixing space in a motionless ideal produces the aspect of "magnificence" the poem celebrates. And yet the human mind seeks structure—wants to form the moving color into a destiny. I disagree with those who see Stevens disposing of theatricality at this point, rebelling against metaphoric deferral and confronting the "first idea" of the auroras. The tragic drama begins with "in a single man contained," when the poet puts his own body onto the stage, which heretofore was all scenery. To know change intimately, not just as spectacle, is to participate in the destruction of the most fundamental trope of the poem—the serpent itself as a figure of change. To figure or name change is to halt it. "He opens the door of his house [the house he has made of this naming] on flames." It is burning inside and out. This is living theater, but theater nevertheless, a tragic drama of the struggle between our embodied, theatrical perception and a principle of innocence we set against it. Ironically, the antitheatrical critics label this as the advent of the postponed "denouement."

Bloom argues that the poet, by containing the first idea in his mind, has mastered the maze. But this spatial contraction of the auroras from wide-wise splash to house fire is not in the nature of mastery, since the frame that would contain time is consumed by it. Stevens is explicit: it is fear, not mastery, he feels as he opens the door, though in the third person it may be cathartic.

Indeed, we are still in the theater in canto VII, broadened again in scale, darkened in shade, and accelerated in scene change. It is common to read the cantos after VII as a shift away from "jetted tragedy." Under the law that "it must change" Stevens reduces the "mystical cabala" behind all the "jettings" to a "flippant communication under the moon," of which he is the impresario. "Destiny" becomes "slight caprice." But if the auroras are returned to an endless decentering, the mind is not enthroned (as Bloom's logic of transumption would suggest) for long. Tragedy reasserts itself within this commedia dell'arte.

The poem's turn to innocence has been read as a route out of tragedy. But innocence (anti-theatricality) is a pastoral contrivance, especially as it is associated with nature in the American landscape tradition, a "being without history" that this poem refuses. Innocence is no less theatrical than malice. Helen Vendler is rightly uncomfortable with this part of the poem, calling innocence "a wish dispelling a dream of malice," but I think Stevens provokes this skepticism. It may be important to recognize what Stevens is bidding farewell to here: not an embodiment but an "idea." Is the idea of maternal transparence discredited, or merely lost to time in its past embodiment? The distinction between experience and idea may be moot, since for Stevens to believe in transparence is to experience it. Yet it is worth remembering this farewell when the idea of innocence and transparence is rescued from time and embodiment later in the poem, extracted as "pure principle." Though the conditions of consciousness limit us and cause us to identify fate with malice, we can posit as "pure principle" an innocent and transparent nature. Yet insofar as the principle enters experience, it is tragic. In the first "farewell to an idea" is a warning about how to apprehend the last illusion of the poem.

For Bloom, this innocence is "fresh imaginative possibility," "casting death out" (*Wallace Stevens: The Poems of Our Climate*, 276). For Joseph Carroll, it is "a teleological principle of sentient relation" (255), mythically embodied in the mother, yet simultaneously associated with the father, the master of the maze, "the origin of space and time . . . and not contained by them." Whatever Stevens may mean by innocence (and I think he asserts rather than explains the notion), it is framed by theater, arises in a drama of desire, and is a matter of effects, not origins. Innocence produces an "idiom" which is subject to time, as is all human discourse. In the poem a narrative is imposed on innocence; it enters time and thus the "tutoyers of tragedy" speak softly once again.

The sense of a tragic dimension to "Auroras" becomes most pointed in allusions to *Hamlet,* the story of Denmark, a northern place where presumably the aurora borealis is most often seen. The parallel between the "naïve pretense of sleep" in the father's theater in canto X, and the innocent state in which the Danes later "lay sticky with sleep," recalls the dumbshow in Shakespeare's play, where Claudius' guilt is mimed. The Danes in "Auroras" do not, admittedly, "live alone" in their bee-loud glade. They represent achieved communal harmony and Heideggerian dwelling in place. But how tenuous it is. In a poem that begins with the specter of the father, we must see these Danes as doomed and their state as rotten. Stevens surely plays Hamlet, the discontent, bringing the wintry feel of death into the hearty land. The mother recalled from canto IV is "still-starred" and everlasting, but perhaps also ill-starred, which may be why, in canto III, her family, like Ophelia, say "goodnight, goodnight" with such regret. "Shall we be found hanging in the trees next spring?" Stevens asks concerning the honeycomb existence, the fullness of bee-ing. It is a question that Hamlet often asks. The question hangs ambiguously; it echoes from Hamlet's suicidal thoughts and the political distress of his world, to resonate with Stevens' own contemporary culture. There is no "innocent" talk of racial brotherhood and motherland in Stevens' postwar world. Heiddeger's ideal of "dwelling" is unredeemable. The stanza anticipates homelessness, as bees abandon their hives and give up the orders they have created, to swarm elsewhere and create anew. But since this is tragedy, a shadow falls on the sense of renewal. Death is outlandish and anti-social, something "only the two [man and Death] could share," for, as Homer tells us, "men live toether, but each man's death is his own." The "tutoyers of tragedy" are speaking "loudly" at this point. Giving up his wish to be at home in the world, Stevens returns to the cosmic vision of the auroras, "like a great shadow's last embellishment," and that "last" tolls the end of vision and the withdrawal of innocence into endless cancellation which the poem can never comprehend. The balance between tragic and comic vision that "Auroras" seeks is rehearsed in the experimental formulas of the final canto. The poet plays Polonius as he reviews the possibilities. How should the drama be classified ("tragical-comical-historical-pastoral, scene individual or poem unlimited . . .")? This work, as part of Stevens' grand Poem Unlimited, settles after many permutations ("unhappy people in a happy world"; "happy people in an unhappy world"; and so on) on a tragic imbalance—"an unhappy people in a happy world"—and exchanges the "hushful paradise" of dwelling in innocent earth for the agonies of battle in "hall harridan." Frost would, however playfully or ironically, make us "whole again beyond confusion" and return us to a womb-like dwelling where the waters of time are restorative. Stevens' vision is one of heroic struggle and fire to the end.

The poet remains true to his northerly landscape, drawing his last scene from *Beowulf* instead of Shakespeare. The phrase "hall harridan" has always grated on my ear, especially as followed by "hushful" and "haggling." It seems "outlandish," ungrammatical, a verbal extremity quite different from others in Stevens. It sounds, indeed, like *Beowulf*, in its multiply alliterative *h*'s ("Hrean weard in Heorote; heo under heol-fre"). The mother's peace is disturbed in the hall of the communal Danes when the hell-dame Grendel's mother attacks:

> She came to Heorot. There, inside the hall,
> Danes lay asleep, earls who would soon endure
> a great reversal, once Grendel's mother
> attacked and entered. Her onslaught was less
> only by as much as an amazon warrior's
> strength is less than an armed man's
> when the hefted sword, its hammered edge
> and gleaming blade slathered in blood,
> razes the sturdy boar-ridge off a helmet.
>
> (*Beowulf*, 89–91)

If in "Auroras" the specter of the sky gives up relentless happiness for the relentless maelstrom of human fate and fortune, this new "fullness" of "all lives" cannot be projected as a spatial transcendence. It reverses the incarnation model. "He" "meditates us," but we first meditated Him, and as in time he was born, so to time he must return. The chiastic "blaze of summer straw in winter's nick" does not warm us; it is an image of consumption, with a tragic grandeur. The imagination that thinks of winter in the midst of summer does not draw comfort from the cyclical and repetitive motions of time. The future is mostly unknown.

Stevens' late northern landscapes undo the pastoral ideal of the "bee-loud glade," and of dwelling in place. They reject as well the Shelleyan sublime, the "bee-thou me" of agonistic transcendence in which the poet yields his identity to a higher power that controls the landscape. The imagination suffers its eccentricities, experiencing reality as a theater of changing scenes, of which we are both creator and audience. But from those fluctuating frames come glimpses of a boreal continuity. Land-scape in Stevens is adequate, not because it captures original nature, but because it brings us into relation with a flux we cannot frame. Karsten Harries has written that "the aim of spatial constructs is 'not to illumi-nate temporal reality . . . but to be relieved of it: to abolish time, if only for a time'" (quoted in Harvey, 206). But if the auroras can be considered a "spatial construct," they would seem to contradict this notion. If Stevens persists in his fiction of a center, still more of his imagination than is generally acknowledged is dedicated instead to the tragic experi-ence of a temporal reality that has none. It would be for later, postmod-ern writers to give up the dream of mastering the maze and thus see time in less tragic terms. Stevens persists in the longing to "dwell" in an inno-cent state, or to "master" the changes of the temporal world. But here Stevens acknowledges that despite the dream of mastering the processes of nature, the fated response to those processes is a mental process of equal rigor.

4

Moore's America

A Place for the Genuine

Marianne Moore is most familiar to readers as the poet of armored animals, creatures who defy our efforts to entail them. Moore is also a distinctive poet of places—and they are similarly elusive. Writing in the midst of the Progressive era's rugged individualism, she offers a posture of humility toward the wilderness. Moore's sense of the frame and the flux emerges in "A Grave" (CP, 49), which describes a seascape in Maine. Like Stevens, she knows her eccentricity and suspects a perspective that claims the center:

> Man looking into the sea,
> taking the view from those who have as much right to it as you have to it
>   yourself,
> it is human nature to stand in the middle of a thing,
> but you cannot stand in the middle of this

Landscape has an explicit political and moral implication for Moore, as well as the aesthetic and ontological implication it has for Stevens. Ultimately, no human has a "right" to the "view." Moore shows how unyielding nature is and how little it resembles us, except as a counterimage of our imperial stance. "The firs stand in a procession, each with an emerald turkey-foot at the top, / reserved as their contours, saying nothing." The view we would take will ultimately take us into its flux:

> the sea is a collector, quick to return a rapacious look.
> There are others besides you who have worn that look—

whose expression is no longer a protest; the fish no longer investigate
    them
for their bones have not lasted.

Landscape, that prospective gaze, in which man dominates over the
scene, must submit to the reciprocal gaze of nature, and ultimately to the
indifferent turning away of death. Yet within this sense of the frame and
of the flux, Moore does create a landscape, one in which nature is com-
pared to itself, and we to nature. For one does not, in Moore, know the
thing in itself, the "colorless primitive" of Stevens' "anti-master man." "A
Grave" (CP, 49) is another "landscape with boat," but without the bal-
cony view. The animal perspective is featured. Trees have turkey feet,
birds "swim through the air at top speed, emitting cat-calls," "the blades
of [our] oars / moving together like the feet of water-spiders." This is a
scene full of movement and transience, representing us in our mortal,
not our imperial state. One cannot "take" a view, one can only give it, and
give up the ghost. Anthropomorphism proves a figure of death itself:

The wrinkles progress among themselves in a phalanx—
    beautiful under networks of foam,
and fade breathlessly while the sea rustles in and out of the seaweed

Moore is famous for her menagerie, but her ideal of poetry puts the
animal "in the middle" of a landscape. In Frost, the American landscape
is converted to a version of the pastoral that reveals its fictional and fleet-
ing character. In Stevens, landscape is a meditative space in which the
shapes made by the imagination respond to the pressure of reality.
Moore's landscapes celebrate the principle of the wild within the frame.
Her landscapes, like her poems, emerge from "raw material" both natu-
ral and cultural. Landscape provides Moore the medium for her fullest
exploration of America, both its society and its geography. Far more
than Frost or Stevens, she draws on the patterns and images others have
made, and creates a landscape of these. In particular, her "imaginary gar-
dens with real toads in them" stand in contrast to the hard and soft pas-
torals that have sometimes stood in for an American sense of place. In
the first part of this chapter I discuss Moore's sense of the frame as it
arises in her refusal to yield to the lure of the shallow image, the illusion
that America is a toad-free, prelapsarian garden.

In acknowledging the frame Moore shows humility about the imagi-
native appropriation of the object, and indicates a world that language
cannot capture. She reveals anxiety about her own and her culture's ten-

dency to become absorbed in the shorthand substitutes for experience, the reductions, simulations, and facile myths, the quick "takes" that convert experience to commodity and distract us from the rigors of reality. The war against the facile constructions of reality must be fought on both sides, of course, since the artist traffics in illusions. The way to salvation for this devout poet is through instruments arising from the fall. In "The Jerboa" (CP, 10–15), for instance, Moore's Depression-era poem of "too much" and the revelation of "abundance" in adversity, we see this ambivalence played out. The poem begins by enumerating the vain luxuries of ancient culture, then moves to praise a simple desert rat who thrives in poverty. What appears at first to be a nature/culture binary turns into something more complex than the praise of animal abstemiousness over human wastefulness. Western civilization presents a contrast: Roman and Egyptian mimicry and distortion, on the one hand, and Hebrew redemption of illusion in the service of divine purpose, on the other. Moore portrays a flawed imperialism that would vainly fix its image on the world with a resourceful mimicry that would draw the landscape into a higher purpose than itself. Pharaoh is ultimately at the mercy of the flooding landscape, over which he ostensibly stands master, whereas exiled Jacob, in the inhospitable desert, makes a pillow of the stones. The colossal imitation of a pine-cone in front of the Vatican may be "contrived," distorting the scale of nature, but Jacob's theft of Esau's birthright, through a trick of illusion ("cudgel staff / in claw-hand") is in line with nature's own work of camouflage. The jerboa "honors the sand by assuming its color." And so the poet's images must serve creation's grace rather than plunder it. Similarly, in surveying the American landscape and culture, Moore will try to sort out "serviceable" illusions, pierced with inner light, from those that skim reality for easy gratification and gain. As we will see in later poems, Moore's meditation on modes of inhabiting landscape entails a reflection as well on racial history. In this poem it enters through the landscape of the African desert, arising as an aside, but establishing the connection between race and place.

Moore's America is a place of constant change and accelerating speed, and she seems just as ambivalent about that quality as she is about the uses of illusion. On the one hand, she enjoys the entrepreneurial energy of American technology and business, and incorporates images of its creative momentum. Nature does not stay still, nor should man. Moore's own poems are structured syntactically, and through imagistic leaps, to catch that sense of speed. William Carlos Williams called her poem "Marriage" an "anthology in rapid transit." On the other hand, American speed is often combined with a sense of rapacity and hurry, a desire for quick takes and facile generalizations. Williams' own landscape poem "Spring and All" presents some of this same conflict—how do we see the dynamic life of nature unfurling when we are speeding by in our car? How can the sense of motion be reconciled with the desire for accuracy? Moore had a vivid feeling for the continent she had crossed by train, as she puts it in "People's Surroundings" (CP, 55), on "straight lines over such great distances as one finds in Utah and in Texas / where people do not have to be told / that a good brake is as important as a good motor." Must we choose between nature's dynamism and culture's momentum? Moore's poems attempt to integrate the world's motions with her own.

Moore's fascination with nature's "fluctuating charm" (CP, 180) and its elusive swiftness sets her against the human impulse to fix it in shallow simulations. Reality is always quicker than our grasp. She admires the swiftness of the ostrich in "He 'Digesteth Harde Yron,'" the quicksilver of the plumet basilisk, the "kangaroo speed" of the jerboa, which defeat our desire to turn nature into still life. Her landscapes, similarly, refuse to stay still within our frames. The appropriate response is not speed of possession, the plunder of time and space, but speed of transformation, "conscientious inconsistency" (134), in which the mind, "enchanted" by its object, adopts its iridescent changes.

That flux affects human affairs as well, and underlies Moore's sense of history and modernity. America's benign myths of origin stand in paradoxical relation to technological mastery through increasing speed and efficiency. America is an unfinished landscape, or a series of landscapes on the site we call America. Our origins do not establish an ultimate dominion, or even set a process in motion since beginnings are contested. Far more explicitly than in Frost or Stevens, then, Moore's temporality reveals the historical dimensions of landscape, and the impact of landscape on history. In the second part of this chapter I take up Moore's representations of American history in relation to place—her emphasis on history as process rather than image, on nature as condition and reflection of history rather than a ground of historical meaning or a proof of dominion. She critiques the tendency to convert historical sites to "sights," spaces of merely touristic collection and facile narrative, static displays rather than scenes of evolutionary struggle and contingency.

American Versions of Pastoral

Moore's famous remark about poetry applies as well to her view of America:

I, too, dislike it.
　　Reading it, however, with a perfect contempt for it,
　　　　　　　one discovers in
　　it, after all, a place for the genuine.
　　　　　　　　　　　　　　　(CP, 36)

But what is the genuine? Could place itself provide the sense of the gen-
uine, an authentic connection to nature? Moore's "genuine" surprisingly
evades the model of American naturalness, the always-future past of the
"first idea" in which materiality and meaning are perfectly joined as "na-
ture's nation." Moore's America, whatever original nature it may retain,
is a dense network of imaginary gardens, some quite materially imposed
on the landscape. If nature is not simply aligned with the genuine, nei-
ther is culture simply aligned with the artificial. But America *is* intri-
cately bound up with landscape and geography. The task of the poet is
not to create nostalgic myths of contact and presence, but to make a
place within this modern condition for a lived relation to the world.

Moore knew America's landscape in modern terms, through its com-
mercial and technological advances, its conquest of time and space,
through the language of advertising and the images of fashion and en-
tertainment. These were for her as much a part of the landscape as were
the mountains and rivers that suggested to English settlers an untainted
Eden. As she shows in "People's Surroundings," Moore knew America as
well in its local and domestic arrangements, in the diversity of its styles,
"the deal table compact with the wall," Shaker simplicity as well as the
"Sèvres china and the fireplace dogs" (CP, 55) of Gilded Age extrava-
gance. She admired efficiency and durability, as well as the ingenuity that
could produce a "paper so thin that 'one thousand four hundred and
twenty pages make one inch,'" but she noted with implicit distaste the
flair for mass production with its "vast indestructible necropolis / of
composite Yawman-Erbe separable units" (55). The idea of the genuine
in America could not be reduced to single species, and would have to ac-
commodate a dense and various life, in which nature and culture were
inextricably bound together. But there were two tendencies of American
life that inhibited the genuine: derivativeness and rapacity. Rapacity has
the tendency to destroy what it is trying to possess. Derivatives are sim-
ulations that bypass experience and present themselves as the real thing.

America's anxiety about "the genuine" set in early, of course. The
country is continually "awakening" from the slumber of derivativeness.
Emerson complains in 1836 that "the foregoing generations beheld God
and nature face to face: we, through their eyes. Why should not we also

enjoy an original relation to the universe?" (*Nature,* 1).[1] Moore was herself a persistent critic of her culture's tendency, as she writes in "Poetry," to "become so derivative that it has become unintelligible" (CP, 267), unable to awaken genuine response ("eyes that can dilate, hair that can rise if it must" [266]). Moore and her generation also worried about a citified and suburbanized American society eschewing its rural and fundamentalist past and living, as Frank Lloyd Wright complained, by imitation "spread wide and thin over the vast surface of the continent" (quoted in Bogan, 1). But America could hardly sustain the idea of the genuine on pre-industrial terms. That "pioneer unprefunctoriness," as Moore called it in "Love in America" (240), must find a modern tenor. To be an American, she quoted Henry James as saying, is "not just to glow belligerently with one's country" (Moore, *Complete Prose,* 321). But civilizing America was not simply a matter of suppressing its wildness and imposing models of elegance and civility. On the contrary, America's uncouth and unbridled spirit was not as large a problem as its tendency to rely on received ideas and images.

I want to approach the subject of Moore's America by way of a 1920 poem called "England" (CP, 46–47) which reveals the relation of landscape to language. England merits the title only as the first word of the poem, not as the last word in good taste. As Moore conducts her Cook's tour of European excellence, she parodies the tendency to identify geography with specific cultural traits. The gravitational center of this poem is America, and while the avowed theme of the poem is that "excellence" knows no boundaries, the agenda of the poem is patriotic (though assertively non-nationalistic). Moore is wary of America's tendency to adopt chauvinistically the very identification with nature and the primitive that has driven intellectuals to Europe and encouraged Continental haughtiness toward the uncivilized American scene:

> and America where there
> is the little old ramshackle victoria in the south,
> where cigars are smoked on the street in the north;
> where there are no proof-readers, no silkworms, no digressions;
>
> the wild man's land; grassless, linksless, languageless country in which
> letters are written
> not in Spanish, not in Greek, not in Latin, not in shorthand,
> but in plain American which cats and dogs can read!
> the letter *a* in psalm and calm when
> pronounced with the sound of *a* in candle, is very noticeable, but

why should continents of misapprehension
have to be accounted for by the fact?

. . .

the flower and fruit of all that noted superiority—
if not stumbled upon in America,
must one imagine that it is not there?
It has never been confined to one locality.

America is a continent, able to encompass all the narrower attributes of
foreign locals. America as a "locality" is marked by regional diversity that
resists reduction to singular traits. America can embrace both a "little
old ramshackle victoria" of slow Southern gentility (in contrast to high-
speed living on the highways going West) and a cigar-smoking vulgarity
of the modern, industrial North. Moore begins by echoing the Eu-
rophiles' complaint about America's lack of refinement (it is as lan-
guageless as it is linksless), but she hints of enjoyment in the qualities
deplored by outsiders. America is a place "where there are no proof-
readers, no silkworms, no digressions" (too much of a hurry). It is "the
wild man's land." But if America is for some characterized by the lack of
nuance and cultural refinement, for others it is about straightforward
naturalness where "letters are written" "in plain American which cats
and dogs can read!" This is an extreme version of pastoral, a wish to
identify culture with nature and thus to claim cultural innocence against
European decadence. In defense against England's preemptive claims,
Americans celebrated their originality. Such a theme of American "natu-
ralness" is illogical on any terms, disdainful or patriotic. Turning the
bizarre but colorful expression "raining cats and dogs" in on itself,
Moore parodies America's notoriety as "nature's nation"; she neverthe-
less celebrates America's idiomatic vitality. It is not, in fact, a language-
less country. Moore's own language is anything but plain; it is full of
digressions (and obsessively proofread). Yet she shows the same affection
that Frost showed for the forceful conclusion, homely aphorism, and in-
ventive idiom of American speech.

A lively debate was going on at the time this poem was written about
whether there was such a thing as an "American language." H. L.
Mencken, a critic of English hegemony but also of American dullness
("no business ever foundered through underestimating the American
intelligence," he quipped), scrutinized the idea of America as a "lan-
guageless country" and explored the truth and misprision in the notion
that America had merely bastardized the mother tongue (American lan-

guage as counterfeit English). It is clear that Moore had read Mencken's *The American Language,* first published in 1919, before writing "England" (1920). The question of the genuine has particular relevance here, as the English evoked the concept in order to abhor all things American, especially its "stolen" language. Mencken identified an American language that was something more divergent than a derivative of English; it was an entire new "stream." While the English expressed abhorrence of American "expectoration" in the "pure well of English undefiled," Mencken celebrated the fecundity and class and regional diversity of a new language—the autonomy of America's new idiom. The book begins by documenting English snobbery about Americanisms, with the first four chapters entitled "The Earliest Alarms," "The English Attack," "American 'Barbarisms,'" and "The English Attitude Today." Moore asks concerning "all that noted superiority" (recognized in the world abroad): "if not stumbled upon in America, / must one imagine that it is not there?" She may be remembering a long passage Mencken quotes from Sydney Smith, which begins: "In the four quarters of the globe, who reads an American book? Or goes to an American play? Or looks at an American picture or statue? What does the world yet owe to American physicians or surgeons . . . ?" (18). In referring to America as a "languageless country," Moore may be recalling Mencken's quotation from Coleridge: "the Americans presented the extraordinary anomaly of a people without a language" (3). Moore admits that "the letter *a* in psalm and calm when / pronounced with the sound of *a* in candle, is very noticeable," and hardly music to the ear trained on the King's English. (She is recalling Mencken's examples of how the English revile American sounds: "missionary becomes missionary, angel, angel, danger, danger, etc.") But why should this mere accident of linguistic history become a summary of national character? With Mencken, Moore rejects a notion of "natural" English, some pure, undeveloping "well" of undefiled words. "The genuine" in language has little to do with purity of origin. The emergence of American speech, like the endless transformation of the landscape, was a sign of vitality in use. The link between language and landscape here is important. Moore identifies the dynamic, evolutionary character of culture with the diversity of nature and dynamism of the landscape. At the same time, by connecting language to landscape she reminds us that it is constructed as well as organic, that it operates as a sign as well as a signified.

If Moore challenged European superiority with a call to American creativity and diversity, she was also wary of how the myth of the American primitive might legitimate American habits of plunder. Affectation and rapacity might seem opposite vices (the one of civilization, the other of savagery), but they are related in that both foreclose experience, and thus "the genuine." As the world becomes something to price and consume rather than to experience and praise, purchasable simulations and traces of reality supplant elusive, recalcitrant actuality. The transformation of nature into marketplace is a fact of modernity, but the poet's role is not in sales (it may be in R&D). Of course poets traffic in representations. So Moore had to negotiate a space for her art that was not incriminated by the case against the fake, the simulated, the derivative—the case she herself was making about the culture at large. Her reality would be a confluence of presences, images, and uses that make up the changing phenomenal world.

America, Ezra Pound complained, was a "half-savage country," and Moore may well be echoing his phrase when she writes, in "New York" (CP, 54), of a "savage's romance." The Progressive era was beckoning America to an out-of-date "romance"—a glamorous master narrative— of the unconquered wilderness and inexhaustible resources. The unruliness of this land, its expanse, its ingenuity, its untamed splendor, stimulated the imagination. Those growing up in America at the turn of the century indulged a taste for Cooper's 1826 romance *The Last of the Mohicans,* with its noble savages. "The hunter, like the savage whose place he filled, seemed to select among the blind signs of the wild route, with a species of instinct, seldom abating his speed, and never pausing to deliberate" (116). But as the hunter displaces the savage, so the consumer displaces the hunter in our cultural logic. The savages are the consumers as much as the objects of romantic fantasy. Is the "New York" of the title and first line the modern city, Moore's new home, or the "wilderness" of the Catskills and the Adirondacks, the site of American nostalgia for origin? The tone of the word "savage" is as ambiguous as its referent and grammatical function. Moore had taught "savages" at the Carlisle Indian School the "civilized" skills of commercial accounting and stenography, and much of her poetry pays tribute to the civilized behavior of so-called primitives. How civilized is a culture that annexes land as it "needs the space for commerce," that has appropriated wildly within the last century? The commercial lust and reckless exploitation of resources exhibited by an urban culture that can only imagine the landscape in terms of its desire for consumption, can indeed seem savage. Moore's imagery demonstrates how fashion culture has adopted the very ways of the savage. New York City is "peopled with foxes," its population parading the streets in pelts and wrapping themselves in "tepees of ermine."

Moore's reversible phrase—the "savage's romance"—replaces the oppositional rhetoric of nature and culture with a reciprocal one. In this way Moore's ambiguous reference to "New York" anticipates and complicates William Cronon's view of Chicago as "nature's metropolis." The links between city and country are intricate and not all one-way. But a reciprocity requires distance as well as association. Moore's poetry maximizes proximity verbally, but then works to reestablish distance, to remind the reader that our images are not reality. The consumer's America is a warehouse for the fur trade "dotted with deer-skins" and "picardels of beaver-skin." New York commercial culture literally skins reality for material goods and self-aggrandizing images, forgetting nature's otherness. And yet it would be too simple to read the poem as the shame of culture against the tragic glory of nature. Nature can be appreciated as well as plundered in the name of culture, may indeed require the lens of culture to be seen at all. In this sense the proximity can be useful. Moore likely admires the imagination of the writer she quotes from *Field and Stream* who compares a fawn's markings to "satin needlework [that] in a single color may carry a varied pattern." He has not appropriated nature for art but rather has appreciated the art of nature. Moore's note tells us that the fawn was "discovered in a thicket and brought to the hotel." Whatever ambivalence she may have felt about this transplantation, she knows it is within culture that its markings can be seen. Moore was a devoted museum visitor, and most of her knowledge of nature comes from books, films, and exhibits. She had climbed Mt. Rainier, but in turning to write about it in "An Octopus" she does not transcribe her experience so much as collect and assemble various representations of it. The "contact" sought by Thoreau and revived by Muir remained elusive; the search for authentic experience must acknowledge the fact of mediation.

These inversions of value and attribution—the savage look of fashion, the refinement of nature—bring the two worlds of "New York" into close proximity through the power of imagination, just as they exist in close association through the power of commerce, in the first, long, embedded sentence of the poem. But in the next sentence Moore works to reestablish distance, to separate the two worlds of consumer and consumed, pointing toward a "wilderness" beyond quick acquisition. Moore is perhaps thinking of her own journey, not from the old center of the wholesale fur trade, St. Louis, to the new one, New York, but her more recent migration, from Carlisle, Pennsylvania, near Pittsburgh and the "conjunction of the Monongahela and the Allegheny," to Manhattan, when she asserts:

> It is a far cry from the "queen full of jewels"
> and the beau with the muff,
> from the gilt coach shaped like a perfume-bottle,

to the conjunction of the Monongahela and the Allegheny,
and the scholastic philosophy of the wilderness.

Romance takes on a new tenor here, evoking the glass slipper and the silk
rather than the leatherstocking. But the conjunction of the Mononga-
hela and the Allegheny rivers is not a romance but a locality existing a
"far cry" from the images of adventure and plunder proliferating in the
brains and bowels of the culture and disseminated through postcards of
"Niagara Falls, the calico horses and the war canoe." (Moore's family
owned an old landscape painting representing the scene of this conjunc-
tion of rivers, leading out into the open west.) But she knows all too well
that, thanks to the New York barons Carnegie and Frick, industrial Pitts-
burgh has grown up on this site. What does Moore mean by wilderness
here? Not, it seems, what John Muir praised and William McKibben
mourns. This is a new kind of wilderness, one of man and nature to-
gether; we can no longer map reality into neat binaries of city and coun-
try, where the city is "near" and the wilderness "far." Even when culture is
geographically close to the landscape, however, it remains distant, other.
Places must be distinguished from their representations. There is a dense
geography and human history behind a "dime novel exterior." The effete
"beau with the muff" and the perfume-bottle-shaped coach might be
signs of urban decadence. But Teddy Roosevelt–neo-primitives, bred on
urban luxury but seeking in nature a cure for the malaise of culture, who
borrowed images of masculine prowess from the backwoods "atmo-
sphere of ingenuity," are not so different. Their barehanded, anti-modern
conquest of nature, of "the otter, the beaver, the puma skins / without
shooting irons or dogs" was a weekend affair, not a real encounter with
the wilderness. Nature is still object, not other. The wealth of the Amer-
ican landscape, celebrated by Henry James in *The American Scene,* cannot
be reduced to "natural resources," to items for conspicuous consump-
tion, gratuitous adventure, or even raw necessity.

This anaphora, "it is not," becomes a structure for the *via negativa* (a
practice of showing distaste) like a negative map by which Moore can
"make a place for the genuine," asserting distance from the simulacra of
New York. The practice of reading and writing New York involves resist-
ance, "contempt" for the quick captions. For the wilderness is its own
"scholastic philosophy," equal in elusiveness to the works of Aquinas and
Duns Scotus with which Moore was familiar, and equal, as well, to the
wilderness of Henry James's prose, which she quotes at the end of the
poem: "It is not the plunder, / but 'accessibility to experience.'" One
would not think of scholastic philosophy as being accessible. But access

is not ownership and experience is not simplicity. Moore's poem imitates this rigor in its suspended syntax, which takes in increasingly complex clauses, full of conceptually demanding details. In the end Moore does reduce the wilderness to a phrase, but it is a phrase that points beyond itself to a depth and density that cannot be fathomed. The poem, like scholastic philosophy, becomes its own wilderness (rather than an image of the wilderness) in the concatenation of phrases. And here we return to the paradox that initiates the poem. For if one aim of "New York" is to establish the distance between nature's wealth and culture's desire, another aim is to refuse the opposition of nature and culture. The wilderness and scholastic philosophy, like real toads and imaginary gardens, become enfolded in a denser reality, a greater wilderness, which is always near and accessible, but also remote, requiring no special charter or protection from the accretions of commerce. One need not travel to the Adirondacks or the Catskills to visit it. This reality, the subject of all Moore's poems, is minutely particular, but "has never been confined to one locality." It can be experienced or ignored; it cannot be occupied.

In "New York" Moore largely "stands outside and laughs" when confronted with the wilderness, as she wrote in her first version of the poem. In "An Octopus" (CP, 71–76) she has at heart our getting lost. While "New York" catalogued the modes of plunder, "An Octopus" tries to convey the immediate experience of the wilderness. It does so, paradoxically, by drawing attention to our mediations. Moore presents a reality that is never circumscribed, which cannot be reduced to an image or a use, and cannot be mastered by a single perspective. She does not so much describe reality as give us an analogous experience in language. She draws a map in order to get us lost. "An Octopus" may well have been inspired by a map—an aerial map, "deceptively reserved and flat," of Mt. Rainier and its eight-armed glacier, included in a park pamphlet. But disorientation is the rule in the expedition that follows the title. The relation of land and sea becomes ambiguous; the poem compares the lowest point of the continent— the life of the sea—to the highest. There are no stable coordinates here:

> an octopus
> of ice. Deceptively reserved and flat,
> it lies "in grandeur and in mass"
> beneath a sea of shifting snow-dunes;

The map can only lie in trying to configure the "grandeur" in which the glacier "lies." And the passage goes on to suggest a distinction between this elusive reality and the frames we put on it:

dots of cyclamen-red and maroon on its clearly defined pseudo-podia
made of glass that will bend—a much needed invention—
comprising twenty-eight ice-fields from fifty to five hundred feet thick,
of unimagined delicacy.

Thus begins a six-page descriptive poem, piling up different languages, nomenclature of the sea, flora, human anatomy, technology, geology, every line of which bears close reading, but which pulls us along in the momentum of its syntax. Here we have radically different regions of nature compared—the cyclamen flower evoked at the site of the ocean creature, the octopus, fuses the flora of Mt. Rainier and the fauna of the underwater world. For whom and by whom is the "pseudo-podia" "clearly defined"? What is clear when we impose the category of a "foot" on either an ice field or an octopus? Mt. Rainier, the poem suggests, cannot be charted; that does not mean it cannot be experienced. Like an octopus the reality spreads out in all directions, and the safe distance of metaphoric abstraction yields to mind-boggling shifts of scale and scene, exuberant lists, densely textured, proliferating images of power and delicacy, that come as close as any modern poem to the American sublime, that aesthetic triumph over mapping. The ambition of the poem, in its accreted quotation, its disarming metaphors and strained syntax, its radical parataxis, its shifts in scale and perspective, is to develop our regard for what is beyond our power to circumscribe, to quantify, and to sell off.

In 1922 Moore visited her brother, stationed near Seattle, and together they made an expedition to Mt. Rainier, which only two decades before, in 1899, had become a national park. Like so many of her contemporaries, then, she had rushed to acquire the wilderness experience, on the "game preserve" of the American Eden. But Moore's poem is not a spontaneous overflow of powerful feeling. She does not indulge in naïve realism or frontier fantasies—old myths of American prioritism, of the wilderness within unleashed by the wilderness without. She does not come "face to face" with original nature. The landscape has been heavily intercepted by a collage of maps and field guides, by human interpretation and representation; it cannot be known independent of these constructions. Moore's way, then, to the American sublime is by heightening rather than suppressing the mediations. Nature has little to do with the wilderness that is legally chartered and protected by park rules and regulations, the wilderness simulation that William Cronon has documented in "The Trouble with Wilderness." But the poet can evoke a

recalcitrant reality through various frames and signposts, one that sub-
sumes us in its power and exceeds our knowledge in its "capacity for
fact." Its "neatness of finish" defies the finish of any pictorial frame. The
glacier and park at Mt. Rainier become emblematic of this elusive real-
ity, a bounded nature exhibiting nature's boundlessness. The poem is
constructed out of quotations from the park manual, along with a wide
variety of sources including the *London Illustrated News* (sea world),
Baxter's *Saints' Everlasting* (spiritual world), and a conversation over-
heard at the circus (social world). We may apply here Gertrude Stein's
remark about the landscapes of America: "I like a view, but I like to put
my back to it." Moore does not invite us to take the view of Mt. Rainier;
it cannot be "taken." A site cannot be fixed as a sight. What the imagina-
tion can do is give us something. Moore creates a distinctly textual real-
ity in collage form that provides an analogy (rather than a simulation) to
the wilderness experience it evokes, a rhetorical sublime to suggest a nat-
ural sublime. Reference to language, and even self-reference, as well as
pictorial representation, overlap. The diagrammatic reality, the "glassy
octopus symmetrically pointed," turns into a fearful symmetry which
"receives one under winds that tear the snow to bits / and hurl it like a
sandblast / sheering off twigs and loose bark from the trees . . . is 'tree'
the word for these things / flat on the ground like veins?" The attention
to flatness again functions doubly here: to challenge our notion of the
relation of the word "tree" with its vertical association to this austere,
faceted reality, this incredible height that flattens all other features; and
also to remind us that our own "smooth" "flat" maps are not the textured
reality they point to. This octopus knocks the map out of our hands, and
the trees themselves, "flattened mats of branches shrunk in trying to es-
cape," are a little like our own feeble efforts to escape nature's magnitude
by mapping it. Put another way, we may try to flatten, or map, Mt.
Rainier, but in fact it flattens all our efforts. The sense that we have
turned Mt. Rainier into a theme park for "those who lived in hotels but
who now live in camps—who prefer to" contends with the image that we
and our maps are just part of the fauna of the place.

Man's will to map the world by coordinating it to his own body,
Moore emphasizes, finds its match in nature's power to deceive. The gla-
cier dotted with flowers looks like the "pseudo-podia" of the cephalopod,
which is itself footlike only to bipeds. And we don't even seem to know
our hands from our feet. The "Goat's Mirror . . . that lady*finger*like de-
pression in the shape of the left human *foot*" (italics mine) "prejudices
you in favor of itself before you have had time to see the others." The

maps we make send us in circles: "Completing a circle, you have been deceived into thinking you have progressed." The octopus on the aerial map is "deceptively reserved and flat," but the real one has the "concentric crushing rigor of the python," and obeys a vaster geometry than ours. The Indian ponies in the landscape are "hard to discern" among the birch trees, ferns, lily pads, and other enumerated flora. Nature may play the prickly host—we are "met by the polite needles of the larches"—but only to elude us. Maps give us a false sense of security too. This glacier is an active volcano and produces an avalanche at the end. Its "reserve" is temporary. Moore is fully aware, in quoting the promotional rhetoric of the park administration, that nature's intention is a human fiction. But our plunder and presumption are more than matched by its mysterious geologic presence that can alchemically transmute verdure into onyx, and that displays spruce trees with the eerie legacy of an American royal family "each like the shadow of the one beside it." Nature is continually erasing the images that it projects; the storm "obliterates the shadows of the fir trees." Man's fraudulence turns on itself as he witnesses miracles he "dare not speak [of] at home for fear of being viewed as an impostor."

Moore takes nature off the map, then, but she knows she has put it in a theater. To remind us of this, a curtain falls at the end of the poem, an avalanche to image the blank page: "a curtain of powdered snow launched like a waterfall." Ultimately this is not a poem about Mt. Rainier. Like other modernist texts, it is presentational rather than representational, and Mt. Rainier itself becomes enfolded in the dense fabric of a poem that is about nothing less than the earth and our institutional and imaginative relationship to it, enacting rather than describing that relationship. We cannot "know nature," in Thoreau's phrase, except through the kaleidoscope of our landscapes. Hence the poem is a compilation of quotations and allusions rather than a first-hand account, like Thoreau's description of Mt. Katahdin or Muir's description of Yosemite. Thoreau's "Contact! Contact!" like Emerson's "original relation to nature" is an elusive ideal, but not just because of modern development. Man has not ruined nature; nature has absorbed man. Indeed, humans become part of the "fauna" of the scene at Mt. Rainier—the mountain guide and the hotel keeper are among the "diversity of creatures" who make their home in this place. While they and the tourists they draw are constructing "Mt. Rainier," then, Mt. Rainier is encompassing them.

As Patricia Willis and John Slatin have shown, Moore's poem asks us to recall *Paradise Lost* and to acknowledge that we have forfeited that "power that Adam had," the power of naming, and of original sight. This allusion has specific relevance to the tradition of the American sublime, of course, and the myth of America as the unfallen Eden. The paintings of Albert Bierstadt and Frederic Church suggested immanence and transparence. Moore's poem acknowledges mediation from the outset, dashing any illusion of an American Adam who might establish an innocent civilization in harmony with nature. Moore's poem insists that there is no easy turning back. A return to nature is not a return to innocence. Rainier has been framed and structured by man; the wilderness, as we conceive it, is a construction. But Moore creates another kind of sublime in returning elusive power to the object—a sublime beyond us, not ourselves.[2] This thrilling encounter with place is intercepted repeatedly by the comic presence of tourists who are "happy seeing nothing," and businessmen "who require 365 holidays a year." The sense that we have turned Mt. Rainier into a theme park for tourists enamored of the pseudo-rigors of outdoor life contends with proliferating details and jolts to our orientation that the contemplation of this place provokes.

"New York" and "An Octopus" critique the rough pastoral of American wilderness discourse and suggest a sublime reality that cannot be reduced to an image or a tag. "The Steeple Jack" (CP, 5–7), written about a decade later, considers the soft pastoral, exposing the dangers that lie within Arcadia. Not only wilderness parks, but also resort towns were a growing phenomenon of the new century. Empson's definition of pastoral as "a partial world depicted as a whole world" suits this poem, in which enumerated flowers display gardens containing much of the predatory animal kingdom (foxglove, tiger lily, spiderwort, snapdragon), without threat, and in which "there are cats, not cobras, to keep down the rats." In this temperate zone we have "the tropics at first hand" without the threat of exotic serpent life, except on fashionable snakeskin shoes. Moore delights in the harmonious blends of the natural and human worlds and values retreat from the centers of modern life. But she is no Norman Rockwell. She brings her urbanity with her, reminding us at every turn that we are not in paradise, that place cannot return our innocence, and that indeed the pastoral world, if we forget the artifice that makes it, may be more dangerous than any other.

Moore was certainly aware of a different role for herself as she wrote "The Steeple Jack." The poet of "New York" and "An Octopus" was publishing in obscure avant-garde magazines (*Others* and *Broom*). She did not cater to a "public out of sympathy with neatness" (CP, 76). Her audience was the New York avant-garde, out of sympathy with the genteel tradition of literary pastoral. But as winner of the Dial Award and editor of *The Dial,* she had become an arbiter of taste rather than its critic, and her audience had widened. Exhausted from her editorship, and from attending to her mother's weakening health, perhaps also retreating from the frenzy of Manhattan brought on by the stock market crash, Moore decided at the end of 1929 to seek a quieter existence in what was at that time still a suburban milieu. Brooklyn had only been annexed to New York City for thirty years when Moore moved there, and it retained an outsider identity. Here Moore returned to the writing of poetry, making significant changes in her style. The poems became more musical, the syntax more relaxed, the pleasures more accommodating. Rhyme enters the work more conspicuously than before, knitting the voice into pleasant sonic patterns. Moore's own language supplants quotation, and its tone is more ingratiating. Had she dropped her vigilance against the temptations of the glossy phrase or the gilded image? Had she succumbed to parochial pieties and surface harmonies? How, Moore asks, might one be "at home" in such a place, open to its genuine satisfactions, without mistaking it for the world? This home differs from the one in the poem "Dock Rats," which she wrote upon moving to Manhattan in 1918; that was a site of transitions, of comings and goings, this, of complacencies and moral slumber. But Moore's poem reminds us that we are "not native" in Arcadia.

Particularly at issue, for this artist who liked elegance "of which the source is not bravado," was how to reconcile aesthetic coherence and moral incoherence. From the beginning of "The Steeple Jack" (CP, 5) she does this by emphasizing artifice, by drawing attention to the frame:

> Dürer would have seen a reason for living
>   in a town like this, with eight stranded whales
> to look at; with the sweet sea air coming into your house
> on a fine day, from water etched
>   with waves as formal as the scales
> on a fish.

Moore conceived a composite place, part Maine resort (she had summered on Monhegan Island) and part residential borough (the steeple jack she names—C. J. Poole—actually worked in Brooklyn, and some of the images, like the stranded whales, are taken from local newspaper accounts). The constructed scene displays the abundance and variety of nature, with all its extremes, refined into pattern and harmony—what the classical writers called *discordia concors*. Pastoral is a form of still life, concealing history and temporality and engaging in illusions of timelessness. The seagulls flying back and forth over the town clock erase time in their shuttle. The "etched" water will not flow. No work goes on in this eclogue, though there are "fishnets arranged to dry." Virgil would have seen a reason for living in a town like this. But Moore's scene is inscribed with *et in arcadia ego*—"I too am in arcadia," says the real toad in the imaginary garden. Our sins wash up like Leviathan on the beach. As Susan Stewart has suggested in *On Longing*, in the modern system of objects, the gigantic is often a metaphor for the abstract authority of the state and the collective public life. If the notion applies here, the stranded whales provide a troubling allegory. Yet this is not a bleak poem, nor is its assertion that "it could not be dangerous to be living in a town like this" entirely insincere. It celebrates the perennial abundance of nature and delight in sensory orders, and the pleasure of things "ambition cannot buy or take away." In another sense hope is affirmed—a hero is present, a student, an artist—and their ideals survive their human habitation.

"About suffering they were never wrong, / The Old Masters. How well they understood / Its human position," wrote W. H. Auden in "Musée des Beaux Arts" (*Selected Poems*, 79). He was looking at some paintings by Breughel, particularly "Landscape with the Fall of Icarus," in which one can barely perceive, in an otherwise placid agrarian scene, the fallen Icarus sinking into the sea. Auden admired Moore's poetry (adopting her syllabics) and knew her "Steeple Jack" well, so perhaps he took some inspiration from this poem as he struggled with the tension between aesthetic pleasure and moral vigilance. Moore places her perspective close to that of another Old Master, Dürer (she had written about him for *The Dial*, mentioning his travel to see a stranded whale). Her view is thus one of a perceptive outsider. To be "not native" to the pastoral myth of place can give one a privileged view, a heightened sensitivity to both its pleasures and its faults. Like Dürer, she is attracted to the extraordinary (eight stranded whales, a twenty-five-pound lobster), and like him, she creates a painstaking but understated formal (etched) order. (The gulls flying over the clock in ones and twos and threes almost image the carefully counted syllables in these matching, sonorous, unaccented stanzas.) But also like Dürer, Moore brings a moral (and religious) sensibility to this scene. To look at eight stranded whales with a feeling for suffering is to go beyond the thrill of spectacle or merely aesthetic response. Surely the "sweet air" is tainted by the moral, not to mention the physical, odor of their displacement, though we tend to hold our noses. From the out-

set, then, Moore creates a tension between the delight in designing pic-
turesque surfaces and the moral compunction to expose a corruption
beneath them, a tension between pastoral and parable.

Whereas "An Octopus" was aimed at getting you lost (the poem dis-
orients you immediately: "an octopus / of ice"), "The Steeple Jack" seems
to want to make you feel at home. Nature is close but does not consume
us; technology is close but does not control us.

> One by one in two's and three's, the seagulls keep
>   flying back and forth over the town clock,
> or sailing around the lighthouse without moving their wings—
> rising steadily with a slight
>   quiver of the body—or flock
> mewing where
>
> a sea the purple of the peacock's neck is
>   paled to greenish azure as Dürer changed
> the pine green of the Tyrol to peacock blue and guinea
> gray.

Easy passage here between the human and natural worlds characterizes
the pastoral. Moore goes on to note the hospitable character of the cli-
mate (again, in contrast to the forbidding Mt. Rainier), which favors a
rich variety of flowers, the fog enhancing, rather than obstructing, their
lush growth. But the mention of the fog serves as well to remind us that
appearances are unreliable—the unsaid is as important as the said in
Moore's method of understatement. Moore has put us on alert. And
soon enough, a storm encroaches on the placid scene.

> The
>
> whirlwind fife-and-drum of the storm bends the salt
>   marsh grass, disturbs stars in the sky and the
> star on the steeple; it is a privilege to see so
> much confusion.

This is written off as more charming Americana, nothing to get ruffled
about, but its "fife and drum" may also recall a revolutionary struggle
and sacrifice that we forget at our peril. Pastoral is the forgetting of time,
but our well-being was achieved in history and can be undone by his-
tory. Moore harbors a special fondness for "the student / named Am-
brose [...] / with his not native books and hat" who appears in stanza 8,
because he is not complacently parochial, does not take this partial

world for a whole world. Ambrose is not the shepherd-insider of the pastoral world, through whom we imagine a life of harmony. That is, he knows not to mistake this retreat for America, and knows that small-town life is not an escape from the corruptions that plague America. Named for a Saint, and the embodiment of Emerson's American scholar, he appreciates the charms of this place while recognizing its imperfections and the artifice behind its placid surfaces. From the distance of the hillside he can delight that "there is nothing that ambition can buy or take away," yet he knows that such ambitious buying and selling drives American life, so recently shaken to its foundations. Here is a respite from Wall Street, not a cure for it. If *he* appreciates locality for itself, rather than for its speculative value as souvenir or natural resource, still, the *place* is not innocent. Ambrose conducts us to the pitch of the church, which, while it is part of the overall picturesque charm of the place, is "not true."

This has been from the beginning a poem about *seeing*. Dürer's stylized gaze conducted us through the first part of the poem, with its etched water, its play of scale, and its enhanced colors. But as the poem turns to Ambrose for direction, a transition occurs. The body enters the scene, since Ambrose, unlike Dürer, is in it. From his hilltop prospect he can miniaturize the world and make it a kind of souvenir (memorizing the antique-sugar-bowl-shaped summerhouse, the mechanical boats), but he must finally surrender the toy-like scenery and confront what has hitherto been disguised by fog. The decorative palette of the poem now turns to stark and unambiguous black, white, and red. Humans, in various social positions, enter the poem, and so does a worker: the steeple jack of the poem's title, the moral counterpart of the artist, placing danger signs even as he "gilds." We are reminded that what is seen has been made, and with that recognition danger and sin become explicit. The "not true" has exposed not just fiction, but falsehood and corruption.

There are other prospective inhabitants of this hitherto empty town, "waifs, children, animals, prisoners, / and presidents," escaping "sin driven senators," all of them creatures who are vulnerable or corrupt. These "simple people" do not ensure the innocence we cling to as a legacy of American small-town life. Rather, this is a place where presidents (Coolidge was in office) evade their responsibilities, choosing not to see or think about the evil in their midst, and thus serving its ends. As Moore turns to the institution of the church, she locates the worst form of hypocrisy (whitewash) exactly where there should be none. But as a pious Presbyterian, she believes that all human institutions are erected in hope, not in innocence. The church may be most susceptible to corruption because presumed most innocent. The columns of the church, sup-

ports for a frail humanity, are "made solider by whitewash" (thus to ap-
pearances only, and not reliable at all). The steeple jack, the very figure
assigned to correct the collapsing steeple, is himself only human and
thus a sinner. (We recall Jonathan Edwards' "Sinners in the Hands of an
Angry God" in this image of a spider spinning a thread. The indelibly
"etched" scene of the artist now becomes as fragile as a web. Ingenious
man is not really in control at all, but a sinner hung by God over the pit
of Hell.) The steeple jack wears the colors of Satan and "gilds" the star
that "stands for hope." Hope is misplaced, it seems, when it is invested in
human institutions, whether they be stock exchanges, places of worship,
or small-town societies. Yet this is not a sermon in the tradition of
Jonathan Edwards, but a pastoral in the tradition of Andrew Marvell.
The poet delights in a world arrayed for sensual pleasure and relaxation,
a world of densely varied vegetation, with "cat-tails, flags, blueberries
and spiderwort, / striped grass, lichens, sunflowers, asters, daisies" (and
so on for several stanzas, some two-thirds of which had been cut to make
this still copious version) and charming human structures—"a school-
house, a post-office in a / store, fish-houses, hen-houses, a three-masted
schooner on / the stocks." Moore's lists are little societies—one notices
the relative modesty of this list of dwellings (where a schoolhouse gets
no higher grammatically than a fishhouse, where a grand schooner, like
a beached whale, sits on stocks), in contrast with the verbal and visual
plenitude of the gardens. Still, man and nature do achieve a kind of har-
mony in this place, at least in moments of detached meditation, when
history is pressed into the background. But this poem was included in a
collection of three entitled "Part of a Novel, Part of a Poem, Part of a
Play," and one feels strongly that a story (narrative is the end of pastoral)
is about to begin.

Whether she is dealing with city or wilderness, sublime or pastoral
landscapes, then, Moore's America becomes a place for the genuine
when she reveals the frames that create "people's surroundings." Because
these environments are made as well as inhabited, they do not offer
places of permanence or grounds of origin. What is true of her animal
poems is true of her landscapes—nature, as it relates to human beings, is
embedded in history.

Landscape and History

These investigations of contemporary America's myths about itself led
Moore increasingly to inquire into American historical origins, especially
as embedded in our sense of place. American ideology reveals a resist-

ance to the idea that "nature's nation" should be subject to history at all. How could a culture grounded in innocent nature be anything but permanent? An incarnate culture does not *evolve;* it is truth revealed. History, for Americans, was becoming a commodity, something we could collect to enhance our image and permit our complacency about the present. By emphasizing historical place we create the illusion that our origins are natural and inevitable, and that historical meaning is a static set of images. But Moore's poetry insists that all human institutions are subject to the contingencies of historical process. And all landscapes are historical, shaped and marked by the human history that has traversed them. She responds, particularly, to the tendency of Americans to convert historical sites to tourist "sights," flattening history with received, abridged images. When history becomes a sight, an object of tourist consumption or national myth, it flattens out. Moore seeks to return a certain depth to history by discovering from the surface its dense network of meanings. Historical sites speak not so much of a sanctified, living heritage as of the profundity of the historical process itself. History is not heroic narrative or divine fiat but a set of contingencies, "what has come about" (CP, 109) in the mingling of human intentions with nature's ways. History is the opposite of still life. Moore is a descriptive, not a narrative poet. But description in her work resists mythic formations. Again, she makes a place for the genuine by reading with a certain contempt.

The triad of poems called "Part of a Novel, Part of a Poem, Part of a Play" included, besides "The Steeple Jack," "The Student" and "The Hero," two poems that examine American distinction without succumbing to American bravado. "The Hero" in particular (CP, 8–9) speaks to this difference between luminous sites and superficial sights. The hero is listed among those variously "at home" in the seaside town of "The Steeple Jack," and it is clear that Moore invests some hope in his presence. But for him to be "at home" is not to be complacent or provincial, but on alert. And he is not a conventional hero of bold feats and reckless courage. Theodore Roosevelt went looking for danger. This hero "shrinks" and does not like "deviating headstones / and uncertainty." Moore's personal hero was George Washington, whom she mimicked with her tricorn hat and cape. But while the popular image saw him crossing the Rubicon, Moore might remember that his strategy was retreat. Washington was, as she said of the hero of another poem, "hindered to succeed." "The hero" here is an appropriate heir to Washington, a type of the Christian soldier "that covets nothing that he has let go." But he is not a "natural," at least not a biological or social, heir to Washington, since his embodiment in this poem is African-American. He is not interested at all in surfaces, the thrilling surfaces of the romantic wilderness or the charming surfaces of seaside retreats. He is intent on "the rock crystal thing to see," "brimming with inner light." In this inward relation toward place and its meaning, he is "at home" even though his racial origin stands continents away. The hero's foil is the "fearless sightseeing hobo" (who is implicitly not at home), the hobo of contemporary tourism; she checks off her list of sights and domesticates historical meaning. "What's this, what's that," she asks, demanding of history that it be named and pinpointed, rather than contemplated.

In an understated fashion, while presenting a contemporary image, Moore introduces here the major struggles of our heritage, the "deeds of war," as Frost called them in "The Gift Outright." These connect us to the land: the revolution and founding of a nation, and the civil war and near foundering of a nation, which continues in a struggle for racial justice. These are parts of the historical landscape that the sightseeing hobo cannot penetrate. For this obnoxious woman, such transforming events are nothing but a collection of monuments. This "hero"—never named—is merely a "frock coated Negro," a park attendant at a national cemetery (Williamsburg) dressed in revolutionary costume. He is invisible to the tourist, part of the background. She addresses her question ("where's Martha buried?") not to this informed guide but to "the man she's with," so unheroic as to have no other designation in the poem. Yet the guide has a "sense of human dignity and reverence for mystery" which his visitor lacks. Ignored by the tourist, probably because he is black, he nevertheless provides the information required: "Gen-ral Washington / there; his lady, here." He is more authentic in his response than she is in her question, though he is "speaking / as if in a play," on the stage of history. The guide has a historical imagination rather than a tourist's curiosity, and sees with an inner light. We might recall that the 1930s, when this poem was written, was a dormant period in the struggle for civil rights. A complacent attitude toward Jim Crow laws prevailed. Many of Moore's poems of this period feature the unheralded heroism and nobility of the black race. There may be some racialism in this attitude, as Cristanne Miller has pointed out (128–166), but it stands as a direct retort to the racism of the time. "Standing in the shadow of the willow," his figure acknowledges that the past is not a "sight" but a mystery that continues to inform the present.

Throughout her poetry Moore sustained an admiration for the natural world that reckoned with the story of humans in it. This is perhaps most apparent in Moore's poems of the South. Moore's visits to her brother in

Virginia inspired three poems in the 1930s, "Smooth-Gnarled Crepe Myrtle," "Bird-Witted," and "Virginia Britannia." Together they form a sort of updated "Notes on the State of Virginia." "Virginia Britannia" (CP, 107–111) looks at landscape through the lens of history and vice versa, more than one hundred and fifty years after Jefferson's account, and more than three hundred years after the Jamestown settlement. It aims for a different kind of seeing than "sight seeing." And it engages in a different kind of historical imagination than that encouraged by Williamsburg pageantry. With the inclusion of this 1935 poem, the title of Moore's subsequent volume, *What Are Years* (1941), takes on a particular American emphasis, expressing not only lyric's traditional meditation on mortality, but a study of history and its meaning as well. The poem has a special implication when considered not only in the light of continued racism at home, but also surging, racialist nationalisms abroad, where nature is used to mask the sinister purposes of power.

"England" had been concerned with a contemporary situation in which America was seen as rough and backward, inferior to all things "abroad." "Virginia Britannia" looks back at the earliest efforts to impose European culture on American land. What was allegorical in Stevens, the question of the relationship between the soil and man's intelligence, becomes in Moore a literal meditation on New World settlement. The poem exposes the provisional and contingent character of dominion, undermining imperial attitudes through the selection and arrangement of details. Neither dominion nor incarnation, but rather adaptability, intermixture, mimicry, and mutability prove the strongest traits in the history of this landscape. The land is not, finally, ours, but we are "the land's" in the sense that landscape determines history as much as history determines landscape.

"Virginia Britannia" starts very much as "The Steeple Jack" does, scanning the scene for curiosities, gathering impressions. Here the poet begins with the broad prospect, the anticipatory sweep of dominion, then moves in to complicating detail and anecdote. But while the language is paratactic and mimics a tourist brochure, Moore wanders away from the official tour, observing the overlooked and what has been much looked at but not properly seen. Jamestown was situated on a narrow sandbar linked to the mainland of Virginia. The poem opens with an approach, in present tense, which simulates the approach of the first European visitors to the tidewater. But the Virginia that Moore beholds is no Virgin Land: the new world has seen an old dominion come and go; historical process quickly imposes itself on landscape. This nature has been "known" by many and for a long time—by man and by animal, the wild and tame of each species, though by none in its totality.

> Pale sand edges England's Old
>   Dominion. The air is soft, warm, hot
> above the cedar-dotted emerald shore
>   known to the red-bird, the red-coated musketeer,
>   the trumpet-flower, the cavalier,
>   the parson, and the wild parishioner. A deer-
> track in the church-floor
>   brick, and a fine pavement tomb with engraved top, remain.
>   The now tremendous vine-encompassed hackberry
>   starred with the ivy-flower,
>   shades the tall tower;
> And a great sinner lyeth here under the sycamore.

The sense of manifest destiny in "Dominion" is immediately qualified by
"Old" and "edges." "Pale" initiates a vocabulary of color that will later
scrutinize racial attitudes throughout the poem; "pale sand," in the con-
text of the whole, suggests the white man's presumption of natural do-
minion in this place. But the colors remain primarily aesthetic here. In
presenting "red bird" next to the "red coat," aesthetically equalizing na-
ture and man, Moore deliberately delays reference to "red skin," which
appears in stanza 10, though the Indian presence in this place is central
to its history, beginning in stanza 2. Perhaps Moore knew that "red skin"
was itself a convention, based not on the natural pigmentation of the
Amerindian but on his bear-grease decorative paint, which the earliest
European visitors mistook for racial essence. What is "natural" and what
is "cultural" or man-made collide and overlap one another from the out-
set, belying presumptions of dominion. The Earthly Paradise of imperi-
alist lore, with its "soft, warm" air and lush, welcoming flora and fauna
must give way to the truth of a "hot" climate where "unEnglish insect
sounds" suggest not just aesthetic diversity but a relentless struggle
against malaria. "Care" has formed the roses, but also the "yew" in the
poem; suffering underlies but does not consecrate dominion. When
Moore later remarks on the "outdoor tea-table, . . . the French mull dress
with the Madeira- / vine-accompanied edge" and other "luxuries," she is
struck by how paradoxically "stark" they seem "when compared with
what the colonists / found here"—a far from nurturing environment
met a far from godly invader. The material "glory" of these Old Domin-
ion grounds is itself now only a replica of a hard-won, genteel past, the
unlikely outgrowth of a morally and physically rough frontier whose
conquest is less than certain or heroic.

The past is written into the face of the present, not as its original and enduring glory but as a conglomeration. The juxtapositions of human and natural inhabitants work here as leveling parody ("the trumpet flower, the cavalier"), especially as the man/nature opposition of the list influences the "parson/wild parishioner" pairing. (The lineation makes us read "the wild parishioner" as "a deer," since he has wandered into the church; but of course the wild parishioner is also the colonial himself, that "great sinner.") From here it is but a deer-step into the church; all boundaries are permeable. The accident of the hoof print claims as much posterity as the careful engraving. Nature itself inscribes this struggle for dominion as the vine encompasses the "tremendous" hackberry that now "shades" the "tall tower." Moore's later imagining of the "strangler figs choking / a banyan" dispels the myth of nature's innocence. The struggle for dominion is natural and nature is neutral, copresent with man, and available to model man's moral life in its graces and faults. Moore expropriates and diverts the pious rhetoric of the past. As the eye moves from the landscape's "edge" to its presumed human center, we encounter a grave: "A great sinner lyeth here" is a period quotation, but the spiritual accounting takes on new direction as the words share church walls with "tobacco crop records." Here is a land of "cotton mouth snakes" and "cotton fields," of "wolf design" on Lawrence pottery, a land far from Eden and still in need of grace. Even Jefferson's picturesque curving brick wall is "serpentine."

The great sinner "awaits a joyful resurrection" (presuming election), but a complex history intervenes, as Moore makes the transition from the subversion of the nature/culture hierarchy to challenge the dominion of one race over another. It is clear in this poem that the Indian represents culture, not nature—he is not "all brawn and animality." Moore introduces the story of Captain Smith, Christopher Newport, and Powhatan, compressing much American lore into a stanza's worth of anecdotal fragments (such as a tourist might gather, but only an artist could meaningfully arrange). The founders are not predestined leaders but "odd" figures, reminding us that all norms are embedded in history. Indeed, the term "odd" and its more flattering companion "rare" recur throughout the poem and become the primary descriptive adjectives for the phenomena of this place from the modern point of view:

> We-re-wo
> co-mo-co's fur crown could be no
> odder than we were, with ostrich, Latin motto,
> and small gold horse-shoe:

arms for an able sting-ray-hampered pioneer—
painted as a Turk, it seems—continuously
   exciting Captain Smith
   who, patient with
his inferiors, was a pugnacious equal, and to

  Powhatan as unflattering
   as grateful. Rare Indian, crowned by
Christopher Newport!

(CP, 107)

Moore alludes here to Smith's unconventional leadership and love of adventure. Captain Smith was an Englishman who joined Hungarians in fighting the Turks, beheading three before being taken as slave and later escaping, only to be poisoned by a sting-ray he lived to consume; his motto was *vincere est vivere,* to vanquish is to live. But this fetishized coat of arms has become an emblem of audacity. Moore also conveys Powhatan's pride, who, when offered a coronation as emperor of Indian tribes and vassal to the English king, replied "I also am a king and this is my land," instead giving his fur crown and cloak to Christopher Newport, who returned with them to England. (Moore probably saw them in the Ashmolean Museum when she visited Oxford as a young woman.) Odd perhaps is Pocahantas with a bird-claw earring, but even odder her cross-dressing as an English lady. History exposes the truth of exchange over the presumption of dominion, where the English spout Latin mottoes and paint themselves as Turks, endlessly posturing and naming counties after English lords while adopting Indian names for rivers, sporting French finery, and importing Andalusian flowers. Assertive identity defeats itself in acts of appropriative mimicry.

A garden is not only an aesthetic arrangement, it is a language, by which historical cultures express their desires and social arrangements (splendor, pride, in the language of flowers). Moore's gardens are eccentric allegorical spaces. Here the poem borders the garden with the human story—the stanza form slides one into the other without transition. History shapes nature just as nature shapes history. The long lists of flora and fauna convey the convergence and struggle of these disparate cultures. Moore records that struggle in her own thematic shaping, the index of scent and size ("dwarf" and "gigantic" recur in the description of plants), but especially, as we saw in the opening passage, in the vocabulary of color. The green propriety of the sculptured boxwoods established by the English colony and their uniformly "white roses" asserted against "unEnglish" (malarial) "insect sounds" nevertheless have tough stems, "thick as Daniel Boone's grapevine," a sign of their adaptation to the challenging American soil.

The "jet-black pansies" and "African violet" mark the presence of the Negro "established"—as the euphemism goes—on the banks of the Chickahominy. "Established" like imported plants, not willing humans, in this post-lapsarian garden, they nevertheless become integral to the emergence of civilized life in Virginia. Moore relishes the image of the black pansy "overpowering" the lesser flora. And in their later resistance blacks are indeed "inadvertent ally and best enemy of tyranny" in a society still, in the thirties, far from righteous. The color of the mockingbird, we are told three times, is "gray," and as "terse Virginian" he is emblem of the confederacy, the assertion of an old South still resentful of the Emancipation that requires it to pay wages to the Negro it employs for gain. (In an earlier version Moore referred to these sharecropper landlords ironically as "the bothered by wages new savages," again checking the presumption of civil community where behavior is in fact barbaric.) We are invited to "observe" the mockingbird, standing blind on a pillar of cupidity. But the mocking bird is also a reminder, as John Slatin has pointed out (208–252), that America is about mimicry more than originality. The primary "native" trait is "endless imitation." The "terse Virginian" adopts the call "of whippoorwill or lark or katydid" in his pursuit of their nests and eggs. He is a figure for a culture "that did not see" the world beyond its own interests, but at the same time absorbed the traits of that world, becoming something else.

As in "England," language is an important feature of dynamic national identity, and language impresses itself especially on geography. Language in this poem develops as nature does, absorbing local and imported words to establish a diverse sense of place. Language is integral to historical process and leaves its mark on the "narrow tongue of land that Jamestown was," not only in the linguistic mix of place names, but in a legacy of contending doctrines. The rival mottoes of colonizers—*vincere est vivere*—and colonials—"don't tread on me" (spoken, Moore reminds us, by a snake)—lead to the wisdom through suffering of the "black idiom" which sees us "advancin' backward in a circle," repeating ourselves through time rather than progressing. "Colonizing" is a way of saying "taking what we please." And in removing the euphemism, Moore subverts dominion.

Moore's own language works against "dominion" through a stanza pattern that overrides syntax and creates a contrapuntal rhythm through

heavily hyphenated adjectives. These absorb rather than enhance asser-
tion. The dense imagery, the propulsion of the list, the quick juxtaposi-
tions, submerge hierarchies and preferences in the aesthetic pleasure of
sensory overload and the overall sense of *discordia concors.* Moore does
not "cradle" "priorities" as the colonists did. She can afford more equa-
nimity. The intricate rhyme scheme (a twelve-line stanza including a
triple rhyme in the middle, a couplet in the penultimate lines, and a
rhyme between lines 3 and 12) gives the poem "an elegance of which the
source is not bravado." The art of the poem is to draw our attention to an
aesthetic order rather than a cultural hegemony or a single-minded cri-
tique. The aesthetic order of the poem does not whitewash moral inco-
herence, but it shows equanimity in its attention to details, reordering
the site to describe the rich entanglement of nature and human purposes
that has brought us where we are.

The poem that began with an approach to the "pale sand" of Virginia's
shores closes with a receding view of the "darkening filigree" of the live
oak's boughs. Naïve claims to dominance give way to this elegant en-
twining, itself yielding to the day's decline. Moore turns visionary at the
end of the poem, but she first locates spirit in the minute particularity of
the sparrow's "ecstatic burst of joy." This precisely identified "caraway-
seed- / spotted sparrow" that "wakes up seven minutes sooner than the
lark" may offer a hope more explicable to the religious Moore than it was
to Hardy in "The Darkling Thrush." The sparrow also reminds us of
mortality and heralds the finale:

> The live oak's darkening filigree
>   of undulating boughs, the etched
> solidity of a cypress indivisible
>   from the now aged English hackberry,
>   become with lost identity,
>   part of the ground, as sunset flames increasingly
> against the leaf-chiseled
>   blackening ridge of green; while clouds, expanding above
>   the town's assertiveness, dwarf it, dwarf arrogance
>   that can misunderstand
>   importance; and
> are to the child an intimation of what glory is.

This "indivisible" is not yet the achievement of liberty and justice for all,
or a Wordsworthian memory of celestial glory. Throughout the poem
Moore has presented Virginia as a hodgepodge, an "inconsistent flower

bed," despite the passion for monoculture of those who thought they held "dominion" over it. The natural cypress and the hackberry, like the historical Indian and the colonist, and indeed nature and man together, become "indivisible" because intertwined in a continual struggle for dominance and survival. And as mutability and mortality rule all living orders and entities, they "become with lost identity, / part of the ground." The imagery of this poem has been structured on a principle of incongruity and intermixture. The "etched solidity" of historical memory and even of nature becomes a fading outline. Here all colors darken, and all proportions are dwarfed. John Slatin is undoubtedly correct to hear Wordsworth in these lines, and thus an intimation of immortality, but the focus of the poem is not on immortality. The expanding clouds suggest the absorptive power of change; the mini-conflagration of the sunset at the end of the poem reminds us not only of God's power dwarfing man's, but perhaps also of the tragic history of the South, the consequence of arrogant dominion. History tells a story not just of origins but of convergences and disappearances, of forces that thought to dominate but ultimately had to succumb, identities absorbed that were once imposed.

Moore revisited the subject of Jamestown in 1957, after a U.S. Air Force celebration of the 350th anniversary of the Jamestown landing. "Enough: Jamestown 1607–1957" (CP, 185–187) retains a frankness, in the midst of cold war ideology, about America's origins: "Marriage, tobacco, and slavery, / initiated liberty." The poem repeats the story of the failed colony, its starvation, the subjugation of Indians, the craving for quick wealth that resulted in neglect of husbandry and pervasive death. Again she contrasts a cultivated garden, lush and seductive to the contemporary visitor, to the unforgiving conditions of early Virginians, whose colony "did not flower," who were not heroic but "tested until so unnatural / that one became a cannibal." But ultimately Moore does not pass judgment on the past ("who knows what is good") and finds room to endorse the celebration. America's origins are "partial proof" that must be renewed by "present faith" in the yet-unrealized ideals of the nation.

For Moore the genuine is historical; it cannot be held in place. Landscapes are framed and mediated, subject to both human and natural flux. But a place can be made for the genuine even in a world that is increasingly mediated and abstracted. That is perhaps why the attitude of contempt must accompany all efforts to represent it. Moore's America is an ongoing project that has no telos; a confluence of presences, images, and uses makes up the phenomenal world. We keep making and unmaking landscapes on the site we call America. Rather than exalt an ideal of what America once was, she expresses an idea of what it might be, "home to a diversity of creatures," not a collection of icons, slogans, and national attributes, not a "dime novel exterior," but a land remarkable for "accessibility to experience."

5

Amy Clampitt: Nomad Exquisite

Poets of the modern period, I have suggested, continually submit the projections of the self to a reality that will not stay still within the frame. Frost's New England figures seek a mirror in the landscape and discover its otherness; Stevens' early personae shrink or expand in relation to the forms of environment. Moore's quotations and descriptive details construct a vision in which the self does not stand in the middle. A mobile self is the consequence of the superfluity of human forms and the dynamism of the physical world. Poets after the modern period began to explore mobile identity as an embodiment, not just a consequence, of dynamic landscape. Elizabeth Bishop makes travel not just a circumstance but a figure of being. Clampitt's nomad imitates the restlessness of nature, relinquishing the taproot of an essential selfhood for the sporadic and rhizomatic movement of a wandering soul. The landscapes of these poets are not just provisional; they are characterized by their beholders' excursive sight.

In reckoning with the frame and the flux, modern poets create provisional landscapes that acknowledge the limits of metaphor and perspective and the transitional quality of human orders. They might allude to a steadying metaphysical axis—Stevens' "center," Moore's "glory"—but their attention remains on the prismatic turnings of mind and world. One finds suggestions, throughout the work of Frost, Stevens, and Moore, that this transitional mode of landscape might be embraced as an identity, not just a condition of vision. It would be the work of a later generation of poets—Amy Clampitt, A. R. Ammons, and John Ashbery among them—to fully explore this identity, to relinquish the center and seek a home in motion.

Amy Clampitt is the least well known of the poets in this study, but she most directly expresses some of the themes and attitudes I am representing here: the restless feeling within the frame, the dynamism of nature, the fragility of the domestic, the connection of landscape and history, the mingling of human and natural orders, the American sense of mobility. In an interview she remarked:

> If I'm asked to describe myself as a poet, what I end up saying is that I'm a poet of place.... I feel a certain kinship with [Elizabeth Bishop's] nomadism, if that is what it is; though I've been based in New York for many years, I feel less and less as though I really *lived* anywhere. Is that kind of uprooting possibly an American tradition? The more I think about this question, the more intriguing it becomes. Whatever answer there may be, I suspect, will have some relation to being native to the Midwest—and having left it. And then looking back. (*Predecessors, Et Cetera*, 163–164)

What can it mean to be an American poet of place so late in the twentieth century, when the fictions of place that formed the culture no longer serve it? If we once spoke of the American landscape in the language of Genesis, we were more inclined by the end of the millennium toward the Book of Revelation. But Amy Clampitt does not slip easily into nostalgic or millennial rhetoric. Like Moore, her major precursor, she resists the version of the past that idealizes geography as a timeless absolute, a lost presence that we can passively lament or naïvely reinhabit. At the same time she protests against an alienated posture that approaches the world as commodity. Her poems reckon with temporary reality and history; she is diagnostic and instructive without becoming didactic. Clampitt portrays a culture of appropriation and exclusion that has failed to take account of its own restlessness, and the natural drift and variety of the world we inhabit.[1] But unlike Moore's hobo, disengaged from place, she creates ad hoc habitations, and a nomadic mode of habitation open to astonishment.

Clampitt's nomadism is more than a theme or ideology, however. It is a way of seeing, a sensibility, an aesthetic which can be distinguished from a variety of other stances available in American literature: the colonizing, the alienated, the touristic, the cosmopolitan, the immanentist, the transcendental. While Clampitt is not a poet of psychological or philosophical complexity, nor of radical formal innovation, her emphasis on the nomadic does accord with certain modern efforts to resist the codification of reality, to think between our frames rather than from within them. Clampitt reveals how poetry might become a guide in developing this nomadic imagination: searching out and crossing boundaries, scavenging, finding value in what has been ignored, setting up formal patterns which she then works to defeat. She suggests how the poem, even within formally crafted structures, might become an extrinsic nomadic unit rather than a despotic unity or a nostalgic retreat.

The nomadic is a way of thinking—situated, but always edging out and moving on. Unlike the cosmopolitan ("Walt Whitman a Kosmos"), at home everywhere, the nomad is at home nowhere, or only in transition. The nomad has a deterritorialized, Heraclitean sense of space, often evoking the atomic level at which existence composes and decomposes ("Nothing truly is except the atom, // the Whole a sieve of particles, its terrors / loomed of shadows' cumber" [CP, 130]). Rather than recodify the world, Clampitt presses against boundaries, examines "life on the edge." The edge of course implies a frame. To be nomadic is not to be formless or without structures; it is, rather, a particular serial relationship to forms. Dynamic "attachments, links, dependencies" (CP, 251) make up Clampitt's human as well as her natural ecology, but these are dynamic rather than secure. She investigates habitats, looks for ways to dwell in experience, yet insists "that no point is fixed, that there's no foothold / but roams untethered save by such snells, / such sailor's knots, such stays / and guy wires as are // mainly of our own devising" (CP, 273). Her frames are windows, sometimes bus or airplane windows; her spaces of connection are rest stops and train cars. But these circumstances are evidence less of our denatured condition than of our natural mobility, part of the "terrain that from above, aboard the hurled / steel spore, appears suffused with vivid / ravelings, the highways' mimic of veinings // underground, the fossil murk we're all / propelled by, for whatever term" (CP, 286).

On the first page of *The Kingfisher* Clampitt ventures out and unhinges domesticity, launching a nomadic career that never rested on its laurels. "The Cove" (CP, 5–6) recognizes the instinct to avoid exposure, to seek shelter in the "snug house" where "whole nutmegs / inhabit the spice rack." As we sit "listen[ing] to Mozart / or read[ing] Marianne Moore," however, we are already open to a world beyond. Even as we venture out, we dodge for cover. A window frame leads to where the eiders in the fog "tip / and tuck themselves into the swell, almost / as though diving under the eiderdown / in a *gemütlich* hotel room at Innsbruck." The play on eiders and eiderdown is delightful, in its suggestion that nature might be our comfy bed. Certainly the landscape Clampitt reveals has an uncanny power, both domestic and otherworldly. Like Bishop's "embroidered nature, tapestried landscape" (*Complete Poems,*

91) Clampitt's scene is done in "ombre and fine stitchery." But as the porcupine with his "needle-tined paddle tail" emerges, like one of Bishop's animals, as a surrogate for the human, one senses the comedy in our anthropomorphisms. We watch the porcupine emerge at dusk,

> to examine the premises,
> and then withdraw from the (we presume)
> alarming realm of the horizontal into
> the up-and-down underbrush of normality.

Clampitt figures the rather clumsy, groping nature of our nomadic instincts in another animal:

> we noticed a turtle—domed repoussé
> leather with an underlip of crimson—
> as it hove eastward, a covered
> wagon intent on the wrong direction.

Yet as the poet's gaze moves out from the "snug-house," to the yard, and finally to the shore, accepting the awkwardness of our attempts at domestic elegance, another kind of vision opens up, one perhaps only available to the exteriorizing nomad. The final tapestry of sea and sky, in indigo, a color the eye cannot perceive, is sublime rather than domestic:

> hanging
> intact, a curtain wall just frescoed
> indigo, so immense a hue, a blue
> of such majesty it can't be looked at,
> at whose apex there pulses, even
> in daylight, a lighthouse, light-
> pierced like a needle's eye.

The lighthouse is there as an ordering principle, the poet's reassurance to us that the life of the nomad need not be terrifying, that we will not wreck on the world's blinding sublimity.

Wallace Stevens was perhaps more of a vacationer than a nomad, but he understood the power of the nomadic sensibility, and his depiction in the early poem "Nomad Exquisite" (CPP, 77) brings us close to the quality of Clampitt's imagination, the way it can "unhand unbelieving."

As the immense dew of Florida
Brings forth hymn and hymn
From the beholder,
Beholding all these green sides
And gold sides of green sides, . . .

So, in me, come flinging
Forms, flames, and the flakes of flames.

Clampitt views nature, as Stevens' nomad does, not for its eternal out-
lines but for its restless, even violent vitality, which brings forth, in be-
holder and poet, a comparable restless vitality of the imagination. Such
an imagination, beholding the world for its "gold sides," its metaphysical
beauty, and its "green sides," its sensuous beauty, responds with fiery
forms. But while an "exquisite" nomad concerns herself with beauty, she
does not build mansions to it. For she is "exquisite" in the other sense as
well: she "searches out" a home in motion.

Clampitt frequently portrays her native Midwest as a soil nurturing
her nomadic sensibility even as its culture, bent on survival, became
parochial. Paradoxically, this land of "settlement" promotes movement,
drift, restlessness. This is not, of course, the vision of the Midwest with
which Americans began. Rather, the Midwest was mythologized as the
vast Edenic garden of the industrialized East, infinitely exploitable, the
manifest destiny of empire on its westward course. An ahistorical sense
of the perceived natural environment as given, timeless, and original
prevailed through the nineteenth century and lingers even to the pres-
ent. But like Moore, Clampitt sets history, natural and human, against
environmental myth, examining the sense of the Midwest in terms of
those who actually lived there and from the perspective of one travel-
ing in the opposite direction. Repeatedly she uncovers a place and people
in flux. Clampitt's "Heartland," which she began to describe in *The King-
fisher,* is not a place of abiding, primordial nature, confirming individ-
ual identity, but an elusive and ephemeral site that we have struggled,
in vain, to possess. An alluvial land full of restless inhabitants, this void
can be framed, sectioned off, clotted with farmlots, but never filled.
From the outset, then, Clampitt asks us to relinquish our approach to
landscape as an escape from time and history, a donor of presence, a
solid ground of Being. We cannot dwell in the heartland, as in the
woods of Walden. Being, in such a place, remains a transitional, restless
becoming.

Clampitt reads geology as evidence of the fluent, metamorphic nature of place. The geology of the Midwest, with its abundant fossils from the Eocene age, reveals a space "half sea half land," as she writes in "Imago," a former ocean bottom (CP, 59). Through this association Clampitt gives a fresh identity to her native place; the "frontier" of American dominion has another story to tell, unflattering to claims and settlements. The prairie schooner "under unmasted coifs of canvas" is appropriately named as it crosses a landscape unyielding as the ocean that once covered it: "Midsummer's welling bluestem / rose so high the wagons . . . / dragged belly-deep in grass / across the sloughs" (CP, 55). As if to imitate geology's dramatic grammar, Clampitt forms single stanzas and even sentences that telescope transformation rather than suppress it (she is a nomad of history as well as geography). Her imagery reinforces this dynamism. In "The Quarry" (55–56) a site of plunder, of raw material for our permanent structures, our banks and government buildings, becomes, for the poet, a space of historical inquiry, a timespace where "Light years / of ooze foreshortened into limestone" leave an unsteady footing in the present. To imagine back in geological terms is not to establish a rock foundation but to discover, literally, that your house is built on sand. Syntax is the sluice of history, washing oceanic past down onto marble-domed present. Such language exposes us to the forbidding anonymity of space which confronted our forebears:

> No roads
> no landmarks to tell where you are,
> or who, or whether you will ever find a place
> to feel at home in: no alpine
> fastness, no tree-profiled pook's hill,
> the habitat of magic: only waves
> of chlorophyll in motion

Clampitt writes specifically of the first settlers, but the syntax and tense leave the scene looming over the present. Even now, the vast horizontal of the prairie space tends to obliterate the pastoral feeling of Adamic belonging, enchantment, dominion. Clampitt notes the fragile markings of the human claim as so many potential fossils: "this festering of lights at night, this grid of homesteads," and today "the frittered sprawl of who we are, / of where we came from." The anthropomorphic surface ("this hardening / lymph of haste foreshortened into highways," this "heartland," the "belly of the future") funnels into the body of De Soto, gold-lusting epitome of human presumption and rapacity, at the end of the poem. His is an Ozymandian fate:

>   Flushed finally
> out of the heartland drainpipe,
> the soft parts of De Soto's body filtered
> into the capillaries of the delta. Will
> some shard of skull or jawbone, undecomposed,
> outlast his name, as the unquarried starfish
> outlast the seas that inundated them?

Against this image Clampitt asks us to imagine the unpresumptuous presences that have crossed this site, rather than lay claim to it: "the lilt and ripple of the dark, / birdsong at dusk augmented by frog choirs / . . . the wickiups / now here, now there." The Indian teepees or wickiups in particular suggest the nomadic history of the place. Images of permanence are a late, imported addition; the gold-topped, marble capitol is a "stilted El Dorado" in this poem in praise of limestone.

The oceanic, nomadic past is an invitation to those called "shirkers" and "misfits" in a midwestern ethos that works to claim, control, hem in, purify, commodify. If the "central fact" of Iowa, as Clampitt proposes in "The Local Genius" (CP, 62), is not Olson's abstract, conceptual SPACE but DIRT, that "utilitarian muck underfoot" of metamorphic earth, mortality, and human imperfection, then the local genius, the neoclassical spirit of place, must be (so prairie heroism prescribes) the Iowan who invented the washing machine. But Clampitt offers a different spirit of place from both Olson's aestheticized SPACE and Iowa's anesthetized DIRT. The nomad, though "far from the hot baths" (344), can nevertheless achieve a "down to earth transcendence."

Clampitt rejects a hierarchical opposition between wild nature and human order, dirt and the washing machine. The nomad, respecting no boundaries, no fixed decorum, even of the inner self, sets her imagination exploring margins, liminal spaces; she thinks beyond the grid. Hence, in "The Woodlot" (CP, 57–58) Clampitt remembers the magical places grown up around the prairie grid, havens from both the brutal horizonal of nature and the rigid social order. "Air, that rude nomad," having made the "fine manners" and neat borders of English gardens impossible, spares growth around the harsh articulations of plow and barbed wire to create this magical, soul-protecting, yet anonymous space where section lines give way to violets, where solid ground and firm identity open up to "a blue cellarhole / of pure astonishment":

>   Before it,
> I/you, whatever that conundrum may yet
> prove to be, amounts to nothing.

This suspension of both individual and group identity is crucial to nomadic thought, its pulsive intensity. This willingness to be awed by a ground which cannot be claimed makes the difference between the nomad and the exile and also between a place for discovery and a territory, a mere site of our imposing desires.

History had always been an aspect of the description of place for Clampitt, but in *Westward* she most directly examines the formation of landscape in relation to the transformation of the Midwest into a structured, agrarian society. The gridwork that defined the homesteads of the Midwest until World War II had to be established, with various interests served and consequences suffered. Clampitt's desire to write a poetry of the prairie came to full expression in the long poem "The Prairie" (CP, 343–358). The poem is a historical, geographical, literary, and personal account of the heartland, a semi-epic of "settlement" and restless movement across a continent. Its vision of environmental history presents the nomadic as a characteristic but suppressed sense of place, which has given way to a feeling of exile. Clampitt was undoubtedly aware of William Cullen Bryant's famous long poem "The Prairies," which represents a vision of the midwestern landscape at the dawn of settlement, when he could "dream" of "the sound of the advancing multitude / Which soon shall fill these deserts." But he is "in the wilderness alone" (*Poetical Works,* 232). From this perspective "these unshorn fields, boundless and beautiful" "stretch, / In airy undulations, far away." The prairie is true to its familiar ocean comparison—its surface "rolls and fluctuates to the eye"—but the "dilated sight / Takes in the encircling vastness," and the motion is circumscribed by expansive vision (228). Bryant anticipates the imminent settlement of the land, without any threat to his boundless freedom. In Clampitt's prairie, however, a population has already come and gone, and the "gardens of the Desert" have proved less than Edenic.

Clampitt's prairie is, foremost, an unyielding absence where settlement is an imposed, enforced condition, not a natural dominion. The prairie is also, like Frost's desert places, a metaphor for the absence within, the cause of restlessness and anxiety within the binding grid of prairie propriety. Against these inner and outer spaces the myth of the self-reliant American Adam, giving name and meaning to the landscape through intellection, cannot stand up. Clampitt acknowledges a deep debt to Emerson, but in this regard she offers a challenge:

> *In self-trust all the virtues*
> *are comprehended. . . .* Self-trust. Man Thinking.

When—my father's father might have wondered—
was Man Thinking, self-reliant, other than
alone in the vast stammer of the inarticulate?
                                        (CP, 347–348)

Clampitt challenges, too, the ahistoricism of Emerson's vision of America. America's individualism and ahistoricism have paradoxically produced a monoculture which views itself as absolute, original, and authoritative. If "all history is epitaph" (in Emerson's phrase from "Experience"), the past might, nevertheless, help to fill the emptiness of the prairie, and of modern life. Clampitt's version of the nomadic accepts "attachments, links, dependencies" even as it rejects exclusionary, despotic social and geographic systems. Unlike the exile and the alienated individualist, the nomad imagines a social web and historical continuities that cannot be codified. The American tendency to shoulder aside what came before, to approach the landscape as if it had no history, to see the dominant order as natural and given, amounts to an ignorance of place and self which "The Prairie" addresses.

"The Prairie" is in many ways a bleak portrait of the Midwest, taken as a site of the human desire for settlement. Clampitt presents nineteenth-century lives as desperately hard, hemmed in, anxious before an un-yielding nature and a merciless social order. But throughout the poem she presents an alternative to settlement and exile, more adaptive to the "tenuity of life," a nomadic way which once thrived on the land. Clampitt never suggests that we turn back the cultural clocks. But the nomadic way of life she discovers in the prairie past has modern possi-bilities, and suggests an intellectual as well as a practical attitude. Far from being merely primitive, the nomadic way of life finds an example in the life of Henry James. Forming a fluent parallel between the landscape and the psyche, Clampitt imagines hidden, unfenced regions of mind and scene, "secret coves" which "the landed, pacing their stiff saraband, / could not have known they harbored." Settled nowhere, imposing no particular pattern on reality, the nomad is best able to discover, beyond the vacancy, a "pattern in the carpet," no barbed-wire geometry but a ro-coco design full of furls and deviations, which has been "trodden under-foot" but may be revealed to the exteriorizing, "unformulating mind."

Clampitt has found an ideal form for her subject, one in which the neat grid of the stanza is overrun by a fluent syntax and a digressive, as-sociative structure, and a "chance fact" is allowed to "leap into place." Three-line blank verse stanzas in eight cantos of 20 stanzas each hold together a bravely nomadic poem which begins in contemporary New

York City, cuts to Chekhov's Russian steppe, then to the American Midwest of a century ago, to California, and back. The poet intensifies this geographic and historical mobility with analogic and metaphoric leaps, as New York's homeless, for instance, recall the prairie's vestigial Indians and both recall the weary warriors of Homer's *Iliad,* nomads all and, in the words of Simone Weil, "far from the hot baths."

Without yielding to a neat plot line, Clampitt does unfold a story here. Her protagonist in "The Prairie" is her Iowa grandfather, born the same year as Chekhov, whose restlessness and anxiety she recognizes as her inheritance. Her grandfather's unsettled feeling, "straying sometimes at dusk in unfenced places," becomes a return of the repressed, evoking the nomadic character of American Indians for whom settlement is a forced, not a willed condition, a paradoxical exile. Against this "dimming memory" of "the species that persisted and that vanished," of "namelessness, of dreamings," the shadow of monoculture always crosses, dealing with the tenuity of life by denying the past and dismissing all that will not fit its structures, that threatens its static preservation, "the puccoon, / the pasqueflower, the compass plant, and vervain" as well as the nomad. One of the sorry contradictions of our history, for Clampitt, is how often our nomadic instincts yield to despotic ones, how individualism leads to parochialism. The underside of prairie heroism, the adventure and daring that brought people to a new land, is the "fencerow patrol" that would conserve the new claims:

> The gossip. The scathing whisper. Party lines.
> Consensus. Stratifyings: oh yes, even in
>
> a place so nearly level, someone to look
> down on—renters; hired men and their unwashed
> progeny; the drifter from nowhere.

In a manifold paradox, it is the nomadic red man who says of the settler: *"the white man does not understand America, / . . . the roots of the tree of his life / have yet to grasp it"* (CP, 346). The obsession with boundaries and parcellings has left the settler detached from the earth. The inevitability of the nomadic way of life on this "settled continent" ("what does it mean?") is apparent at the end of the poem when a different kind of Indian, "an old deaf Mexican" migrant, returns to supplant the "settlers" who once "put a beleaguered foot down against the shiftless" but have since drifted off.

———————

"Dimming memory" is a kind of refrain in this poem of history and erasure. One would not expect the nomad to be the custodian of the past, yet without a stake in monoculture, without its relentless purposiveness, the nomad is more open to the palimpsest of the landscape. It is the nomad, finally, who tells the story not only of the excluded, but even of the "overlaid procedure, forethought, accumulation" that designed the prairie grid. "To be landless, half a nomad, nowhere wholly / at home, is to discover, now, an epic theme / in going back" (CP, 358). This odyssey is a testament to the human and natural ecology, "the linked, perishable, humming webs" that define and redefine place. Clampitt's sense of place is deeply ecological; it defies the totalizing impulse that has characterized other American visions of landscape. But she conveys an image of ecological patterns that features the dynamic, fluent, even superfluent ("perishable") quality of those patterns.

If Clampitt's experience of the Midwest positioned her for a nomadic sense of place, what was formative has become characteristic of her vision. Yet a nomadic sensibility is not a necessary result of being native to the Midwest. Until Clampitt, our primary bards of the Midwest were the "deep image" poets—Robert Bly, James Wright, William Stafford, and others—and their sense of place is quite different from hers. As their epithet suggests, the deep image poets worked by selecting a scene or image and delving into it symbolically. Like Clampitt, they resist the model of landscape as a sweeping vista, of the imagination's relation to place as imperial and detached. But in supplanting transcendentalism with immanence they create an unconscious sense of place with little particularity to it. Where William Carlos Williams' fixed gaze might aim at objectification, the deep image poets moved toward an intense subjectivity, understanding Williams' dictum "it is imperative that we sink" in a new way. Immersion, for both, has a vertical force rather than pulsive intensity. Stupefaction becomes a form of revelation. These poets often heightened their effects by using simple sentences and the "language of ordinary men," but without discursive content or logical connection. Atmospheric images—night, shadow, empty roads—also placed feeling over intellection. The deep image poets tend to represent the Midwest as an emptiness, but a ghostly, elegiac emptiness, not one that casts doubt on the poet's romantic desire for presence.

Nothing could be further from Clampitt's connection to landscape. Her ordering of the earth involves networks, webs, lateral connections among nerve centers. As if directly addressing the deep image poets, she declares "depth isn't everything" and thrives without a taproot like the spruce which "hold[ing] on / spreads its underpinnings thin . . ." (CP, 117). Where a deep image poet will sink into a well of meanings and sur- mises, Clampitt will imagine outward, will exteriorize the image. Where they tend to stage meditation in a single scene, her mind refuses to stay put, creating a landscape out of associated fragments. Sometimes she moves through a paratactic structure (variations on a theme), as in "The Spruce Has No Taproot" (117), where her mind bounds from cats to cinquefoil to roses and back to cats; sometimes she moves by association, as in "Urn-Burial and the Butterfly Migration" (132). Experience, scenic or otherwise, is always at once highly specific and broadly connected, not through obvious contingencies or purely metaphysical leaps, but through reaches of the known or observed. The connections tend to foreground particularity rather than funnel into general principle, so that the effect is more digressive than inductive. Sometimes the move- ment is metaphoric, with those surprising bounds of connection which Frost called "fetching," as when a pile of defunct cars is "lasagna-layered" or a lindenbloom suggests a stately "bell-pull." This is the joyous no- madism of the restless imagination which refuses decorum and wanders freely from one order of reality to another. For Clampitt, the Heraclitean and metamorphic nature of the world stimulates these adventures in language.

Clampitt's syntax operates like her vegetation, linking highly disparate images in the loose clasp of the sentence, forming a temporary, expedi- ent unit (a rhizome) rather than an abstraction or a deep-rooted unit:

> a gathering in one continuous,
> meshing intimacy, the interlace
> of unrelated fibers
> joining hands like last survivors
> who, though not even neighbors
>
> hitherto, know in their predicament
> security at best is shallow.

(CP, 117)

No poet since Marianne Moore can sustain longer sentences, pressuring subordination and closure without abandoning the rules of composi- tion. Typically, the syntax drives a thought that will not stay put, so that sentences end (or only seem to end) somewhere other than they began. Clampitt varies her syntax, as an artist uses different brush strokes to evoke different moods. "London Inside and Outside," for instance, piles in clauses that give the poem a dimensionality of present and past (the perceived and the remembered), indeed, of outside and inside, within a single surface. Typically, the initial point of view is that of the nomad, looking back at a former domicile:

> Looked back on happily, the ivy-hung,
> back-wall-embowered garden of our
> pied-à-terre and domicile in Chelsea
> seems oddly like some dream of living
> halfway down the well that sheltered
> Charles Dodgson's Elsie, Lacie
> and Tillie—with those geraniums
> in urns, that lily-of-the-valley
> bed not quite in bloom, those churring
> ringdoves, those thrushes murderously
> foraging for earthworms: an exterior
> so self-contained, a view so inward
> that though at night we'd note
> faint window-glimmerings eclipsed by ivy,
> we seemed to have no neighbors either
> to spy on or be spied on by.
>
> (CP, 253)

By the end of the stanza, through the twists of syntax that break down the dichotomy of outside/inside, we are drawn back in, but invited to look out. The syntax and thought structure of the poem reveal both Clampitt's homing instinct and her wanderlust. Other ways of being inside and outside at once have arisen in the stanza as well, through observation and association—the Dodgson book, the geraniums in urns, and so on. The syntax lends itself to the compact, British feel of the place, an unterrifying exposure of inwardness that continues throughout the poem. This is one kind of pulsive intensity in Clampitt, but there are many others. For her, landscape and language are linked as structures open to mobility, restless in their frames.

Like Marianne Moore, Clampitt replaces depth with an at times almost rococo surface. Yet Clampitt's nomadic style is distinct from Moore's accumulative one, at the level of syntax and imagery alike. The complexity of Moore's prismatic syntax is built around constant ironic qualification and double negation; the absorption of quotation from various discourses; circumlocution; extrapolation pulled in by epigram;

digression disciplined by moral purpose. It is a poetry that takes in the world from the vast reading room of a Brooklyn apartment. Clampitt's syntax wanders, pursuing the course of a memory or an association, a variation on a theme, interweaving experience and reflection, fonder of the dash and the parenthesis than the semicolon. Clampitt's premise that "our home is motion" seems to derive most directly from Elizabeth Bishop. Clampitt's eye roams over scenes without establishing itself as either transcendent or stationed. In Clampitt's "Midsummer in the Blueberry Barrens," for instance, the syntax is relaxed and the poem is all foreground, dominated by present tense. It makes a striking contrast to the inside/outside dimensionalities of "London."

> Away from the shore, the roads dwindle and lose themselves
> among the blueberry barrens. The soil is tired;
> what little there was of it in these upland
> watersheds wore out years ago.
>
> (CP, 266)

The deceptively aimless manner recalls Bishop, as does the relaxed syntax, designed to hold back an apocalyptic dread. The dread follows the beholder to the luxury of the shore, where the resort houses are, and hovers around the figure of St. John the Baptist, whose feast day is celebrated. But this is not a day for martyrdom. Like Bishop, the nomadic Clampitt skirts but avoids apocalypse. Yet there are differences here as well. Bishop's is an excursive and interrogative vision, a gradual sublime, in which the landscape's meanings lean out but are never fully grasped or articulated. She tends to abide in mysteries and tonal ambiguities, to turn the questions of observation inward. Clampitt's imagination is more likely to establish a footing in her subject, however tentative, to set up makeshift structures around it rather than rely on the cumulative effect of peripheral vision.

If "depth isn't everything" for Clampitt, neither is height. Perhaps because her young eye fed on the midwestern prairie, there are no mountains, no steep and lofty cliffs. Hers is a "down to earth transcendence," "airborne, earthbound." Her fence-sitting meadowlark supplants the soaring skylark. She eschews a rhetoric that scales up to the vague and the lofty, that experiences wonder only in the vast or the obscure, that builds a scaffolding when there is so much wonder near the ground. She finds the sublime by staring not at the sun but at a bog of insectivorous plants, in "The Sun Underfoot among the Sundews" (CP, 15). But if here a "wilderness swallows you up" and the ground is not stable, this sinking is entirely conscious and real. Clampitt needs no surrealism to experience mystery; the world already turns itself upside down. There is plenty of depth in surfaces—so much, in fact, that "you start to fall upward."

Scavenger that she is (hence her interest in birds, seeds, berries), Clampitt finds value in surprising places. But she also unpacks associations and allusions, blithely investing the world with the conscious human purpose which makes it habitable. Indeed, there is an instructive and even allegorical aspect to Clampitt's verse, but the thought is not fixed to the thing in any monolithic way. On the contrary, for Clampitt the overflow of verbal invention and association may be the shortest way to opening the silence, not the silence of the tongue-tied and the unexplicit, but of the world's word-surpassing variety.

The world is always tied to words for us; we relate to nature by naming it. Silence is not an alternative to language but a condition of landscape itself, in that it does not speak. Clampitt respects this silence without submitting to it. Like many nature poets and poets of place, Clampitt is fascinated with names. Her botanist's precision is one of the joys of her work, and there is little sense in Clampitt that the world can be brought into poetry through the vague gesture, the symbolist's nod; it demands precision. She is an advanced student of nomenclature. But naming is a form of claiming and classifying which cannot accommodate the world's ultimate silent being. That must be approached, not through the inarticulate moan, but through exhausting the resources of the language. Hence in "Botanical Nomenclature" (CP, 16) Clampitt relishes the various names that have been given to "'that pink-and-blue flower / you find along the shore'" and the myriad associations these different names call up. Each name is a perspective which gives the plant an identity, different from the other names, and none can quite embrace "the mirroring / marryings of all likeness." For the nomadic poet bearing witness to the web of names, imposing no nomenclature of her own, each thing is uniquely itself, yet universal.

Names do not merely classify; they embody lore. As Moore's "Virginia Britannia" makes clear, we name places in order to claim them, to stamp ourselves into them, to memorialize. The landscape retains the names even as it casts aside the identities. Clampitt takes up Moore's story of John Smith and Powhatan, turning to the layers of narrative around the story of Powhatan's daughter, "Matoaka." The stories fade away until we must feel that

> Awe,
> in all the stories

we tell ourselves, is finally
what's durable, no matter how
we mollify it, no matter how our
pieties keep changing.

(CP, 372)

The permanence we feel in landscape derives from its role as a site of our will to remember. The landscape refutes monoculture not only by its natural variety but by the diversity of names attached to it. Language and landscape are indeed tied, not because nature is a book, but because names create a residue of our ephemeral orders. The earth is cross-hatched with the frames we variously laid over it in time. A meditation on names is thus a lesson in the transience of all descriptions; geographic names register the passing of cultures, divinely authorized as they may once have seemed. In "Matoaka" (CP, 369–376) a meditation on geographic names, Indian and English, becomes a lesson in humility, not only for the patriarchal European culture that colonized the native one, but for the contemporary culture which presumes to judge its past, to deconstruct and rename. But the landscape opens a silence for the poet where the names have pressed into it. Lake Matoaka, bearing the tribal name of Pocahantas (christened Rebecca when she was imported to the English court—"what she called herself by then is not recorded"), becomes a site of meditation on the unnamed, unnameable life we all share:

to stroll thus
is to move nearer,
in imagination, to the nub,
the pulse, the ember of what she was—
no stranger, finally, to the mystery
of what we are.

(CP, 376)

It is the privilege of the nomad, approaching the world without designs upon it, to feel this pulsing identity.

We have seen how, in Clampitt, landscape is deeply involved in historical and political realities. The earth is crossed with the various contending populations and their landscapes. Place names and other language sediments are the residue of those crossings and conflicts. If Clampitt's vision involves the political relation of language and landscape, it also involves a calculus of ecology and economy. But just as Clampitt refuses a simple opposition of nature and speech, so too she has a subtle reading of how man's entrepreneurial energies might become aligned with nature's dynamic systems. Her environmentalism is one with her nomadism.

Clampitt defines her nomadism against a prevailing tendency of American culture to homogenize and commodify, and to ignore or exclude whatever cannot be commodified. She implies that a culture concerned only with commodities inevitably stagnates, as in the "stilted El Dorado" of Iowa's capitol. In "The Prairie" she sets the image of Chekhov's money-burning Jew against the emergence of the American West as "essentially a customer." "What I see from my own peculiar perspective, as a writer of poetry," she argues in the introduction to *Predecessors, Et Cetera,* "is a conspiracy all around to stamp out the sense of living continuity, to stamp out singularity, to do away with everything that's not a recognizable commodity" (165). She celebrates what is ignored by monoculture: beachglass, sea mouse, salvage, pokeweed. The nomad, who lays claim to nothing and carries little baggage, is particularly positioned to appreciate this singularity of things, to decommodify the known and draw attention to the imaginative value of what has been ignored. Where the alchemy of the commodities market would turn hay into gold, Clampitt does the opposite, rebuking permanence in "Stacking the Straw" and making the harvest monuments stand for the transience of all human achievement, intellectual as well as material.

A great deal of Clampitt's poetry directly protests the commodification of landscape, the slash and burn of enterprise, which seeks an opening for its lusts, but threatens the imaginative openings that nature provides in its delicate ecological balance and diversity of life. The legacy of Jefferson's America in Clampitt's "Notes on the State of Virginia" (recalling Moore's critique as well) is ecological destruction:

>   mercantile
> expansion, the imperative to
> find an opening, explore, exploit,
> and in so doing begin to alter,
>
> with its straking smudge and smear,
> little by little, this opening in
> the foliage, wet brink of all our
> enterprise: the blur of bays, the
> estuarial fog at sunrise, the glooms
> and glimmerings, the tidal waters.
>   (CP, 282)

Will our homogenizing enterprise stamp out the essential mystery of things? The "brink of all our enterprise" may suggest a danger, a limit we have reached, beyond which nature will be destroyed by enterprise in the sense of commercial technology. But Clampitt allows another sense of "brink"—an opening; and of "enterprise"—an adventure or risk, in which the artist may invest some hope as well as place a warning. Nature is the "brink of enterprise" for the poet and for culture generally because it is a source of renewal and creative inspiration; the wild acanthus becomes the prototype of the Doric column. If we destroy this opening to renewal, we risk our own exhaustion. In "Marine Surface, Low Overcast," for instance, Clampitt praises the virtues of that most uncommodifiable entity, fog. Here, as elsewhere in *The Kingfisher,* a series of economic puns highlights a reality which enterprise cannot construct. The descriptions are pitched to our love of the crafted, the delicate, the expensive: "Laminae of living tissue," "aluminum, furred with a velouté / of looking glass" (13). The mist exceeds human ingenuity:

> no loom, no spinneret, no forge, no factor,
> no process whatsoever, patent
> applied or not applied for,
> no five-year formula, no fabric
> for which pure imagining,
> except thus prompted,
> can invent the equal.
>
> (CP, 14)

Clampitt is strikingly unsentimental about dwelling, and she refuses to identify nature with home. Human economy is designed to resist the tenuity of life, to control, hoard, or convert to gold. Hence while the capitalist's enterprise may seem ruthless in what it destroys, the conservative instinct behind it may be fundamental, even for the poet. Its emotional equivalent is elegy. In "Camouflage" (CP, 40–41) an encounter with a killdeer's nest is presented in an equivalent language of luck and lucre:

> It seemed at first like a piece of luck,
> the discovery, there in the driveway,
> of an odd sort of four-leaf clover—
> no bankful of three-penny greenery
> but a worried, hovering, wing-dragging
>   killdeer's treasury—

The economic metaphor might seem here to mark a difference rather than a similarity with the commodities market, but as "luck" turns to Darwinian chance and the cards are stacked against what we invest with feeling, we take on some of the same reckless attributes as the "enterprising" capitalist. "We'd have turned that bird's / entire environment // upside down to have preserved them." This, certainly, abbreviates the paradoxes of the modern ecology movement. Nature's economy is spendthrift, as the "broken-wing pageant" which follows the nest scene makes clear. Camouflage itself is but an evolutionary accident, the babies "a casual handful of dice, squiggle-spotted by luck / that made them half invisible." We, too, are subject to nature's spendthrift economy, but our emotional economy emerges from memory ("not part of the shorebird's equipment"):

> For a day, we couldn't quite afford
> that morning's black discovery.
> Grief is like money: there is only
> so much of it we can give away.
> And that much grief, for a day,
>   bankrupted our economy.

This apparently anecdotal poem opens up a large question that occupies Clampitt repeatedly, about the economy of elegy for the nomadic sense of place. In traditional pastoral elegy the landscape is both a responsive site in which the poet enacts his grief, and a counterpoint to loss, a space of memorial permanence and of nature's regenerative powers. Clampitt's elegies tend to emphasize movement across a landscape, not only the traditional processional movement of the bereaved, as in "A Procession at Candlemas," but the inevitable drift and dissemination of the earthly which death confirms rather than arrests. In "Urn-Burial and the Butterfly Migration," for instance, the "rest for the body's residue" in this settler's burial ground is "friable" and yields to the nomadic ways of dandelions, immigrants, and butterflies, to "that unrest whose home— *our* / home—is motion" (CP, 132–133). The high rhetoric of the poem ennobles an untranscendent, inconclusive vision.

Clampitt's elegies make clear that the nomadic vision is by no means a facile or callous one. She is really only "half a nomad"; she has the homing instincts of the pigeon. The feeling of exile and the longing for a permanent home are inescapable human feelings. Like Frost, she recognizes that the retentive impulse is as important to life as the excursive one. But no actual return home can eradicate such feelings, as "Black

Buttercups" makes clear. There is an anxious as well as a joyous side to
the nomadic existence, but Clampitt chooses it as one chooses necessity
rather than delusion.

Clampitt's most consistent critique of the elegiac sense of place (so in-
congruous with the nomadic impulse) occurs in a series of meditations
on vacant lots in *What the Light Was Like*, *Archaic Figure*, and again in
Westward. In these poems one feels the play of memory and longing
against the pull of change. The vacant lot is conspicuously a modern,
even postmodern, space, the opposite of a wilderness or a garden, no vir-
gin land or terra incognita but a commodified space filled and emptied
out, to be eventually filled again. Having been "based in New York City
for many years," Clampitt has had a special vantage point by which to
correct the ahistorical view of American landscape as open space; rather,
it is cleared space. As a site the vacant lot marks the nomadic nature of
humanity. The repetitions of lost time in "Vacant Lot with Tumbleweed
and Pigeons" (CP, 172) ("two summers / and a winter solstice since") re-
call Wordsworth's "Tintern Abbey" ("five years have passed"). The
poem's stop-time hyphenations ("a not-yet-uprooted / tumbleweed,"
"the / soon-to-be-obliterated stations / of nostalgia") recall Elizabeth
Bishop's "Poem" with its "yet-to-be-dismantled-elms" (*Complete Poems*,
177). Clampitt's poem enacts the erasure it describes, as it moves in
twenty-eight lines making two sentences, from memory ("The rooms
gone, hallways and stairwells / air") to the sense of forgetting ("the roof-
less staircase of outmoded custom") to the forgotten ("the dispossessed,
the razed, / the triste, the unaccounted-for"). But the poem most resem-
bles Frost's "Hyla Brook," with its layering of nostalgias in which imagi-
nation literally writes value onto the blank landscape. In Clampitt the
tumbleweeds and pigeons become the surrogates of the imagination and
of writing:

> the ricepaper
> of the first December snowfall
> inscribed with a not-yet-uprooted
> tumbleweed's whip-limber pyramid,
> spare, see-through, symmetrical,
>
> an evergreen in one dimension, each
> brushed-in, accidental grass-stroke
> beside it letter perfect.

Writing's "evergreen" against the bleak oblivion of time is a transient if
delicate way of marking out a "station of nostalgia." The homing pigeons

return in dwindling numbers, like dimming memory, in "Progress at Building Site with (Fewer) Pigeons." In this poem Clampitt's imagination is turned less on the dismantling of the past than on the uncertain evolving of the future, the new writing on the vacant lot. Yet the poet does propose a kind of foothold available to the nomadic sensibility.

Amy Clampitt is often described as a "naturalist" and admired for her wonderfully detailed descriptions. Her critique of American exploitation of land and lives, and her own celebration of wild things as they resist domestication, make her a plausible subject for the "ecologically oriented" critic. But the objects of Clampitt's adversary energies are not domestications and constructions, or even the struggle for domination, but stasis, monoculture, and commodification. Like the nature she constructs, Clampitt is a "fanatic" and a "mobile opportunist," compulsively creating structures and abandoning them in a restless, fugitive motion. She is attracted to the fugitive things of nature that find a foothold in non-native ground, things that travel and adapt. The garden ideal, like the wilderness ideal, has little appeal for this poet who admires the tenacious weeds that spring up everywhere and are never quite eradicated. What she loves about wild things is their affront to neatness and decorum. She goes out of her way to find aesthetic value where it cannot be commodified or exchanged for simulacra (calendar art, Disney parks, even poems).

In this context Clampitt's poems on vacant lots offer particularly interesting examples of this contemporary pastoral, recalling the resilience of Stevens' late poems of poverty such as "The Plain Sense of Things." Eliot offers a contrast: the "vacant lots" of his "Preludes," where old women gather sticks, suggest apocalyptic emptiness. For Clampitt, they are an opportunity to fill, especially in "Vacant Lot with Pokeweed":

> Tufts, follicles, grubstake
> biennial rosettes, a low-
> life beach-blond scruff of
> couch grass: notwithstanding
> the intermingled dregs
>
> of wholesale upheaval and
> dismemberment, weeds do not
> hesitate, the wheeling
> rise of the ailanthus halts
> at nothing—and look! here's
>
> a pokeweed, sprung from seed
> dropped by some vagrant, that's

seized a foothold: a magenta-
girdered bower, gazebo twirls
of blossom rounding into

raw-buttoned, garnet-rodded
fruit one more wayfarer
perhaps may salvage from
the season's frittering,
the annual wreckage.
                    (CP, 329)

If the vacant lot is a landscape without inherent meaning, it is still a po-
tential habitat. What is a Texas pokeweed doing in New York City?
Dropped from some vagrant's pocket, it has taken hold on this surpris-
ing site. Here is a mode of survival, a way of living, amidst the weeds and
interglinting dregs, which real estate, with its gaze set on scaffolding,
cannot recognize but which poetry, in its resistance to commodity, can.
The vacant lot defines a new sense of landscape and of place: no longer a
site of our nostalgia for power, presence, or permanence, the vacant lot
defines landscape as a space of temporary habitation.

It is interesting to consider the meaning of the word "vacant" here. It
has a double significance, both empty and available, and this ambiguity
suggests a contrast between human and natural "use." The scene is "va-
cant"—between human constructions—yet in natural terms it is full.
This fullness is not represented as the return to a primal condition so
much as a natural opportunism, matched by the poet's own inventive-
ness, creating a pastoral landscape out of this scene of weeds and debris.
For man and nature alike this vacant lot is a "site," not an essential place.
Nature here is parallel to the social, creative, and decreative world of
man, but antithetical to its system of commodification, offering an alter-
native mode of circulation and exchange. The parodic character of the
natural scene suggests resemblance to the energies that produce social
orders. But there is a difference. In its alliance with nature's construc-
tions, this scene offers a counterexample to the economy of real estate
("we think this is a vacancy, but look, it is not vacant but full") and im-
plies the possibility for mobility (lateral as much as vertical) unrealized
in public life. Nature in this poem represents an alternative use of the va-
cant lot. But the ultimate focus of the poem is not on this alternative
construct but on the general superfluous expenditure that overrides
each of these uses.

The first stanza of "Vacant Lot with Pokeweed" gives us a sort of low-
grade organizational vitality of "lowlife" (in a social and a perspectival

sense) couch grass—a rhizomatic rather than a vertical, rooted presence—
of "grubstake" rosettes (like those "prospectors" borrowing supplies on
the promise of returns), enterprising despite the appearance of negation
in the "intermingling dregs / of wholesale upheaval." There is a kind of
defiant irony in the "rise of ailanthus" out of these dregs, the "tree of
heaven" which stinks to high heaven. Clampitt is not just trumping Don-
ald Trump. The scene suggests both an alternative cycle of exchange to
one based on commodification (real estate) and a fable of the struggle
toward dominance and the transience of all ascendancies.

As Clampitt's vision roams around this disorganized or low-organized
space, this "vacant" lot, the eye settles on a focus that gives it a new defi-
nition and a place to invest the lyric energy. Clampitt too is a prospector
and discovers, or creates, a landscape. The pokeweed has humble origins
(its seed having passed through a bird's gullet), but having "seized a
foothold" (which is just what the poet's gaze—"and look!"—has done
within the vacancy of the lot) it ascends to majesty with its regal "garnet-
rodded" (sceptered) fruit. The pokeweed has transformed the vacant lot
into a "bower" with a "gazebo"—a *hortus conclusus*. But this is not the
Rhodora pleading its own excuse of beauty in a raging world. Nor is it an
example of the meek inheriting the earth. Another poet would stop with
the pokeweed and sentimentalize the survival of natural beauty out of
cultural "wreckage," or the ascendancy of "natural" aristocracy over that
which is constructed. But Clampitt has no investment in preserving this
particular arrangement. She has a "wariness of going along with any-
body's program whatever" (CP, xviii). While the economy of Clampitt's
nature is not involved in commodification, it does suggest a structure of
entrepreneurial expansion and obsolescence, and it does, insofar as the
poet designs it, become abstract. The "annual wreckage," "the season's
frittering," is that of nature and culture alike. The poet returns her land-
scape to "the season's frittering" where it is broken into fragments and
dissipated to make room for a new landscape vision, a new filling of the
vacant lot. Whatever is "salvaged" (not monumental) is salvaged in a
transfigured form, as a "wayfarer" (some vagrant bird) consumes the
fruit and discards its waste elsewhere. By representing nature here as an
entrepreneurial force that moves in when real estate moves out, Clampitt
locates both nature and culture within a general superfluity, but this also
allows her to create tension within the parallel, since the vagrant and
wayfaring ways of these natural inhabitants are recalcitrant to the stan-
dards of propriety and property. When the margin moves to the center,
when a weed bed becomes a garden, it is a mark of superfluency, not re-
verse hierarchy.

Clampitt runs considerable ethical risks in conceiving nature as an entrepreneurial force, which she does frequently. Tradition prefers to offer nature as an innocent space to be violated by man's exploitative enterprise, or protected against it—a space of permanence or annihilation, not of transition. Shouldn't she deplore "wholesale upheaval and / dismemberment" the way nineteenth-century poets deplored enclosure? Clampitt chooses, instead, to praise adaptability, and a superfluity that defies the division of the world into owned "lots." "Something there is that doesn't / love a Third Avenue tenement," she writes in "Real Estate" (CP, 169). That "something" may be a human rather than a natural force, but it is not thereby disdained. She has little sympathy for "the Holdout tenants / . . . gesticulating by storefronts . . . adapted only to an anxious present" or the old pawnbroker dusting off her ancient umbrellas. Clampitt will not traffic in nostalgia, nor wax sentimental about the "birdcage" fire escape about to be torn down. It signifies entrapment in attachment to place. Instead, the entrepreneur who rents a U-Haul and carries all the pawned stuff "off somewhere" wins her applause. She knows, as in "Progress at Building Site with (Fewer) Pigeons," that the constructions of the present, which will themselves become the cages of another time, are hard to recognize as home. But it is the concept of home that must be modified, as she learned from long reading of Elizabeth Bishop.

Clampitt—Quaker descendant, tenant advocate, McCarthy campaigner, refugee from the provincialisms and neighborly fences of midwestern life—is sensitive to the damage of entrepreneurial energy when it involves the machinery of ownership and property, driving out what can't pay or what can't be priced. She relishes the unbrokerable life of nature as a kind of revenge on such restrictions. In "Kudzu Dormant" (CP, 283), for instance, she admires the way nature slips out of the management of human enterprise and pursues its own superfluity. Much of her irony, like Frost's, is built upon such disruptions of the nature/culture boundary. Amidst the "debris of enterprise that's slipped / into the lap of yet another / annal of the poor" the "overdressed daffodil prospers," flagrantly, against all the negations and rigid tastes of the civil world. The personification also allows that "the poor" themselves might enjoy a superfluous expenditure, rather than merely being superfluous, thrown in with the other waste products of the dominant culture, or mere sufferers of history's abuse, cast-offs of a selective legacy. "Like the daffodil," kudzu presents a counter-current of enterprise, a "rambunctious eyesore, / entrepreneur (as most are) / from away off somewhere." It is not part of an authentic Southern lineage of place, but is a foreign "opportunist" like the mockingbird in another poem, who is "ready to expand its range where / there's an opening." Clampitt enjoys praising kudzu as an outrage to proud roots and elevated tastes, like some makeshift circus: "ropes, pulleys, shawls, / caparisons, tent curtains . . . strung / above the raw, red-gulleyed / wintering hide of Dixie." The poem offers an implied retort to the Fugitive poets and their natural aristocracy, those who would take their stand in the abiding cultural roots of agrarian Dixie, in retreat from the appalling drift of modernity. She knows that kudzu was brought in from Asia to enrich worn-out soil and protect against erosion, and that it has exceeded its use. (As David Worcester points out [112], the quintessential Kentucky bluegrass was a similar import.) As a "panacea rampant," kudzu has become a "charming strangler" choking out the nostalgic charm of the plantation park it was supposed to revitalize. Clampitt chooses "on principle [to] . . . admire it green," a life form that will not be contained. The entrepreneurial spirit (as she construes it in nature) is for Clampitt an antidote to something much more threatening: the various forces against mobility, whether in idealized "roots" that reject impurities, or impersonal control and homogenization, in the name of laws, tastes, traditions, or class structures.

The nomad cannot afford to waste anything. The backside of civility is therefore a place in which to dwell. In this sense again the nomad can be a kind of entrepreneur. While "wilderness" has little appeal as a concept (she prefers birds, weeds, common wildflowers, and rhizomes to Adirondack vistas or forests primeval), the waterways and shores (those superfluencies) get special attention from Clampitt. They are (in "Notes on the State of Virginia," [CP, 282]) the "wet brink of all our / enterprise: the blur of bays, the / estuarial fog at sunrise, the glooms / and glimmerings, the tidal waters." If she observes that with our "straking smudge and smear" we have begun to "alter the face" of this presence "little by little," it is not clear that "enterprise" should or can cease, that the face should be immobile. But she awakens in us a desire that there will always be an "opening in / the foliage," an unconstructed, uncommodified space. Thus, as we saw, "the wet brink of all our enterprise" has a double sense, evoking excitement and anxiety, opportunity and disaster. In her parody of the pastoral elegy (and especially of "Lycidas"), "The Reedbeds of the Hackensack" (CP, 165), Clampitt relies on questions, some rhetorical, some unanswered, to formulate her response to the dying New Jersey waterway. The question that she frames through the example of the reedbeds is the same one that Frost poses through his oven bird, "what to make of a diminished thing," and like him, she isn't ready to settle for grief and rage. But in focusing on the reedbeds she finds in nature a trope for her own poetic response, one that refuses the fraudulent, high-toned lament of a society whose "civility" thrives on the very practices that have destroyed what it would mourn for, which turns its back on what it has despoiled and uses rhetoric to distance itself from its object. "What's landfill but the backside of civility?" Culture tends to destroy its natural resources, then idealizes them in memory. But to call landfill the backside of civility is to refuse this dissociation. Clampitt settles in to consider "scummed maunderings that nothing loves but reeds," and writes a sestina (a mock-elegant form, but also the counterpart of recycling and regeneration) protesting the "fraudulent civility" and admiring the uncultivated reeds (with their "fluent purplings," "the rathe, the deathbed generations") as a "forsooth civility" from which she might draw more inspiration than from the "laureate hearse." She reminds us that this is not an anti-poetic or pastoral of the low, a campy celebration of the "snugly ugly." Nor is hers an *esthétique du mal.* Just how far this "scrannel ruth" can take her she isn't sure:

> Is there a poetry of the incorrigibly ugly,
> free of all furbishings that mark it fraudulent?
> When toxins of an up-against-the-wall civility
> have leached away the last patina of these reeds,
> and promised landfill, with its lethal asphodel
> of fumes . . . ?

"We love the things we love for what they are," as Frost said of "Hyla Brook," and what they are includes our poetic idealizations and our memories, maybe even our despoliation. But Clampitt also imagines a point at which the landscape ceases to be even the "faded paper sheet" on which the imagination writes, a point that obstructs the superfluous power of the imagination, a brink of enterprise that has only a void on its other side.

In some ways the poem marks a limit to faith in nomadism, and to the mobile identity, but a limit is not a recantation. The moral here is not to avoid human construction but to avoid the old opposition between nature and culture that allows certain places to be the middens for our creative waste, others to be marked off as pristine arcadias. All places are landscapes for which we bear responsibility.

6

A. R. Ammons: Pilgrim, Sage, Ordinary Man

A. R. Ammons, more than any other poet of his generation, has attempted to make a home in motion. He took his lessons from the shifting terrain of sand dunes, the eddying of the sea, the irresistible force of the wind. But if Ammons provides the fullest exploration of mobile identity and fluid landscape, his is also the most varied. To identify with motion is not a simple thing. What does it mean to make a home in motion? What do the landscapes of such a persona look like? The self does not give up its retentiveness easily, and the world's movement can suggest a variety of patterns. Clampitt, perhaps as a result of the relative compression of her poetic career, takes on the role of the nomad early and pursues it, through considerable range. But as we move through the landscapes of Ammons' long career, we find that mobile identity includes a changing understanding of what it means to belong to the flow. And as his image of the mobile self develops, so too his landscapes alter in their structure, scene, and representational character.

Nature, for Ammons, is all about flow. In this, it has often been pointed out, he is thoroughly Emersonian.[1] The poet, Emerson wrote, "sees the flowing or metamorphosis" and "flows with the flowing of nature" ("The Poet," 20, 21). "There are no fixtures in nature," and "the quality of the imagination is to flow and not to freeze" (34). These sentiments reverberate throughout Ammons' work, coming to crescendo in his long poem *Sphere: the Form of a Motion*. But Emerson's transcendental identification of a real self with the All is continually tested in modern literature, where metamorphoses do not lead inevitably to wider, integral being, and where superfluity leads to backup. Evolutionary processes are not all ascensions; discontinuity and disintegration may leave a shattered person rather than an enlarged, impersonal identity; sliding surfaces may imply a soulless world. How, Ammons' poetry asks, shall the modern poet stand (or walk) to behold the flow? What is its impact on landscape? This poet of mobility improvised a variety of stances during his long career, most prominently the pilgrim and the sage. In his final phase Ammons broke with Emersonian idealism and the transcendental impersonal, presenting the fully embodied mind of the ordinary man.[2]

Ammons' abiding theme is motion as it mediates the one and the many. But in each of these overlapping but sequential phases, Ammons understands the theme differently, and constructs a different relation between self and nature. In the first phase, Ammons writes fables and parables in which he wanders into a highly ritualized, elemental wilderness, non-human but spiritually animated. The animism protests against a grasping rationality. These are poems of an anxious cogito, looking for validation of the self and, ultimately, a home in the world. This desire remains in tension with a sense of motion as dispersal. In this phase, then, Ammons retains the fiction of a disembodied, noncontingent consciousness that can locate itself within the infinite, but this fiction is continually on trial, and in tension with the life of the self at the center of these lyrics.

In the second phase Ammons' stance is more detached and prophetic, his language more gnomic and didactic. Ammons gives up animism for scientific discourse, even as he continues to entertain a religious rhetoric alongside it, and to evoke the sublime. Thus he creates an impersonal authority at once rational and visionary. The speaker apprehends processes, organizations, and ecological networks rather than focusing on particular units or entities. The frames are not local or representational, but conceptual. Hence Ammons can contemplate entropy without real exposure; since there is no investment in an experiential frame, entropy is simply the means of motion. Though "scope eludes [his] grasp" (CP, 151), he has identified with the motions he describes; he has, like Clampitt, made a home in motion. Particulars exist here as representatives of the many, and the geography is ultimately a geography of mind, uncharted and dynamic, endlessly traversable, but implicitly (through the spatial metaphor) whole and abiding. The pilgrim poems are future-oriented, looking for an apotheosis of wider being. These poems of the prophetic phase dwell in a continuous present. They appear more pragmatic, the walk metaphor conceding to perspective and provisional vision, but their acknowledgment of limit is framed in a rhetoric of endless renewal and possibility. Ammons may declare that "the overall is beyond me" (151), but it is still very much alive in synecdoche, which evokes a grand dynamic unity overriding local transitions. The aesthetic is Whitmanian: more centripetal and centrifugal than truly decentered.

In his third phase Ammons is neither pilgrim nor seer but ordinary man, and the poems are much more concerned with the contingent and partial. Here Ammons confronts the past, especially as it exists as debris in the landscape of the present. There is, of course, a sublime of the ordinary, as Stevens knew, and as Ammons' *Garbage* brilliantly demonstrates. The visionary figure has become the man on the dump, the beerbelly in a bulldozer, turning the incendiary surface of a huge mess. The language of awe and of the transfiguring flame is one channel of lyric energy. But it doesn't really do the job. *Garbage* is dedicated "to the bacteria, tumblebugs, scavengers, / wordsmiths—the transfigurers, restorers," not to the visionaries, and a considerable portion of the poem is involved in imagining the lowly work of local transfiguration.[3] This constitutes the primary work of Ammons' last phase of writing. The overall falls away as a referent, and the poems focus on local transition and adjustment rather than the overriding or even microcosmic shape of flux. Ammons' emphasis on the ordinary is not a form of domestication, however. Indeed, the ordinary is strange, uncanny. It is here, paradoxically, that Ammons is least "at home" in the world, at least in an ideal sense, for the ordinary is associated with human limit and mortality.[4] Nature in this phase involves the body directly, its entropy part of a cycle that excludes the accompaniment of a transcendental self. Mind itself is embodied and cognition is behavior and navigation, not a mirror of the world. Entropy is still understood in relation to ecological cycles, but the language of evolution, with its dynamic of retention and waste, and its material account of human behavior, brings a new emphasis. The voice of the ordinary man is the most personal in Ammons' work. The world is truly decentered, but the poem is centered in a finite, unfixed self. Home is not in a sublimated"motion" but in "the writing of this poem." "Home is where the doodle is" (SV, 34).

The figure of the pilgrim initiates Ammons' work and occupies him well into mid-career. Nature is the scene of the pilgrim's search, but it is not the object of that search. Ammons' directive to readers in *Ommateum* to avoid literalism and impressionism should continue to inform our reading: "the imagery is generally functional beyond pictorial evocation of mood, as plateau, for example, may suggest a flat, human existence, devoid of the drama of rising and falling" (SM, 5). Landscape, for Ammons, is parabolic. Natural ecologies model behavior in other affiliated spheres—psychological, economic, aesthetic—and instantiate a pattern of being that overrides distinctions between the natural and the human. "These poems, then, mean to enrich the experience of being; of being anterior to action, that shapes action; of being anterior to wider, richer being" (SM, 5). It is precisely these affiliations that draw Ammons to nature, and it is in the examination of such affiliations, rather than in the primacy of the natural world, that he can be read as a "nature poet."[5]

In these poems the lyric subject approaches landscape in the desire to locate voice and thus identity within the world of the not-me. Voice is the manifestation of self ("I say, therefore I am"),[6] but voice must be given away for the self to participate in integral being. Voice is experienced as a unity that must be dispersed into plurality in order, paradoxically, to attain a wider unity.[7] Motion is the traversal between the one and the many. The poems vary in how they structure these rituals of relinquishment, but each encounter repeats it. Indeed, existence seems to require such repetition. The opening poem of *Ommateum* introduces us to this anxious cogito:

> So I said I am Ezra
> and the wind whipped my throat
> gaming for the sounds of my voice
> (CP, 1)

The poem's elemental landscape, consisting of the sea, dunes, and night, is not so much a place as a condition of dispersal in which the wind is the agent and the antagonist of the poet's fragmented, separate selfhood. The opening line hints at that fragmentation, where the "so" suggests ongoing narrative, a prior origin to which the self might return. "I said I am Ezra," the poem implies, because I doubted that I was, because the condition of individual existence is contingent and partial. Indeed, nature besieges the voice almost immediately, its authority ultimately cast to "the dunes of unremembered seas." The middle of the poem presents images of fragmentation and dispersal (broken fields, ripped sheets) associated with the location of self in the body, where the voiced identity has no power and "falls out of being." In "turning" the poet surrenders but also tropes, establishing the authority of the self in a new connection to the world. The struggle to merge the partial with the infinite can be heard in the verbs, which suggest reciprocal motions: "the words were swallowed up" or they were "leaping over." Indeed, the prepositions of the poem (up, over, into, in, from, among) propel the voice beyond its singularity into a potential, infinite destination. In the end the "I Ezra," which had been separated from the infinite and threatened by dispersion, goes out to it, regaining poetic authority while embracing fluent being.

> so I Ezra went out into the night
> like a drift of sand
> and splashed among the windy oats
> that clutch the dunes
> of unremembered seas

Each of these early poems presents a version of this narrative, the effort at an articulation of the self. In place of objective validation, the poet finds temporary release from singularity into infinite, dynamic being. The variations in the poems derive from the obstacles encountered in the transition from one to many, and the rotating structure of unity and brokenness. Individuated voice opposes nature's motions, so the pilgrim must throw away his voice in the enumeration of particulars. This becomes itself a meaningful vocation for the pilgrim-self, his way of intersecting with the infinite, so it must repeatedly "gather up" the "pieces of [the] voice" (SP, 3) in order to throw them away again. Nature "answers" the poet's call not because it has spiritual force but because the poet's voice has dispersed itself among the elements, split itself off from an initial self-identity. But again the structure of the poem promises a larger, redeemed identity. Like the "night" and the "unremembered seas" of the first poem, the "unwasting silence" in "The Pieces of My Voice" portends something beyond fragmentation and dispersal: an integration, through the death of a singular self, into a transcendental whole.

Again and again in these poems the pilgrim exposes himself to the transience, erosion, and fragmentation of nature (figured as wind, sand, sea), in order to be gathered up into a voiceless infinite. Each poem plots this movement differently, but it is often mapped according to a vertical/ horizontal logic, with the self as a force for "building up" or "running down" while nature "goes by" "sidewinds," and levels (SP, 3). In advancing this ritual Ammons draws on an alliance but also a distinction between the voice-I and the seeing-eye. The former defines an original unity, which must become dispersed. The latter defines an expansive consciousness, which can collect what is scattered. But there is no sacrifice of visionary power in these rituals of self-sacrifice. "In the Wind My Rescue Is" articulates a pleasure in release from the ordering, hierarchical mind, but the images of multiplicity and extension that form the first and third stanzas depend on the central image of gathering. The pleasure of caprice informs the "loose dreams" and "unknown tongues." In yielding human power to the erosive force of nature, Ammons projects a new identification of the self with freedom from the partial and restrictive structures of individuation. It is a movement out of singularity and location into the wider parabolas of bliss. Death here is not a "terminus" but a transit to the infinite:

> I sat in my bones' fragile shade
> and worked the
> knuckles of my mind till
> the altering earth broke to
> mend the fault:
>
> I rose and went through.
> (CP, 69)

Similarly, we find in "Mansion" (CP, 75–76) that a "ceding" of the self to the dispersing wind is also a "seeding" of the self into a transcendent position, a higher "mansion" of consciousness. A fictional bargain, even a kind of courtship, takes place in this poem between the self and the wind, which enacts the movement from one, to many, to one again. Sight expands identity as consciousness projects beyond the body and stands outside it, "watching" from an extended location. The languages of brokenness and redemptive unity merge in the puns. The body has already been identified with the landscape ("tree of my bones") when the poet says to the wind:

> stroll my dust
>   around the plain . . .
> and when you fall
>   with evening
>
> fall with me here
>   where we can watch
> the closing up of day
> and think how morning breaks

A binary logic (close/open, fall/rise, think/watch, cede/seed) organizes the movement from brokenness to redemption, suggesting the struggle to overcome part/whole tensions.

In each of the poems I have discussed so far, indeed in all of the pilgrim poems, Ammons builds a narrative or meditative structure out of this problem of the one and the many. Literally, each poem involves a crisis or impasse—the individual voice threatened by the outer world, access to the infinite blocked by embodiment, and so on—which the lyric subject tries to overcome by an adjustment of his understanding or positioning of his self. In "Hymn" (CP, 39) the horizontal intersection of the self/scene dynamic is referred to a perpendicular intersection of an I/you, where crisis in the one/many is transfigured. The pattern of the stanzas inscribes this transition. The convergence and reciprocity between the end of the first stanza—"up farther than the loss of sight / into the unseasonal undifferentiated empty stark"—and the end of the second—"with all the soul of my chemical reactions / and going right on down where the eye sees only traces"—suggest an identity of one/many that leads to the unifying rhetoric of the abstract couplet: "you are everywhere partial and entire / You are on the inside of everything and on the outside" and to the interpenetrations and conflations of scale figured in the particulars listed at the end of the poem: "the sweetgum has begun to ooze spring sap at the cut," and reciprocally, the vaster soul becomes antlike, entering the chasm of the bark.

The stance of the pilgrim, then, defines a specific relation to the landscape. Nature is not a dwelling place (the voices in these poems are specifically exposed), but a scene of instruction. No encounter is definitive; rather, the adjustments enacted are ritually repeated and the pilgrim-seeker is both visionary and penitent. An interrogation of the idea of home also gives a modern emphasis to Ammons' nature poetry.[8] For the Romantics "home" was the name for an original condition of transcendental being that we might rediscover in our attachment to nature. Modernist writers described a pervasive condition of homelessness arising as man is severed from his myths. More recently, writers have inverted the logic of home and homelessness, undermining myths of original belonging and defining "home" as a space of provisional, creative ordering. Ammons' "For Harold Bloom" (*Sphere*, 1), which in its placement at the end of his first *Selected Poems* suggests a conclusion, proposes that man's "home" is social and cultural, not natural. "Goodbye, I said, goodbye, nature so grand and reticent, your tongues are healed up into their own element and as you shut up you have shut me out. I am as foreign here as if I had landed, a visitor." Nature doesn't need or care for our longing, hence offers us no belonging. Within the human community, and within discourse, our meanings take place, though they may be fundamentally "about" our relation to nature, our longing. But while Ammons "returned to the city and built a house to set the image in," it is not obvious that he can "dwell" here either.[9]

Two particularly homeless poems of this pilgrim period point to the fictional and formal, as opposed to representational or experiential, nature of this ideal of unified being. It obtains, to use a Romantic word Ammons revives, in "longing." Cognition may not prove the existence of the self, but neither can it throw off the discrete self in a transcendent unity. Like "For Harold Bloom," the earlier "Gravelly Run" (CP, 55–56) repudiates the pilgrim's earlier animism. The ritual throwing off of the cogito ("I don't know") and submission to the "victory of stones and trees" cannot unburden the self. The dream of a transcendent identity, "as if birth had never found it / and death could never end it," depends on the very extension of that identity onto the "body" of nature ("stone-held algal / hair and narrowing roils between / the shoulders of the highway bridge"). It is but a step from the human body to human institutions (cathedral, "green religion"), and from there the whole inventive structure collapses back into detached particulars. No knowledge of the thing in itself replaces the dream of integral Being. This poem reverses the one/many/one paradigm, entertaining unity in its center, but framing it in entity. This time the instructive voice is not the wind's, but the poet's only: "hoist your burdens, get on down the road."

"Cascadilla Falls" (CP, 206–207) offers another study of the one/many examined in terms of the cogito, the central matter of the pilgrim's encounters. But like "Gravelly Run" it sets the stage for a reconstruction of the lyric subject as sage. The poem is still a kind of parable, but Ammons introduces a realist effect by naming the site and evoking a scientific discourse of vastness. The poet comes to dwell with the infinite in terms that affirm the engendering power of the self. The landscape refutes his narrow authority, projecting a decentered, plural reality of "motions" beyond volition and consciousness. While the poem narrates a failure on the part of the lyric subject, its form restores a one/many harmony.

> I went down by Cascadilla
> Falls this
> evening, the
> stream below the falls,
> and picked up a
> handsized stone
> kidney-shaped, testicular [. . .]

The opening lines of the poem show the cogito turning in on itself. Knowledge leads to unknowing, and unknowing threatens identity. Anthropomorphic thinking presents a potent ("testicular") self; the stream flows from the body (projected onto the "kidney-shaped" stone). But as knowledge becomes inconceivable except in mathematical terms ("800 mph earth spin . . . 30,000 mph of where the sun's going"), it threatens to overwhelm this initial identity. The stance of the lyric beholder and natural historian yields to the superperspectives of science, and knowledge is severed from experience and mastery. Ironically, the metaphors, which initially empowered the speaker, now threaten him. The stone, having been associated with the body of the speaker, comes to "dead rest." At the same time, the dropping of the stone delimits the orphic power of the speaker; he relinquishes metaphor, returning the stone to its stoniness.

The scientific language should not distract us from the classic elements of the poem—the falls and stream as figure of many/one and stasis/motion, the sky as a figure for the infinite or higher unity, the poet gazing at the sky and crying out when his knowledge fails him. The "turn" toward the sky is itself a trope (like his turning from the wind in "So I Said I Am Ezra"), though a trope of supplication. He pauses here ("stood still") in the collision of the one and the many, an incongruity figured in the contradiction at the end: "I do / not know where I am going / that I can live my life / by this single creek." But the disavowal of knowledge is in another sense a move toward integration. He "doesn't know," but he "can live." In dropping the stone the poet symbolically relinquishes his hold on a narrow unity, abandoning it to "other motions," to the torments of multiplicity.

I have suggested some of the narrative and imagistic elements that contribute to this movement. The representation of motion reinforces the crisis, as the imagery of falls and stream defines a directional flux quite different from the rotational order of the universe. The prepositional energy of the poem suggests the pilgrim figure seeking transcendent integrations—we start with "by" (location), move to "up" (appropriation, as in "take up"), then "into" (integration, assimilation), "around" (circulation/displacement), and move to "of" and "into"; "to" and "from" imply a crossing marked by "over," then "to" moves out again, pulled back to "by." These prepositions of location and dislocation, of placement and anticipatory transcendence, mark out Ammons' poem as modern in its intense tension and bidirectional pull between one and many, finite and infinite. Yet the poem in its whole structure does satisfy the paradigm/myth, as it moves from individual to cosmic to their juxtaposition at the end of the stanza. Indeed, the movements toward this culmination are sequential, since this is a narrative; its syntax is transitive, not substantive. Each stanza represents a state, dramatized by end words—the "and" of the first stanza breaking out of the narrow unity, entering multiplicity; the "haul" indicating a turn toward wider unity; the "dropped" indicating the failure to reciprocally take that universal into the self; "broke" given a line of its own to accent the failure of the initial unity; but the "turn" suggesting not only a trope but a supplicant's openness to the infinite. "Oh" is a variation on "O" apostrophe, uttered to the sky by all poets. The end of the poem shifts to present tense and moves out of the narrative into the reflective. The "single creek" at the end of the poem has plurality inside of it, becoming the form of motion. The word "live" is carefully displacing "know" here. Thoreau went to Walden to "know life." Ammons must be satisfied to live it. But to live life by a single creek is to live in relation to all the multiple motions of the universe.

As Ammons wrote in his introduction to *Ommateum* (SM, 5–6), these poems are "dramatic presentations of thought and emotion" which "mean to enrich the experience of being." The poems give up "partial, unified, prejudicial, and rigid" orientations for a "many-sided view of re-ality" and "an adoption of tentative, provisional attitudes," but their aim is for a new, expansive oneness "of wider, richer being." The emphasis in the pilgrim poems is on this widening rather than on any provisional at-titude or pluralistic understanding. The desire to assimilate world to mind remains a valued impulse, though one that is inevitably frustrated, for "the unassimilable fact leads us on." In "Staking Claim" and "Plun-der" we recognize the world's recalcitrance as a route to the sublime in that the "total" is not calculable or effable but infinite. Discrete human forms are measured against the "roundness and withdrawal of the deep dark" (CP, 83), and the imagination pursues this darkness even as the possessive mind relinquishes it. In the meantime, a "bucketful of radiant toys" (83), that is, poems, allows the infinite, through metaphor, to pen-etrate the finite.

Ammons' pilgrim landscapes, then, are a version of paysage moralisé, exercises in the expansion of being. The flux represents a way of break-ing out of the limits of a prior frame, as if one could choose flux over frame. Ammons will return to the stance of the pilgrim throughout his career, but beginning with his second book a different stance begins to emerge, one that is relatively impersonal, comprehensive, and didactic. Where the medium of the pilgrim poet is ritual gesture, the medium of the sage is abstract proposition and example. The revelation of pattern dominates here over the articulation of self. Problems of identity fall away, and the self becomes a node of consciousness through which the shape of the world reveals itself. Where nature in the pilgrim phase is variously the ally or antagonist of the poet's will, here it is the embodiment of dynamic design, often articulated in abstract titles. Critics have emphasized Ammons' interest in "ecological naturalism," and certainly the greater particularity, the assimilation of "facts" from the biological and earth sciences, and especially the emphasis on cycles, habitats, and cooperative behaviors in the natural world, resonate with developments in the environmental movement. But the natural environment is not the subject of these poems so much as a resource for exemplifying and troping their subject, which is "the form of a motion." This can be seen in human ecologies as well as in nature, as the poem "Mechanism" (CP, 77–79) makes clear: "Honor a going thing, goldfinch, corporation, tree, / Morality: any working order." The goldfinch becomes the intermittent focus of this poem, the exemplar of "mechanism": "chemistries, platelets, hemoglobin kinetics, / the lightsensitive iris, the enzymic intricacies of control." This is no Romantic warbler, no "blithe spirit," in fact no spirit at all. The goldfinch is "not a great songster." But this gold flitterer does provoke an epiphany ("isolated, contained reactions!").[10]

But Ammons draws on natural imagery to give authority to his vision of pattern, and to remove it from the social and psychological attachments it inevitably has when embodied in human institutions. There remains an experiential element to these meditations in which knowledge is a process, incomplete, and subject to the shifting conditions of observer and observed world. But an expansive, visionary posture and a generalizing impulse prevail. The prophet-subject identifies with motion rather than being subject to it. Ammons' particular challenge is to reconcile this Thoreauvian idea of dwelling with his Emersonian emphasis on motion. "Can we make a home in motion?" he asks throughout his career, and explicitly in *Sphere: The Form of a Motion.* To imagine "the form of a motion" is to imagine it as a whole and thus to identify with it.[11]

In this middle phase Ammons is not seeking a home because he has made a home in motion. In these poems he begins to identify the text and the landscape as parts of a dynamic patterning where mind and world, thought and its object, become intertwined. Neither is firmly grounded in the other. Thus the power terms that propel the narrative of subject/object relations in the pilgrim poems fall away. Although Ammons remains attached to a figure of "mirroring mind," it is clear that the model of cognition is not really the mirror but something more mobile and improvisatory (rather than ritualized, as before). Mapping may be the operative term for what the mind does, rather than mirroring, if we accept the map as an instrument of navigation rather than an objective diagram of reality.

Designed though it is to convey a Whitmanian plurality, the prophetic stance remains selective in the nature to which it attends. This phase is initiated with "expressions at sea level" (CP, 134), not visions from mountaintops. Ammons grew up in the mountains of North Carolina, but from early on he eschewed the iconology of the mountain, which in our culture has signified stability and endurance, remote imperial power, sublimity and transcendence. The early poems of dispersal involve a repeated dismantling of hierarchical organizations. A poem still in the pilgrim mode, "Mountain Talk" (CP, 182), makes this preference explicit, glancing at the "massive symmetry and rest" of the mountain and its "changeless prospect," but rejecting its "unalterable view," and Ammons repeats this in *Brink Road:* "I have always felt, / as one should, I think, shy / of mountains" (BR, 40). In this middle phase Ammons does not need to dismantle hierarchical orders because he has set his gaze where nothing builds too high. In giving the seashore a central role, he follows an American tradition of leveled, horizontal relations, of many as one, and of a permeable boundary between stability and chaos. The seashore is precisely not a home, though it may be a habitat. It provides a simple, generally uniform, horizontal image with a maximum of local change and adjustment. It thus becomes an ideal figure for a decentered world. It is in this gnomic phase that the colon arises as a major signature of Ammons' work, a sign with multiple, ambiguous signification, marking permeable boundaries, tentative sponsorships, and analogical possibilities. Similarly, the preposition "of" emerges in this phase to create metaphors yoking concrete and abstract terms, and to override the subject/object dichotomy.

Ammons' walk poems, central to this phase, are in a sense what the pilgrim poems grow into. The sage's poems are not emblematic (they do not convey idea by reducing and abstracting image), but analogical. The sage moves freely in and out of a representational scene, geography of mind and geography of landscape, text and referent, allowing for the play of contingent vision without restriction to a narrow perspective. In the pilgrim poems the one/many relation is experienced as a crisis or problem, whereas the walk poems present this relation as a primary dynamic of form. The pilgrim figure seeks a home, whether by mastery or by submission; he seeks to colonize or become accepted into the infinite. The prophet figure in the walk poems already identifies with the movement he conveys. Since the one/many is not a problem to be resolved but a reality to be apprehended and experienced, these poems are less sequential/narrative than serial/reiterative. Because the speaker identifies with the movement of reality, he does not need to discover it in a teleological process, but rather enacts it in an improvisatory process.

"Corson's Inlet" (CP, 147–151) is not a poem of place, except in the sense that cognition is phenomenological and must inevitably "take place." The poem begins in a thought/sight opposition familiar from the pilgrim poems, but the shift into present tense overrides the distinction, eliding the outer geography with the poem's mapping, the "geography of my work." Description and analogy are held apart in the inconspicuous shift in tense (past for description, present for analogy), but the experience of the poem is of an easy flow between them. The descriptive aspect of the poem places the body within the scene, insisting on perspective ("the news to my left") and allowing for an element of surprise ("to stab—what?"). As we shall see Ashbery doing, Ammons is reworking the ancient Western metaphor of thought as a landscape, showing that its "ground" is shifting and uncertain, with a "moving, incalculable center" or no center at all. The opposition between mind and nature is really an opposition between one map and another or one aesthetic "idea" (hard-lined) and another (fluent), though we have identified these as artificial and organic.

The "geography" in "Corson's Inlet" features small, multiple, local orders and centers of flexible, low organization, which are transitional and entropic. It highlights event over discrete object, and attends to relations rather than entities. Images of retention and flow suggest an ecological vision. The mind as an omnivorous agent is present only in surrogate figures of "swallow and siege" such as the "young mottled gull" that "ate to vomiting," an emblem for the inside/outside interpenetration. The ecological scheme promises constant renewal, a way of trumping death. But Ammons is tempted by a teleological rhetoric even as he eschews it. "The overall is beyond me" and is "the sum of these events I cannot draw." At the end of the poem he creates closure by a thematic refusal of it ("there is no finality of vision"), satisfying the mind's need to refer particular experience to an infinite scope. He projects a state of transcendent being even if he does not provide a narrative of transcendence. Indeed, the poem does map out the conventional structure of an initial unity (blocks, boxes, binds) released into the freedom of plurality and rounding to a new, expansive unity of being. This tendency to evoke an infinite unity at the end, without claiming a "final vision" for the poet, is even clearer in "Saliences,"

> where not a single thing endures,
> the overall reassures, . . .

> earth brings to grief
> much in an hour that sang, leaped, swirled,
> yet keeps a round
>   quiet turning,
> beyond loss or gain,
> beyond concern for the separate reach.
>
>   (CP, 155)

One feels that the poem's rounding off is troped here, despite the clamor against the "separate reach." The abstraction of the language removes us from the choices and limits of landscape, evoking a rhetoric of process and evolution disengaged from the process itself.

Because Ammons is constantly announcing his own practices, criticism has seemed very redundant. But in the behavior of the poem, rather than in its subject matter or discursive content, we find aesthetic and emotional satisfaction. "Poetry is action," and "poetry recommends," by its behavior, "certain kinds of behavior" (SM, 57). Ammons' reflexivity is itself a particular kind of poetic behavior. "Terrain" (CP, 89–90), for instance, after launching a description by way of analogy ("the soul is a region without definite boundaries"), enters into the second term, forgetting its sponsorship. But within that second term the one/many dynamic, which is the real subject of the poem, is reiterated in landscape terms. The soul/body or self/landscape dichotomy is transposed into a network of landscape relations, and duality vanishes. The gnomic proposition that opens the poem yields to a perceptual/experiential model as the poet uses present tense to bring forward the landscape, reversing tenor and vehicle. The "like" in line 5—"It floats (self-adjusting) like a continental mass"—recalls us to the initial metaphor, but the sponsorship of simile is weak and yields altogether to description which enfolds simile rather than extending it: "river systems thrown like winter tree-shadows." Nature's internal resemblances displace a Cartesian model of mirroring mind. The correspondences of soul/region convert to correspondences within the geography itself—"where it towers most / extending its deepest mantling base." The second stanza of this poem adjusts the intersections which have become too symmetrical, so that "floods unbalancing / gut it, silt altering the / distribution of weight." "Weight" brings us back from illusion to the presence of the poem; we feel the weight not in the referential silt but in the "nature of content"— the weight of the "soul" which is the subject of the poem. This extraordinary interpenetration of consciousness and its object returns us, cyclically, to the poem's opening, but only momentarily. The poem seeks other means of mapping the one/many/one paradigm. The images of imbalance are followed by images of dissolution:

> a growth into
>   destruction of growth,
>   change of character,
>   invasion of peat by poplar and oak: semi-precious
> stones and precious metals drop from muddy water into mud

The region is coming apart into multiplicity and separateness (after the earlier symmetry and correspondence). The landscape endures a kind of crisis of multiplicity and separateness—"whirlwinds move through it / or stand spinning like separate orders: the moon comes: / there are barren spots: bogs, rising / by self-accretion from themselves." But if the orders that initiate the poem are entropic, the stanza recuperates with a structure of collision moving toward the "poise" of "countercurrents." The stanza divisions mark an overall pattern presiding in the shifts in focus and organization. The stanza I have quoted moves away from the large geographic model of continental plates and river systems to a more local model of "habitat." The "region" is now far more liquid—it does not just contain lakes and rivers and marshes but is itself "a crust afloat." In this model the sponsoring unity ("the soul" or "continental mass") gives way to "a precise ecology of forms / mutually to some extent / tolerable"—a strange phrase in which precision and approximation must somehow become compatible. But at the same time this "precision" moves to an increasingly imprecise language, a mysticism of "the soul" quite different from earlier geological references. Description turns back into heightened metaphor and visionary stance: "foam to the deep and other-natured: / but deeper than depth, too: a vacancy and swirl: // it may be spherical, light and knowledge merely / the iris and opening / to the dark methods of its sight." The word "still" cues the poem to rest in the interpenetration of imagination and earth: "the moon comes: terrain." This gesture marks the poem's unity—providing a double refrain, one internal to the poem, one echoing the title to complete a cycle.

As "Terrain" indicates, particularity in the prophetic phase derives from enumerative rather than descriptive rhetoric. Ammons does not ask us to visualize a landscape, even when a poem is tethered to a place or a concept stimulated by a specific geological or geographic formation. The most eloquent example is "The City Limits" (CP, 320), which realizes vision in form. The relation of one and many inheres in the play of the unifying syntax and pluralizing diction. The heavy enjambment

works with the lexical diversity to maximize freedom in form and to cre-
ate the sense of expansion the poem wishes to convey emotionally. What
Randall Jarrell said of Whitman applies here: Ammons' lists are "little
systems as beautifully and astonishingly organized as the rings and satel-
lites of Saturn" (*Poetry and the Age,* 126). Here the polarities indicate
not only range, but tension resolved, dualities overcome—good and
evil, life and death, nature and culture, high and low. Collisions in the
diction ("natural slaughter," "storms of generosity," "gold-skeined wings
of flies") have a liberating effect within the constancy of "the radiance."
Collisions become chords in the one/many harmony. The coordinating
conjunction "or" creates an array of oppositions held in tension: "snow
or shale" in textural or "rose or lichen" in visual parallel. Not too much
is made of these arrangements. They remain local and metamorphic,
yielding to other terms of connection. Similarly, the anaphora that
binds the list shifts its position in the line so that litany does not be-
come harangue. While the poem is meditative and reiterative, it does
define a cause-and-effect logic, the present participles and present tense
throughout making the transition from "when" to "then" cogent and
compelling. This narrative is carried out in relation to a subject "you" of
"when you consider" and an object "the radiance" that merge as "the ra-
diance" becomes one with consideration itself and hence with the poem,
which supersedes the "I" to achieve a more dynamic cognition. Indeed
the subject position shifts again, embedding the many in a kind of
polyphony. At the end, in place of "you," "the man" appears, whose spir-
itual condition this time is an effect, not a cause, of the transcendental
paradigm.

The pleasures of the prophetic phase are many, and it is still the phase
readers most associate with Ammons. It delights in the endless renewal
of form in substance, the rediscovery of pattern in particulars. "Scope is
beyond me" (CP, 151) not because the beholder's vision fails but because
motion is the essential nature of this pattern. We engage in the pleasure
of gnomic utterances fleshed out and altered in inexhaustible example.
What this mode gives up, largely, is the self's direct, experiential engage-
ment with the life it beholds. Motion remains theoretical, a matter of
spectacle rather than impact. For all their apparent spontaneity and con-
tingency, these are poems of thoughts more than thinking. By making a
home in motion, in its form, the sage evades its force.

It is perhaps inevitable that the pilgrim should become the sage, and
there are clear continuities between the two stances. In the first, land-
scape becomes an occasion to enact the expansion of the self into the

flux; in the second, landscape becomes a space in which to reconcile the one and the many. But Ammons writes *Snow Poems* against the sagacious stance of *Sphere*. Out of this new, rough, improvisatory, impious, and anti-transcendent language of *Snow Poems* comes Ammons' new poetry of the ordinary man. Here the poet becomes truly embedded in the provisional landscapes evoked rhetorically in earlier work. Of course in a sense Ammons adopted this pose throughout his career. *Tape for the Turn of the Year,* for instance, with its daily account of whims and weather, hardly suggests philosophical authority. But within the offhand rhetoric is a strongly didactic and generalizing impulse characteristic of the prophetic phase:

> don't establish the
> > boundaries
> > first,
> > the squares, triangles,
> > boxes
> > of preconceived
> > possibility,
> > and then
> > pour
> > life into them, trimming
> off left-over edges,
> ending potential:
> > let centers
> > proliferate
> > from
> self-justifying motions!
> > > (TTOY, 116)

In *Snow Poems* he qualifies: "I don't insist / on the meaning, only the facts" (SP, 10). He names predilections and possibilities rather than revealed truths (however provisional). Slippery phonemes and chiasms sabotage propositions ("whorey bottom / or bottomless horrid" [SP, 16]); lists amass words more than things, subverting propositions; double columns divert linear reading. This is poetry of the mind in and on the body—the human body (sexual, mortal) and the body of language. Broad laws of physics and geology, so important to Ammons' middle phase, play little part in this raid on matter and manner.

In this last phase of his work Ammons increases the element of transition and adjustment, in contrast to the encompassing continuities of the earlier work. The poet is more fully situated in the landscape, often doing some kind of simple work. He enters perspective, orients the mind to a particular alignment of reality, and then abruptly alters it. Where the prophetic voice continues, it is now the voice of Proteus. As Ammons writes in "A Poem Is a Walk":

> You remember that Proteus was a minor sea god, a god of knowledge, an attendant on Poseidon. Poseidon is the ocean, the total view, every structure in the ocean as well as the unstructured ocean itself. Proteus, the god of knowledge, though, is a minor god . . . It was presumed that Proteus knew the answers—and more important The Answer—but he resisted questions by transforming himself from one creature or sub-stance into another . . . But the vague question is answered by the ocean which provides distinction and nondistinction. (SM, 14–15)

In mid-career Ammons stays close to the ocean (hence the shore po-ems), and to Poseidon, even as he traces out the "provisional stabilities" and "saliences" that form the waves and dunes. But in the later work he is more interested in Protean metamorphoses. Shifting thoughts and orientations take turns in the foreground. Poetry, Ammons writes, is "a linguistic correction of disorder" (SM, 9), not the disorder of the world corrected by art, but the disorder of a former idea which has lost its power through the introduction of new fact. These poems are indeed "linguistic corrections" in this sense, often marked in the middle by tran-sitional conjunctions like "but," "still," "yet." The model of the poem as epistemological quest is least relevant to this last phase of Ammons' writing. Increasingly, he thinks of poetry as exemplary action and be-havior rather than epistemology. Landscape is now a scene of action rather than an object of contemplation or the backdrop of an ontologi-cal struggle.

As the poet withdraws from the extremes of sea and wilderness, and from the frontiers charted by science, he turns his attention to the everyday, but always astonishing, world of his backyard, his greenhouse, and his local environment. There are fewer lists in this phase because the imagination is less voracious. (*Garbage* is the exception that proves the point, since the lists there imply waste and disorder rather than unified plurality.) In place of the prophet's expansive rhetoric, Ammons offers more focused descriptions. Nature in this phase is local, ordinary, and thoroughly mixed up with the human. We are part of nature (the mind inextricably embodied), and "nature" is our construction (we shape it vi-sually and invest it with value and meaning).

The prophetic phase is broadly ecological in its thinking: "*ecology* is my word: tag / me with that" (TTOY, 112). From this natural philosophy

Ammons derives a "moral order." But later Ammons is less willing to be tagged. He will not let "the man from *Audubon* . . . profile, defile, or maybe / just file" him. "First we artificialize nature / then we naturalize artifice" (GL, 198). He tends to place environmental pieties in a historical perspective:

> our destructive rage
> against the unmercifulness of nature has
> put us in need of saving environmentalists, who
>
> have perhaps never happened
> upon a nest of rattlers: we had to
>
> tear down half the woods to have a door to keep
> the wolves away from: don't tell me that
>
> fetches of wind and slugs of rain erode the
> fields; where is the cabbage to come from
> (GL, 182)

If he imagines nature often as a cooperative system, it can also be a "nest of rattlers." It includes cooperative interactions of stable, cyclical ecosystems, but also the dynamic, competitive, and one-directional changes of evolution. Both patterns map existence for Ammons.

The visionary phase involved matter and energy as material for the abstract form of motion. Later Ammons focuses more on "motion's holdings" (SV, 57), retentive structures, than on motion itself. As he turns his attention and adapts his stance to the ordinary, this amassing, schematizing tendency gives way to a greater sense of materiality. The material may seem ethereal as it descends into microscopic organization, or as substance converts to energy, but while the world is endlessly metamorphic, it is less easily transfigured to a metaphysical state. In *Snow Poems* Ammons begins to talk about trash. The mortal body, in particular, resists transcendence. Ammons comes to terms with death rather than overcoming it.

In the pilgrim poems, death of the self is a vehicle by which the soul or consciousness enters a more expansive state. In the sage poems, death is part of a larger motion to which the mind aligns itself. But for the poet of the ordinary and for the poet as ordinary man, death is real and not merely transitional. The landscape is not an evasion of but an encounter with death. Rot, compost, garbage, bodily decomposition, the "low" forms of scavengers and parasites, come into the foreground. It is the body, not the mind, which dwells in motion. Where oneness had been held to a transcendent, abstract realm before, the realm of the soul or radiance, here it is the realm of matter. The embodied mind has the authority of experience, but not of transcendental vision. "The spirit dies, but the body / lives forever, run out of its limits // though and caught up into others" (GL, 7). Ammons often represents the soul or spirit as fragmentary and intermittent.

This shift in Ammons toward materialism aligns him more with late Thoreau—the author of the Journal—than with Emerson.[12] Though he is "not a palpabilitist," he is nevertheless increasingly a poet of matter who unifies the world not at the level of ideas but at the level of substance and energy. Ideas, in this late phase, are finite and multiple. Thoreau had great faith in the seed and so does Ammons, who sees independent but interactive agents establishing the unity of life. If death is superseded it is not through transcendence but through transformation, the Darwinian principle of the world's unending flux.

Throughout the pilgrim and prophetic stages one feels, despite the constant balancing of one and many, that oneness is the goal of cognition even as it is restive within any partial reach. Plurality is in a sense what the pattern must endure on its way to a greater roundness. Synecdoche infuses microscopic detail and refers to the grand metaphor of all reality. In his sense of the All and its laws of motion superseding particulars, Ammons follows Emerson. But in the late phase he reverses the paradigm: oneness is nodal and intermittent, not comprehensive. Parts do not as readily confer a whole. Nature is an organic unity, but the embrace of the mind in the configurations of landscape is fleeting and finite. Reality is, in a sense, always local, always decentered, hence subordinate to plurality. This, too, draws him closer to Thoreau. But in his late acknowledgment of loss, and of the accumulative force of the past, Ammons removes himself even from Thoreau.

Ammons' sage, like Emerson and Thoreau, lives in a continuous present because he has made a home in motion. As we have seen, "Tomorrow a new walk is a new walk" (CP, 151), without a trace of the past to muddy it. Cycles are renewable and risk is without consequence or any sense of real loss, in the Emersonian sequence of horizons. *Tape for the Turn of the Year,* for example, includes the occasional childhood anecdote, but conveys no sense of loss or waste. While some interest in habitats and cooperative systems carries over from the middle phase, the concept of change in the late work is couched much more in evolutionary terms of extinctions and adaptations. In later works Ammons deals, more than before, with the past, and with the accumulations of yesterdays. The past is not redeemed as living memory, or easily metamorphosed into today's fresh orders. It lingers as debris, as bits of unfulfilled order, as loss. ("I have a life that did not become," Ammons begins in "Easter Morning" [CT, 19].) This is another anti-Emersonian aspect of the new work. The past has no authority, but neither is it easily brushed aside. It accumulates as "garbage," "and there is no way, finally, to throw anything away" (SV, 11). These poems explore a variety of responses to death, including mourning, but what they almost never do is evade death. Transfiguration and redemptive possibility remain strong impulses in the late poetry, but their work is more exposed, more strenuous, more provisional, and more uncertain.

These aspects of late Ammons emerge in *Snow Poems* but come to full, eloquent expression in his remarkable "Ridge Farm" (SV, 1–41). That this will be poetry of adjustment and discontinuity rather than continuous motion he tells us in canto 5:

> recalcitrance, fluency: these:
> too far with one and the density
> darkens, the mix slows, and bound
> up with hindrance, unyielding, stops:
> too far with the other and the bright
> spiel of light spins substanceless
> descriptions of motion—
>
> always to be held free this way,
> staggering, jouncing, testing the
> middle mix,
> the rigid lines of the free and easy
>   (SV, 5)

This is poetry of staggering, jouncing, testing; life achieves its freedoms in breaking apart held orders. Little shocks and surprises assault the imagination, not just the unforeseen, peripheral detail that widens scope (as in "Corson's Inlet"), but reversals, even grotesque reversals, as when a dead mole appears in the watering can with which the poet attends to an abandoned but resilient plant. Indeed, it is in the ordinary that Ammons finds the truly strange. This creates landscapes which surprise rather than endow the beholder with a sense of authority or autonomy.

Ammons puts greater faith in description in this period. Some of the most eloquent passages of "Ridge Farm" are purely descriptive, removing discursive content to embody pattern in image. Tension is rife:

The lean, far-reaching, hung-over sway
of the cedars this morning!
vexed by the wind and working tight

but the snow's packed in, wet-set,
and puffed solid: the cedars nod to
an average under gusts and blusters:

yesterday afternoon cleared the
sunset side of trees, the hemlocks
especially, limbering loose, but
the morning side, the lee, sunless
again today, overbalances:

the grackles form long strings
of trying to sit still; they weight
down the wagging branchwork snow stuck
branch to branch, tree to shrub,
imposing weeds.

(SV, 3)

The poem starts with a weight, a double weight in fact, of ice and grack-les. But the second, bird-weight carries with it the possibility of lift. The cedars are lean and far-reaching, yet "hung-over." The enjambment makes that hangover a form of freedom, overriding a boundary. Wind seems an agent of this stress, but a narrow unity sustains itself since "the snow's packed in." The movement of the cedars, "limbering loose," arises in the recollection of yesterday's afternoon sun, but the dullness "over-balances" with its unifying force, connecting branches, tree to shrub, shrub to weeds. But again, "imposing weeds" suggests the possibility of a disruption of this grim order. Since "imposing" begins a new line it takes on the value of a verb.

Thus, while weight and confinement, the burden of ice and snow, dominate the opening canto, we anticipate transition. Ammons sets imagination at the brink, like a composer introducing half a cadence. We await the completion of the pattern in the movement. A partial, retentive oneness must break out into a more expansive vision. The last canto of "Ridge Farm," culminating a longer, closing movement, evokes "light" as a discontinuous but perennial presence. It "breaks out" in fresh configu-rations, closing the cadence with a descriptive passage that stands against the first for its redemptive possibility.

... yesterday I
looked upbrook from the highway and

there flew down midbend a catbird to
the skinny dip, found a secure
underwater brookstone and began, in a
dawnlike conclave of tranquility, to
ruffle and flutter, dipping into and
breaking the reflective surfaces with
mishmashes of tinkling circlets.

(SV, 41)

The poem that began in ice ends in a brook. A line of restless grackles has become a single catbird finding a toehold. But the sequence does not suggest a continuity of today and tomorrow. The poem begins with "this morning" and ends with "yesterday." This is not an Emersonian prophet of unimpeded radiance. Circles suggest unity, but they arise in a myriad of "mishmashes," not horizons expanding out from the eye. Faith is located in plural, intermittent outbreaks of light.

The images above maximize the interpenetration between order and disorder, tranquillity and flux, one and many, rather than schematizing plurality into abstract patterns and motions. We arrive at the brink of revelation. This brink is reached often, in various configurations. The final stanza is anticipated, for instance, in section 26:

there is something about
a redbird flying down
into
the brook bed, the stone-deep ditch,
and lighting on a washed-out root,
the brook meanwhile throwing mirrors
everywhere—light, mirror, bird, stone

(SV, 20)

These moments follow regularly upon images of mortality, in this case the death of the mole. What the poem does not promise, however, is a transition into a vision of the overall. This is a "real brook" of "deep enleafing" and "certain bends," yet the "tinkling circlets" suggest the imagination glimpsing visionary possibility.

For late Ammons, as for late Stevens, another poet of the ordinary, reality includes the imagination. "If you don't eat the imaginary potato . . . your real capacity to imagine illusion lessens" (SV, 7). Ammons' poetry is especially anti-pastoral in this late phase, testing the pastoral's comfortable balances with frank images of intrusion and threat, disease and despoliation. Nature and man are co-contaminants. But the debunking rhetoric gives way throughout "Ridge Farm," and in later poems, to luminous moments in which the imagination finds some reciprocity with the material world: "still ponds, swallows / plinking them with fine lines . . . nipper fish catching / a chink in the mirror as a / web." In earlier work "nature" was a stable referent, for all its motions, a thing separable from the human configuration of it, something to which the mind went out. But here "nature says nothing— / it has nothing to say" so the poet "fills nature with my unintentionality," tropes its nothingness. Of course there is ordinary nature: the sexual and mortal body, material being. But Nature, as the transfiguration of the ordinary, is a necessary illusion: "Bernie said he wasn't much interested / in nature but if we didn't have it we'd have to / think of something to take its place."

On the one hand Ammons acknowledges the sublimations that go into our pastoral construction of nature. "I love nature especially if there's / a hospital nearby and macadam or / glass in between." We separate ourselves from integral being by denying death, by dividing ourselves from death: "I like nature poetry / where the brooks are never dammed up or / damned to hauling dishwater or / scorched out of their bottoms by acids." But such declarations are set against an insistent confrontation with "the real" as it is known by the nose: "spilldiddlings from the / assholes of filthy sheep." And it is just such denials that lead to abuses: "We can horse deeply in with / irresponsibility's ease; that's what / they say: / I'm afraid nature's going to send the bill: it usually does: / ferocious tallywhacker."

In "Ridge Farm" Ammons represents landscape as more than the externalized view. It is the wind "getting into and up our coats," the rain "prickling us." The beholders are then a part of what they see. These sensations are a reality check, but in the sense that mind and external world roll together: "why test the mind on the reality stone: / nothing will be determined but that / mind, too, terribly flows and stalls." As the mind moves through its shifting landscapes it discovers and creates the "radiant nodes" that make "Ridge Farm," despite its imagery of decay, a joyous poem. *Glare,* Ammons' most unflinching confrontation with the ordinary, nearly relinquishes those redeeming moments of luminosity and coalescence that characterize "Ridge Farm," and even the mock-sublime of "Garbage." The poem refuses sentiment, illusion, consolation; it looks at death as the final funnel. Glare is not radiance and contains no tincture of the sublime. It's even a little menacing. "Ridge Farm" kept the visionary element alive in local glints and glimmers. "Garbage" found it again, in the burning embers of trash. But where are they when the light of day is so intense? In *Glare* we arrive at "the sum of too many things to think about," and the "invisible" is no longer a depth in landscape but a "slice" "between the going away and coming round again" (GL, 243–244). An often endearingly humorous but hardly ingratiating voice tells the truth about oneness—that it's down and out, not up and through: "In time all the stories become the same story; / the energies play out and the hole at the end / contains everything" (243). Yet the poet swerves (with a "meanwhile") from this totalizing void, acknowledging "joy" that can "break out anywhere" (243) The "Strip" which names the first half of this long poem is Ammons' sign of the infinite, not a transcendent cycle of generation and decay. This once sublime pattern, this "invisibility," may be an "opacity" (244). The transcendental "Overall" reduces to "the sum of too many things to talk about" except in the jerky, improvisatory, discontinuous, crude, and anxious mental registers of "Scat Scan," as the second part is called. *Glare* is not an epistemological poem at all. It is ordinary in the sense that it claims no position of mirroring mastery. It is, rather, a record of the embodied mind.

Ammons has shuttled regularly in his long career between long and short poems, an alternation that reflects his fascination with the one/many relation. Thus, while the long poem *Glare* ruminates on the large movements of being into nothingness and back, *Brink Road* registers local moments of transition. Frames are faceted and mobile; poems are triptychs and diptychs. The mathematical one/many dynamic of the sage gives way to a series of freeze frames or "stills" (a favored word) that will not assimilate into a grand pattern. *Brink Road* is Ammons' fullest exploration of the poetics of adjustment. The poet as ordinary man abides through shifts of orientation, more local and episodic than paradigmatic. The poems repeatedly move from a burdened or dispirited state to one that observes and enables ongoing. Vision is less about truth than about belief. The poet reconfigures nature in order to make spiritual adjustments. Indeed, the eye is less reliable than before as a vehicle of knowledge and renewal; the imagination corrects the eye's narrow disclosures. Where the prophetic poems celebrated a continuous present, the late poems acknowledge holding patterns and impulses, the human desire to keep what belongs to time. Mobility involves wreckage and debris—the present scene overlain with the shards of past structures. The image of the stream runs throughout these poems as a figure by which the mind might train itself to mobility, but the overall experience is of transition rather than fluency, of perspective rather than transcendence. In their emphasis on adjusted vision these poems take us back to the pilgrim poems, but their focus is no longer on cognitive authority. Identity seems to be something inevitable but unfixed, like temperament, rather than an essence in need of transcendental proofs.

Ammons employs a similar poetic structure to convey each of these transitional moments. Each short lyric is divided by a conjunction (but, still, meanwhile, whereas, even) that reverses or redirects the logic of an initial image. Rather than conveying a continuous present, the poems register abrupt transitions in being, set against a background "unity of void." The opening poem of the volume, "The Sense of Now" (BR, 3), serves as a template of others.

> Rock frozen and fractured
> spills, a shambles,
> and tiers of time pile into,
> shatter through
>
> other tiers or angle up
> oddly, brightly lined with
>
> granite or talus, a jumble,
> "metaphysical debris":
>
> but the stream finding its
> way down a new hill spills
>
> along the right ledges, shifts
> the schist chips about and
>
> down with becoming coherence,
> and moss beds down ruffling
>
> shale edges dark gray
> to green, and the otter
>
> drinks from sidepools
> almost perfectly clear.

Surprisingly, the sense of now is not one idea but three, without obvious summary or confluence. The paratactic poem is edgy, jumpy, and restless in its movement through these orientations. Indeed, in the first frame disorder is the principle ("fractured," "shambles," "jumble," "debris"). The sense of now includes the past; a former order has collapsed. What appears is "oddly" configured, not obviously patterned. The term "spills" suggests waste, which "piles up" in an accumulation without coherent design. The abstract summary—"metaphysical debris"—is itself discontinuous, the quotation marks highlighting the disjunction. But the phrase brings into focus the abstraction latent in the rocks as "tiers of time." The second frame features motion over its effects. "But" marks a shift in which the "spills" of the previous clause becomes libation more than waste. The movement from solid to liquid allows the "becoming coherence" (lovely and emergent) to gather agency. The mind does not make a home *in* such motion, however, only beside it. The poem has moved from wreckage to fluency and will close in figures of tentative dwelling. It shifts again, now to the "moss" that "beds down" on the shale. An organic image, the moss softens the figure of retention, converting "gray" to "green." The otter, like a surrogate for the poet, partakes of the liquid element through the sidepools (now rock and water, retention and flow, converge). The sense of now is a still moment "almost perfectly clear." Qualifiers of this sort characterize the last phase of Ammons' work. He does not celebrate incompleteness as evidence of the infinite, so much as proof of human limit. Human concern, as he puts it in "Ridge Farm," is "a frail butterfly, a slightly guided piece of trash" (SV, 41).

Fragmentation rather than continuity characterizes human concern, as these three-part poems suggest in their structure. The next few poems in *Brink Road* repeat, with variation, the structure of adjustment established in "The Sense of Now." In "Picking Up Equations" (BR, 4) we again begin with images of wreckage ("storm toss") until the "still" marks a transition to a recuperative moment. Then the broken branch reveals a new logic in the wind's agency; fallen branch becomes "shadow" or trace of the wind's movement, part of the "arc including everything" but known only in its local bends and angles. This geometric/algebraic mapping of the one/many/one paradigm removes the imagination from the emotional weight of the opening, with its sense of exposure and danger. One might be relieved at the pruning of "last year's drought-wood that died way up in the branches," but the human need for shelter against hazard, the ordinary condition of existence, enforces a warning against too easy an embrace of motion: "a nick on the noggin could drop you . . . or you could just be / dazzled and wander off down the road, wild." The imagination retreats from this anxiety to a retrospective relation to change.

In each of these poems Ammons, the ordinary man, seeks an acceptable balance rather than an absolute truth, some sort of phenomenological "regularum." Thus in "Establishment" the eye produces "invitations, deceptions" and indicates translucence while the mind asserts "hard rock." A third, closing image integrates mind and eye: "rock grain" is "cracked and felt into" by "tense roots," a figure of idea taking hold as phenomenal truth and vital ongoing.

Each poem begins, then, with some image of necessity blocking creative ongoing—a rockslide, a storm toss, an impenetrable ridge—but makes an adjustment to refuse terminus and desolation while allowing for tentative order. The pragmatist principle that "belief at any cost serves life" is enacted in the poetry by the imagination turning always toward some angle of vision that will affirm—affirmation is something life requires more than knowledge. So in "Standing Light Up" (BR, 12) Ammons begins with avalanches of stone, mud, and snow, cast off in a "but so what" that turns abruptly to an affirmation of spirit. He offers checks on the imagination of disaster that might follow from a greater investment in a particular order. But the poems are not breezy in their losses either. They evoke, as in Frost, a lyric keeping. Such adjustments are not as facile as the conjunctions suggest, however. Ammons strains the syntax to register the work of restoring flow and contriving new order. Even the syntactically awkward title marks this strain. Contractions and possessives in the poem add to the confusion, indicating how objects separate and reattach in a network of associations and events: "what outleaps / the insides of summits thunder's rumble has / never jarred." The refusal of "jarring" forces is itself achieved by the phonic over the grammatical or semantic orders, making us "halt and listen."

These linguistic strains remind us that our orientations are under construction—they are not passive discoveries but behaviors that preserve life. So for instance in "First Cold" (BR, 15) a first patterning of "white on white," of snow on petal, is aesthetically satisfying but sterile. The "milling" of life in seasonal change produces in the imagination of the beholder a new patterning, of gold on gold, bees and the sun. The descriptions provide a "shifting dynamics between artifice [. . ./. . .] and emergence"("Next to Nothing," BR, 144)—between one construction of reality and another emerging as "motion / undermines meaning with meaning"("Flurries," BR, 73). Motion is not just theoretical; Ammons conveys it by moving from one form to another. To hold is human, Ammons seems to recognize in this volume, and to change is natural. Human adjustment is then the appropriate response to nature.

The poem "Fascicle" (BR, 10), while it does not launch or conclude the volume as it might, tells us something about lyric poetry as Ammons understands it in this phase of his career.

> There's a rift of days sunny (not too windy, not
> too cold) between leaf- and snowfall when
> raking works: away on a weekend, you could

miss it and rain could sog everything slick-flat
or gusts could leave no leaf not lifting
off the ground: stick

around the house, a big sheet ready, a strong-caned
rake strung tight, and catch the sun
just when it stills the air dry: that's likely

to be before some cold front frost-furring
the saw-edged leaves glistened brittle, clouds
tightening the horizon: then the white leaves fly.

The model of poetic activity is not the pilgrim's quest or the prophet's visionary excursion, but the simple, domestic work of raking leaves. Whitman stands silently in the background of the poem, and Stevens, "after the leaves have fallen," but Dickinson prevails. This one-sentence "fascicle" is something less audacious, more contingent, and less transcendental than Whitman's *Leaves of Grass,* less barren than Stevens' "plain sense of things." The lyric gathering is not comprehensive; it arises in a "rift" (marked by the parenthesis). Again, the sense of loss and failure haunts the poem ("sog everything slick-flat"; "no leaf not lifting") and must be dispelled. The gathering at the center of the poem is entirely transitional. It belongs not with cosmology but with the domestic images of the house and the bedsheet (the phrase "strong-caned" left at the end of the line anticipates chair, not rake). A "catch" of the sun, or holding of energy, makes the dispersal at the end not a failure (as it is logically, and in terms of the poem's narrative), but a release. Liberation comes when "the white leaves fly" after the "tightening [on] the horizon." The thrust of all these poems, what makes them ordinary, is their attempt to overcome the fear of death through images of gathering and release. The leaves are "white" presumably because of the frost, but as the domestic "sheet" suggests a paper so the "white leaves" suggest as well a literary dispersal, something countering the death this image also projects. The poem could not end with the success of the catch. But that success allows the final dispersal to become double, overcoming the desolate, anxious language of the poem's opening.

In Ammons' last phase we see a landscape poetry finally loosed from Emersonian idealism (or pragmatism, as Richard Poirier calls it). Ammons answers the Over-Soul's call to theory with the compelling, tangible struggles of the ordinary man to put himself on the side of motion and flow. Death must be transfigured, and it is transfigured, not through confident reference to a transcendental vision but through exercise in "the giving up of oneself away," through "simplicity and the breaking surf" (GL, 243). That breaking surf slaps against the edges of our land-scape, changes its contours, whether they are coastal expanses or inland backyards. All our configurations of reality, for Ammons, are built on sand. And there's a kind of ambivalent pleasure in watching the tide carry them out.

7

John Ashbery: Landscapeople

The "metaphysical debris" that piles up around the "sense of now" in late Ammons is everywhere in the poetry of John Ashbery. Where Ammons works with juxtaposed freeze frames, Ashbery works with flowcharts, building the shifting ground into the very structure of every landscape. As his *Flow Chart* makes particularly clear, one cannot really *think* the continuous present even though one is always thinking *in* it.

> Sad grows the river god as he oars past us
> downstream without our knowing him: for if, he reasons,
> he can be overlooked, then to know him would be to eat him,
> ingest the name he carries through time to set down
> finally, on a strand of rotted hulks.
>
> (FC, 3)

Consciousness is, for Ashbery, a "swift-flowing alluvial mud" in which we, and our landscapes, take form, are flooded, and then different "painted monsters" are born. That mud, though, is made from Bergsonian backwash, the sediment of memory and expectation. On it we build imaginary gardens "with huge blue and red flowers and solemn birds that dwarfed / the trees they sat on," gardens which "need never give way to the fumes and crevasses / of the high glen." We imagine that we have discovered a final, comprehensive vision, that "all will be correct as in a painting / that would never ache for a frame" (FC, 8).

> All's aglow. But we see by it that some mortal
> material was included in the glorious compound, that next to

nothing can prevent its mudslide from sweeping over us
while it renders the pitted earth smooth and pristine and something
like one's original idea of it, only so primitive
it can't understand us.

(FC, 9)

The primitive once again eludes the frame, flooding our formation of landscape.

The formation of landscape (the shapes the mind gives to the physical world in the poetry of Frost, Stevens, and Moore) shifts to the correspondent formation of dynamic identity in Clampitt and Ammons. In Ammons' analogical mode the parallelism between world and mirroring mind often slips into a single integrated surface (as in "Terrain" and "Corson's Inlet"), but scenic and expository modes prevail. Ashbery goes farther. Consciousness *of* landscape has become, for him, indistinguishable from consciousness *as* landscape. And it is almost impossible to gain a footing in this "spongy terrain" (FC, 10). While Clampitt is the nomad and Ammons, finally, the ordinary man, Ashbery is the Cheshire cat or the Brer Rabbit of American poetry—a trickster figure, a prestidigitator always shifting ground and throwing you off balance. He may be the Piranesi of landscape, taking to an extreme Frost's "directive" to get his reader lost. His disappearing paths and slippery topography, his shifts in scale and perspective and subversions of narrative sequence all point to his larger interest in the nature of thought and knowledge, the relationship of mind to environment and the play between temporal and spatial awareness. "Everything is landscape," he writes in *The Double Dream of Spring* (1970), a volume that takes its title from the surrealist landscape painter Giorgio de Chirico. And we are "landscapeople" (AWK, 116), our identities inseparable from the "outsides" we inhabit. We are "outside looking out." Yet the landscape is never quite transparent—a patina seems always to be forming on it. Consciousness arranges and is arranged by the world that slips away into history. Ashbery accelerates this process so that consciousness becomes itself the landscape, or perhaps, the timescape in which he meditates. As we move through the shifting labyrinths we make of the world and of ourselves renegotiating boundaries at every step, a creative absorption substitutes for the deferred sense of transparence. Like de Chirico, Ashbery offers us decentered landscapes with many perspective lines, which both undercut the ideal of a timeless subjective vision, and open new possibilities for reverie in temporal extension instead of spatial depth.

In focusing on landscape in Ashbery I mean to shift attention away somewhat from the predominant view of his work as language-centered. The poet's syntactic and rhetorical strategies for resisting conclusion and hierarchy, his polyphonous pronouns, his homonymic play, do invite a notion of the poem as a site of purely linguistic transactions. The relationship between Ashbery's disarming sentences, as syntactic and grammatical units, and his tumultuous landscapes, as mental pictures, is an interesting one, not quite causal or analogical. Rather than focus on Ashbery's linguistic surfaces, we might think about how the contours of landscape, for him, form a grammar subject to particulars that press against the promise of a stabilizing system of nature. I want to stress that landscape imagery in Ashbery's poetry cannot be reduced, as Marjorie Perloff has suggested in *Poetic License,* to the parodic trappings of Romantic discourse. One can certainly find affinities between Ashbery's work and the paintings of Mark Tansey, those heavily inscribed landscapes, at once allegorical and hyperreal, in which his figures pursue the primitive within an inevitable condition of belatedness. Tansey's sense that landscape is a language does not reduce to the idea that it is a merely linguistic surface. Both artists evoke the mystery of the textually constructed landscape, the end of the line of the book of nature. But Ashbery's work does not, finally, lead us to the detached spatiality that Fredric Jameson has described as postmodern (154–181). Landscape is, rather, a fundamental, generating trope of knowledge in Ashbery's poetry, attractive, I believe, because it insistently invokes an observer and his environment and draws out assumptions of knowledge within our everyday accounts of what we know. Ashbery's poetry sets out to present the feeling of our contemporary landscape of knowledge—unsteady, even cataclysmic, full of trompe l'oeil and obscurities but occasionally luminous. His work remains deeply tied to the meditative tradition of landscape reverie and allegory from Dante to Stevens. But Ashbery explores for consciousness uncharted "spaces" in which temporality is dramatized rather than suppressed.[1]

Mark Johnson and George Lakoff have demonstrated the extent to which "knowledge is a landscape" is indeed one of the metaphors we live by, just as sight is our Enlightenment term for understanding (*Metaphors We Live By*). There is no obvious necessity in this metaphor: as Anne Salmond has shown, the Maori of New Zealand speak of knowledge as treasure, as food for chiefs, as a magic cloak ("Theoretical Landscapes," 82–85). In speaking of knowledge as a landscape, we both accept perspectivism and claim grounds beyond perspective. Landscape is our trope of knowledge because it makes the knowledge seem to be "of" something, not an entirely self-enclosed system. At the same time, "landscape" in Ashbery displaces "nature" as an epistemological trope, and retains a sense of incompleteness and mediation in our forms of knowledge. Landscape, "a portion of land that the eye can comprehend in a single view" (*Webster's*), is engaged but incommensurate with an environment in which space is not absolute, a reality of shifting tectonic plates that can never be mapped, a "ground" that is not stable.

These shaky conditions of landscape do not leave Ashbery in a stance of skepticism, though certainly skepticism is his starting point and drives his vision. There is more to the world of Ashbery's poetry than shallow irony, blank parody, corrected banality, commodity fetishism, and decrerative emptiness, though all such qualities can be found there. If knowledge is a landscape, landscape is a space for dreaming, epistemology a form of reverie. He approaches "vision in the form of a task" ("Fragment," DDS), sometimes even as a burden or compulsion. If his imagination is spatial, its means of expansion is to feature "time's way of moving sideways out of the event." If he resists converting the incomplete or unsaid to a metaphysics of the ineffable, he continues to pursue the charge of unaccommodated thoughts and makes a landscape of that pursuit. And if in retrospect our search for transparence, crashing through landscape after landscape, itself looks constructed, like a golf course "with a few natural bonuses left in," the balm of "pale Alpine flowers" lingers to keep alive the dream, our "chief work" ("A Wave," W, 70).

Ashbery's topography is a complex one, shaped not only by rivers, mountains, trees, islands, capes, peninsulas, storms, and clouds, but by many a farm and field of grain, barren plains, lakes, and ruined cities. I cannot undertake here an iconography of Ashbery's landscapes, which anyway keep changing: pastoral, sublime, suburban, and bureaucratic. In *Some Trees* (1956) Ashbery tended to prefer pastoral landscapes, but he moved toward imagery of the sublime in *Rivers and Mountains* (1967). In *The Double Dream of Spring* (1970) he introduced the paraphernalia of popular culture and suburban fancy into rural scenery, leading to the abandoned picnic grounds of *As We Know* (1979). *Three Poems* (1972) initiated the trope of the journey. *A Wave* (1984) represents perhaps his most varied terrain, continuing the motif of a journey, starting from "home," lured by an ideal of mindlessness, but driven on through a landscape of deserts, beaches, orchards, and steeply shelving hills in its Sisyphean ascent. *Flow Chart* (1991) abandons vertical tropes, though it clings to geographic ones; the River God presides and we live on oozy ground. But throughout all these and later volumes and their various topographies, Ashbery's landscapes are dynamic, temporally inscribed and constantly redirected; they involve dramatic shifts of scale and proportion, so that the trivial or odd rises to become the dominant and monumental, the corner becomes the center. They tend to be multiple as well: while we are establishing one perspective line, another is emerging to claim our attention. They collapse into billboards or shrink to postage stamps. But there is always, within these landscapes, a principle of ground which our cognition cannot fix, a sense of reality which our constructed landscapes may block out, but which also drives their creation and decreation even if it is "so primitive it can't understand us" (FC, 9). Ashbery is not a poet of the void, though he occasionally passes through an "invisible terrain." Even in *Houseboat Days* (1977), where the poet is like Noah, afloat on a flood brought down by degenerated systems, he can build on a reality of water; and eventually the ground presents itself, awakening the Orphean poet. "Data banks," Lyotard has said, are "nature" for post-modern man (*The Post-modern Condition*). Ashbery has, along these lines, been portrayed as a poet of the post-technological sublime, of information overkill, of discourse speaking to discourse, where the observer and the environment collapse into simulacra. Yet, while the bureaucracies of language set up formidable facades, there are no data banks in Ashbery, no computer networks or videos, and only one warehouse. Throughout his poetry, architectural pinnacles spin up in our sight, but are mostly seen in ruins, if at all. Landscape in the broadest sense survives its various scene changes. In Ashbery's most recent book, *Hotel Lautréamont* (1992), the sycophantic self reports to Control about "our example, earth" (HL, 18), but it remains the example we inhabit even if we can't live like Thoreau.

It is difficult to say anything very empirical about so abstract and elusive a poet as John Ashbery, but I want to cite a couple of biographical facts that have indirect bearing on my subject. This so-called "New York City poet" was raised on a farm near Rochester, New York. Memories of this childhood, which surface throughout the poet's career, present a complex anti-pastoral continually yielding to pastoral yearnings. This "North Farm," this "patchwork of childhood north of here" (W, 1) makes a regular symbolic appearance in his work as the ambivalent homestead in which the prodigal son can never quite settle, which he will not recognize when he finds it. Ashbery is a vigorously homeless poet (like Lautréamont, who lived his brief life hopping hotels). He tracks the mental journey of our search for home even though he is less than confident that such thinking is enough to summon us into dwelling. The middle distance, itself a result of our perceptual and cognitive makeup, never comes into focus, never becomes a location, but recedes as in Zeno's paradox. This is not a poet who has put aside pastoral, who has banished its pleasures and settled for a completely urban reality. Although Ashbery's book jackets until recently stated that he "lives in New York City," he in fact spends most of his time two hours away in the relatively rural Hudson, New York. He lives just down the road from the former property of the luminist painter Frederick Church, whose house, "Olana," was designed so that each window would frame a perfect landscape. (Ashbery, like Baudelaire, whose "Paysage" he translated, is very fond of window views, which mark the negotiation between mental and environmental landscapes.) But it is Ashbery's literary interests, more than his rural background, that have led him to continue examining the pastoral mode. His first volume, *Some Trees,* included a number of pastoral reprises, most notably the title poem. Ashbery's approach to pastoral exemplifies the ambiguous distinction of nature and landscape. Here, the trees "arranged by chance" seem like a given reality, though as figures for lovers they suggest how an intentionality becomes a surround. By the end of the poem the spell is over and the artifice which has receded reappears, reminding us that the "arrangement" was only that, not a transparency.

The term "landscape" is a deliberately porous one for Ashbery, for whom it can mean either environment, painting, or, more often, both at once, since our landscape is etymologically and practically a shaping and framing of the land. Indeed, sometimes it is unclear whether the poet is describing a painting or imagining an actual scene. Ashbery for a long time made his living writing art criticism, and some of his favorite painters have been landscape artists. I will explore the dynamics of the term "landscape" in Ashbery—his sense of the mind as an uncharted, metamorphic terrain, his sense of environment as mediated, framed, and proportioned by concepts out of step with it.

"Litany" (from *As We Know,* 1979), a long, two-column double monologue that resists dialectic, text and gloss, or any stable opposition, actually ends up revealing many of Ashbery's predilections. In the passage that I will study the "author," a kind of aesthete, tells us about paintings, "things that are important to him," while the voice of the other column rambles in a more three-dimensional, moralized landscape. As always, it is hard to tell just what investment Ashbery has in anything he "recommends"—yet it is toward the sentiments to which he is most prone that the poet directs his irony, and the sentiments often survive in an invigorated form:

> [. . .] Almost all landscapes
> Are generous, well proportioned, hence

Welcome. We feel we have more in common with a
Landscape, however shifty and ill-conceived,
Than with a still-life: those oranges
And apples, and dishes, what have they to do
With us? Plenty, but it's a relief
To turn away from them. Portraits, on the other
Hand, are a different matter—they have no
Bearing on the human shape, their humanitarian
Concerns are foreign to us, who dream
And know not we are humane, though, as seen
By others, we are. But this is about people.
Right. That's why landscapes are more
Familiar, more what it's all about—we can see
Into them and come out on the other side.

(AWK, 49)

Ashbery is here talking about "pictures," of course, not natural land-
scapes; thus he can celebrate rather than regret their contrivance, even if
he smirks some at the naïve appeal of illusion, the false sense of owner-
ship, the "other side" as the fiction of the vanishing point. There is of
course a wonderful perversity in calling landscapes more "humani-
tarian" than portraits or those strange/familiar metonymies of still life
that reveal our domestic and social arrangements. But the dream of self-
transcendence, of forgetting our humanity, our existence in time, place,
society, is the human appeal of traditional landscape. Ashbery asks how
we might engage this aspect of our humanity without falling prey to its
devices and delusions. In his landscapes we never do quite come out on
the other side, transcendental or otherwise, though he is always alluding
to it; landscape leads into landscape. But there is a great deal of room for
reverie in this method.

In painting, one-point perspective allows the feeling of "coming out
on the other side," through the vanishing point around which the "well
proportioned" landscape arranges itself. As Andrew Ross has pointed out
in *The Failure of Modernism*, much of Ashbery's poetry approaches the
problem of the self through a critique of Albertian perspective: a bodi-
less, metaphysical self contrived for the beholder of isomorphic space is
exposed as a fetish (161–206). Ross's emphasis is more on the skeptical
side of Ashbery, whom he calls "doubting John Thomas." I see this skep-
tical figure as the initiator of further ventures into environment. In the
early semi-autobiographical poem "The Skaters" (RM, 34–63), Ashbery
evokes the hard reflective surface, with watery reality just beneath it. This
is the surface of art, with the markings of our various glides and traver-

sals etched into its glass. Impatient with the snowfall of memory and association and the entropic dartings of the skaters—thoughts driven by the need for novelty—Ashbery invokes the orderly landscapes of art:

> (Viz. "Rigg's Farm, near Aysgarth, Wensleydale," or the "Sketch at
>   Norton")
> In which we escape ourselves—putrefying mass of prevarications, etc.—
> In remaining close to the limitations imposed.
>
> (RM, 47)

Ashbery's parodies of the art historian here mock the yearning to escape our transience and confusion through art, to order life by the principles of art, but he also shares the susceptibility: "How strange that the narrow perspective lines / Always seem to meet, although parallel, and that an insane ghost could do this" (36). It is the "insane ghost" of Albertian perspective, who insinuates his way into our desires, that Ashbery addresses: "it is you I am parodying / Your invisible denials" (42)—denials of time, of the frame, of the body of the beholder. We do not escape our constructions, but Ashbery's strategy in "The Skaters" is to subvert the hypnotism of the vanishing point by deranging it into an anti-mimetic "*bigarrure* of squiggly lines" (36). The work of construction overtakes illusion. This is not the end of the story but the beginning of a new effort. Inspiration here is "a great wind" which "lifted these cardboard panels / Horizontal in the air" (36), not to reveal bare reality or expose an abyss, but to set the panels down in a new arrangement.

Yet behind all the cardboard panels "The Skaters" retains a sense of fluent, "pre-existing, pre-seeming" (34) pre-landscape space, a phenomenological, "shapeless entity" (35) in the "evidence of the visual" to which the child, in this surprisingly Wordsworthian poem, is "devoted" but which is "replaced / By the great shadow of trees" (35) that make it a landscape. Perhaps Ashbery is even alluding in some way here to Wordsworth's skater in Book I of *The Prelude,* who sees the landscape spinning around him, confusing fixed with moving objects. But what in Wordsworth may be read as a mere perceptual experiment of induced motion against the confidence in a stable, substantial landscape and integrated self, is in Ashbery a more habitually swirling condition.

Later in "The Skaters" Ashbery in his New York apartment takes on the identity of Crusoe—paradigm of the solitary lyric observer—and tries to order the world around his island as if it were a painting: "One's only form of distraction is really / To climb to the top of the one tall cliff to scan the distances." That mastering prospect, though, remains illusory: the vultures below "look like bees," but will, he knows, be "rending me limb from limb once I have keeled over definitively." The eagles "always seem to manage to turn their backs to you" (55). Nevertheless, he persists in viewing the world as a sublime landscape:

> Sure enough: in the pale gray and orange distances to the left, a
> Waterspout is becoming distinctly visible.
> Beautiful, but terrifying;
> Delicate, transparent, like a watercolor by that nineteenth-century
>   Englishman whose name I forget.
>
> (RM, 55)

This scene won't stay still, either, of course:

> . . . Now the big cloud that was
>   in front of the waterspout
> Seems to be lurching forward, so that the waterspout, behind it,
>   looks more like a three-dimensional photograph.
>
> (RM, 56)

As the realism and turmoil of the scene and the coming storm drive even the vultures to their nest, Crusoe, tempted as he is to let this landscape turn to environment, to "linger on in the wet" of pure awareness, decides he "really had better be getting back to the tent." Our constructed landscapes don't stay in place, but neither can we do without them. To "linger in the wet" is not really an option, though we may peer out of what he calls in another poem "wet casements."

Ashbery favors scenes that feature hazard, climatic change, or digressions of line ("prolongations of our reluctance to approach") as if they could resist the patina with their inner dynamism or digression, as he tells us in "Litany":

> Pictures of capes and peninsulas
> With big clouds moving down on them,
> Pressing with a frightening weight—
> And shipwrecks barely seen (sometimes
> Not seen at all) through snow
> In the foreground, and howling, ravenous gales
> In the background.
>
> (AWK, 48–49)

Such pictures, obscure in foreground and background, presenting their elusive middle distance, work at the limits of landscape as fixed space, though all their turmoil is of course framed and controlled, the hazard put at an aesthetic distance.

At one level these are probably tacky imitations of Turner, and Ashbery's pleasure in them has an element of camp. But the poet's way is often to recognize the essential emotion even in kitsch (and vice versa) and to redirect it toward more rigorous forms. Indeed, a double register of the luminous and the homely can be felt throughout Ashbery's poetry, and marks the course he lays between skepticism and reverie. Ashbery commented about a group show at the Whitney Museum: "The urge toward grandeur is there, co-existing with the intent to subvert it, through a dead-pan, no-comment rendering. It is true that just plain solemnity will no longer do, the days of Bierstadt are no more" (Ashbery, "1976 and all that," quoted in Wilson, *American Sublime,* 217). But if Bierstadt is out, the genre of landscape, as Ashbery has shown, is inexhaustible. A great deal of the grandeur of Ashbery's poetry comes from his dreaming in time-space and the allegorical adventure it always seems to carry, even as the deadpan rendering tends to make the space a shallow one. The decreative, subversive side of Ashbery, the skeptical side, is itself part of what makes him a dreamer, for as he has said of minimalist art, "the dream of escaping from dream is itself a dream" and "dreamers" "are insatiable expansionists" (RS, 12). The major means of expansion—since the Romantics used up natural space and the modernists, aesthetic space—is time.

> ... By that time
> Space will be a jar with no lid, and you can live
> Any way you like out on those vague terraces,
> Verandas, walk-ways—the forms of space combined with time
> We are allowed, and we live them passionately,
> Fortunately, though we can never be described
> And would make lousy characters in a novel.
>
> (AWK, 85)

We would make lousy characters presumably because our lives don't obey the rules of plot and point of view. These are fragments, of course. Ashbery's poems do not depict scenes; they represent thinking in time. These are stops along the way as he traverses the shifting ground of his mind. It is difficult to discuss whole poems because he creates the feeling that the frame of a poem, like the frames of landscape, simply marks off an interval of the flux.

The most fundamental difference between Ashbery and a Romantic or Transcendentalist poet would seem to be the metaphysical basis for topographical reverie. "I no longer have any metaphysical reasons / For doing the things I do," he writes in a poem pointedly titled "The Preludes" (AWK, 91). Alluding to Wordsworth as much as Eliot, Ashbery implies that one prelude will never suffice for the endlessly redirected journey he is on. But Ashbery is not an entirely gratuitous dreamer either, and his poetry is based on the premise that we never really give up "the prospector's hunch": "The reasons were not all that far away, / In the ultramarine well under the horizon" (AWK, 91), and in fact the metaphysical is never, it seems, gone for good—"all that we see is penetrated by it"—"a presence that is elsewhere" ("As We Know," AWK, 74). We dwell in our constructed world and are constructed by it ("this space" we call our landscape is a "checkerboard / [. . .] Trapped in the principle of the great beyond" ["Statuary," AWK, 76], and we are its pieces, its "landscapepeople," its "staffage"—those tiny brush-stroke figures the apprentice puts in). Those little figures in the landscape often natter insidiously to the poet about his entrapments (landscape, if not language, speaks man, they say), but he only half listens. His non-alienated half is already ahead of the game, aware of his part in the production of the "charge," as in "The Picnic Grounds":

> Will the landscape mean anything new now?
> But even if it doesn't, the charge
> Is up ahead somewhere, in the near future,
> Squashing even the allegory of the grass
> Into the mould of its aura, a lush patina.
>   (AWK, 98)

Ashbery both invests in and undermines the mythology of presence with such phrases as "the mould of its aura," something we manufacture, then worship. If the "allegory of the grass" told us of mutability ("all flesh is grass"), the "charge" is stronger; it can turn mutability to transport (hence Whitman's *Leaves of Grass*). Ashbery is yet one further step ahead. His creative passions go toward beating that charge, even as it arises in himself, to the horizon of a landscape, anticipating the next illusion, exposing the "lush patina" on the luminous moment. But the effect of such doubling back is as much to intensify as to detonate the charge. So the tortoise of consciousness wins the race with time by hopping on its back.

While an ironic hum persists throughout Ashbery's poetry, there are, in fact, "pellucid moments." Such moments stand in contrast both to the snowfall and raging gales of the immersed beholder's unorganized awareness, and to the checkerboards and grids of fixed perspective. They tend to be associated with landscape description, and involve a subversion of linear thinking or a "narrative moratorium," as in "A Wave":

> And what to say about those series
> Of infrequent pellucid moments in which
> One reads inscribed as though upon an empty page
> The strangeness of all those contacts from the time they erupt
> Soundlessly on the horizon and in a moment are upon you
> Like a stranger on a snowmobile
>
> (W, 81)

Of these contacts "nothing can be known or written, only that they passed this way." The language here conflates the moment of knowledge or explanation ("in which one reads inscribed as though upon an empty page") and the "contacts" with reality supposedly explained (the snow like the empty page, the stranger like the invisible inscription). Such moments tend to be horizontal and self-referential, folding back into the constructed landscape of knowledge, yet they are charged with strangeness, not beyond knowledge but ahead of it. Thus in "A Wave" Ashbery remarks that "knowing" (as opposed to knowledge) "can have this / Sublime rind of excitement, like the shore of a lake in the desert / Blazing with the sunset" (W, 70). Knowledge, that mutable fruit, becomes less important for itself than for its anticipatory effects, its rind. This is barely a landscape, empty and approaching night. The lake is Ashbery's (as it is Auden's and Stevens') favorite trope of reflection—here in its primary form, before even the trees have been arranged around it to turn reflection into landscape, the pellucid moment into knowledge. Such biblically charged wilderness and desert spaces develop rapidly into abandoned picnic grounds and crumbling cities. Yet "If it pleases all my constructions / To collapse, I shall at least have had that satisfaction, and known / That it need not be permanent in order to stay alive" (W, 70).

This horizontal charge arising as in a rearview mirror is not sublime and will not jump-start us into eternity (as certain forms of catechresis can do in poets like Hart Crane or Charles Wright). It remains embedded in time, even drawing fuel from time. So Ashbery's "pellucid" moments are often calm rather than ecstatic, registers of transience and appearance that confound narrative logic. They are less epiphanal than telescoped visions, as in the following passage from "A Wave" in which we briefly emerge from an accelerating series of changing landscapes into a glassy moment of meditation:

> . . . anybody
> Will realize that he or she has made those same mistakes,
> Memorized those same lists in the due course of the process
> Being served on you now. Acres of bushes, treetops;
> Orchards where the quince and apple seem to come and go
> Mysteriously over long periods of time; waterfalls
> And what they conceal, including what come after—roads and roadways
> Paved for the gently probing, transient automobile;
> Farragoes of flowers; everything, in short,
> That makes this explicit earth what it appears to be in our
> Glassiest moments when a canoe shoots out from under some foliage
> Into the river and finds it calm, not all that exciting but above all
> Nothing to be afraid of, celebrates us
> And what we have made of it.
>
> (W, 76–77)

The descriptive passage (which almost forgets the allegorical purpose that launched it) collapses together spatial and temporal variation, treating them as one. The trees mark out various landscapes that have meant something—have borne fruit—from time to time. The waterfalls seem natural, and also, as in Wordsworth, timeless, though Ashbery would stress that this is the "waterfall effect" in which the eye tires in its gaze on ceaseless motion. Yet they too conceal the social, the transient human arrangements which the flowers of speech aestheticize. All this is both cast off and gathered up in one vision, one temporalized landscape. This timespace gives a qualified feeling of reality ("this explicit earth"), but also of illusion ("what it appears to be"). So in the mirror of our "glassiest moments" the canoe shoots out like an explanation, but one that ultimately "celebrates us," and what we made of the earth, not the earth itself. We pause in such spaces where, as Ashbery writes in "Polite Distortions" (AG, 62), "the laundry / Of our thinking will be spread out on bushes and not / Come to tempt us too much"; these are sunny moments when the "vast shadow" of causal logic pulls in momentarily.

One of the absorbing, if frustrating, qualities of Ashbery's meditative poetry is the uncertainty of its representations—part anecdotal, part dream vision, part allegory, depictive and diagrammatic by unannounced turns. "The flowers don't talk to Ida anymore" and "mirrors fall from trees," yet symbols persist. Ashbery often presents himself as a poet of "paysage moralisé," but the landscape, the moral vision, and the terms of their connection are all in flux. He does not simply map thought and feeling onto unstable, dynamic elements in a landscape (volcanoes, storms, clouds), though he does include these. Such fugitive and cataclysmic images do not by themselves undermine an overall fixed spatial vision. In Ashbery's mapping the levels of reference themselves are unstable since there is no extra-textual system (historical, biblical, or psychological) to fix them. Frost might "have at heart your getting lost" in his journey poem "Directive," but the terrain is easily mapped to certain subtexts and concepts. Ashbery's allegory leads into Scheherazade-like, serial reverie which turns back into allegory when we least suspect it. Since knowledge is landscape and landscape is a kind of dreaming, the boundaries between allegory and reverie are naturally open. This is not to say that Ashbery holds any surrealist faith in the truth of the unconscious; he is actually more interested, I believe, in the shapes that a conscious, discursive rhetoric can make, following a serial rather than a sequential procedure.

While I cannot index the complex iconography of Ashbery's landscapes, I want to look more closely at two of his most obsessive variations on the perpendicular: rivers and mountains, and trees. Not surprisingly, Ashbery shakes these traditional metaphors by their roots, placing their symbolic structure and pictorial integrity in question.

The opening lines from his poem "Rivers and Mountains" have the virtue of being contained enough to illustrate these points about allegorical levels and perpendicularity of thought. Throughout the poem, and indeed the volume that bears its name, Ashbery weaves his way unpredictably among levels and referents, including map, terrain, nature, city, writing, thinking, land, and sea:

> On the secret map the assassins
> Cloistered, the Moon River was marked
> Near the eighteen peaks and the city
> Of humiliation and defeat—wan ending
> Of the trail among dry, papery leaves
> Gray-brown quills like thoughts
> In the melodious but vast mass of today's
> Writing through fields and swamps
> Marked, on the map, with little bunches of weeds.
> . . .
> So going around cities
> To get to other places you found

It all on paper but the land
Was made of paper processed
To look like ferns, mud or other
Whose sea unrolled its magic
Distances and then rolled them up
(RM, 10)

The "assassins" are out, presumably, to get the "president"—that is, the presiding thought or precept, which the poet serves. The military maneuvers and cartographic manipulations throughout *Rivers and Mountains* have to do with ideas competing for our attention, insights growing conventional and losing their appeal. Thought is dramatized as a spatial struggle. Later in the poem their tiny camp, which seems to exist on the map itself,

. . . had grown
To be the mountains and the map
Carefully peeled away and not torn
Was the light, a tender but tough bark
On everything.
(RM, 11)

So the landscape on the map undergoes a metamorphosis to the point of breaking through to another dimension, a dimension itself not "reality" but its "tough bark." The poem moves along this landscape of thought to various momentary promising orders and ideals that get usurped, various Romantic and Symbolist transports which turn into institutional structures—tax assessment areas, seminaries, and so on—at which point they are "not worth joining" and the ox of desire has pulled the cart away. Ashbery subverts the linear narrative he invokes; here he introduces uncontextualized characters, specific but non-mimetic scenes, seeds of plot that are never resolved. The poem is driven by an overall trope of imagination and writing as a landscape. But no thematic or spatial stability replaces the dissolving narrative.

Throughout the volume *Rivers and Mountains* the poet undercuts the tendency to the vertical, to raising our camps to the skies until we think they are as natural as mountains and believe the prospect they offer to be truth. In the poem I have just discussed the mountains turn out to be a wet dream, and the phallic analogy is not incidental. The vertical thrust of desire continually falls back into the horizontal in this flexing perpendicular. Ashbery does not simply chart a perpendicular model of thought—permanence against flux, culture against nature—but makes a dynamic, temporally driven axis in which monuments tumble, rivers seem to rise "into the dusk charged air," and lakes become the sites of skyscrapers. This early habit of casting all the features of the landscape into flux and competition for centrality and proportion, and particularly this manipulation of the perpendicular, are persistent features of the poet's work.

If knowledge is a landscape, ideas are trees (a landscape consisting of many). The logical sequence of roots, trunk, branch, leaf and the teleological process of growth are, as Deleuze and Guattari have pointed out, the model of Western thought.[2] Their alternative botanical model of the rhizome—that horizontal, subterranean, nodal stem that sends up shoots—provides an enticing image for Ashbery's poetry. But his own inclination has been to work with the landscape metaphors that already preside over our thought, and reimagine those. Hence from his first volume, *Some Trees,* the tree has been a major iconographic feature of his work. The first idea is, of course, the Tree of Knowledge, and it is under this tree that the pastoral and epistemological traditions of landscape form a partnership. The tree of knowledge promises us unity (despite its branching), rootedness, shade and protection, and, above all, ascent toward heaven. But in Ashbery's poetry the tree has dropped so many seedlings, each with its own assertive stem and precarious limbs, that we are now in a forest of symbols so vast that we cannot see it for the trees. (Though we may glimpse the treetops, we cannot escape landscape.) But the point (perhaps of all anti-pastoral poems) is the inevitability of the desire for home, for innocence, for a retreat from multiplicity. "What a pleasure to lie under the tree, to sit, stand, and get up under the tree!" he says in "Variations, Calypso and Fugue, on a Theme by Ella Wheeler Wilcox" (a poet of the Joyce Kilmer generation and faith). "But all good things must come to an end, and so one must move forward / Into the space left by one's conclusions" (DDS, 24).

If the dream of home is one side of the pastoral ideal embodied in the tree, the other is the dream of transport. "Too Happy, Happy Tree" (AG, 44–45) is a paradoxical commentary on the history of an apostrophe, how it persists and gets reinvented. The immediate source of the title and of several lines in the poem is Keats's "In drear nighted December": "Too happy, happy tree, / Thy branches ne'er remember / Their green felicity." But all of Keats's poems of transport—"Ode to a Nightingale," "Ode on a Grecian Urn," "On the Sonnet"—are evoked. From Ashbery's late vantage point it all seems as predictable as it is irresistible—what, his poem asks, will the postmodern version of transport be, "cooly meditative, /

Choosing to tour the back lot" and anyway, "how much branching out can one take?" This contemporary fatigue of transcendence, in its attenuated forms, leads to an end-of-the-line moment, marked in climatic change, glacial moraines, hurricanes, shipwrecks. The poet's seismograph registers such cataclysmic moments as if they were the hiccups. These are "fulcrums" "of inevitable voyages to be accomplished or not." The poem which began with arboreal transport now focuses on the tree-lined but horizontal ground, on our own condition as involuntary seekers in history: ". . . one lopes along the path / Thinking, forcibly," the very search for versions of transport which will tease us out of thought, an enforced condition, a kind of blindness. "And by evening we have become the eye, / Blind, because it does the seeing." We are back within the problem of the observer, the ideal having evaded us, the self "sloughed off"; "we have become the eye," but one far from transparent.

By retaining the trope of landscape, Ashbery preserves, in however qualified form, a notion of the observer and a notion of what—somewhat tongue in cheek—he calls earth or nature. I have to step lightly here; in Ashbery the plank of reason crosses a swamp. "Nature," he observes, "forces us into odd positions and then sits back to hear us squawk." He seems wryly on nature's side in this matter. The conditions of our perception and cognition (including metaphor) are self-certifying and determine the reality to which they seem to draw attention. Hence, for instance, the rose is "always miming freshness tracked by pathos." Ashbery's art criticism strangely echoes Constable in its evocation of nature as a model for the artist. But what is unlike Constable is his resistance to the dichotomy of reality and illusion. Nature is an artist working for certain effects, especially realism, of course. Nell Blaine's landscape paintings are, Ashbery says, sensuous but also astringent because "even at its most poetic, nature doesn't kid around" (RS, 238). The trouble with environmental art, he writes in a review, is its "tremendous competition from nature" (RS, 343). Of Pierre Bonnard he writes: "his paintings are unfinished, in the same way nature is. They seem about to change, just as light is always on the point of changing" (RS, xv). All of these remarks, out of context as they are, show Ashbery's insistence on nature as a referent of unsolid ground. To name knowledge after nature, even in this bracketed way of landscape, is to view it as creative, inexhaustible, based on a "ground" that is always changing, a ground that can also be explored, worked and reworked, viewed from many different vantage points and traversed on an infinite series of pathways.

Ashbery's poetry may be an alternative to the abandoned subjectivity of the lyric observer, but it is not an easy or firm alternative. He writes in

"October at the Window" (AG, 33–34) of the literary history of land-
scape reverie:

> In the dim light of the early nineteenth century
> Someone travelled there once, and observed
> Accurately, and became "the observer,"
> But with so much else to do
> This figure too got lost, charged
> In the night to say what had to be said:
>
> "My eyes are bigger than my stomach."

This is Ashbery's starting point. There is an easy wisdom such a starting
point might lead to: "One must always / Be quite conscious of the edges
of things / And then how they meet will cease / to be an issue, all other
things / Being equal, as in fact they are." But such a complacent post-
modern relativism will never satisfy the dreamer: "But do these complex
attitudes / Compete successfully with the sounds / Of bedlam," where
the dreamers of the past go on "observing" in an effort to bring the world
into the imagination? The play of frame and flux could easily thin out to
a mechanistic habit, the "observer" becoming a producer of landscapes
exchanged like slides in a slideshow. But the "dreamer" persists in imag-
ining a reality beyond the frame.

It is no accident that Ashbery has come back several times in his career
to the figure of John Clare, who ended up in Bedlam. Even as his reflec-
tions on Clare take a tone of modern superiority, there is in them a
strong empathy for "the observer" seeking to pass out of his knowledge
into a self-forgetful concentration on nature. Ashbery shows much less
patience toward the more famous Romantics with their "high-minded
notions of the self and the eventually winged purposes of the self." Clare
resisted converting the landscape to a prospect for visionary flight. Writ-
ing of his pre-enclosure home of Helpston, Clare adopts, his critics have
argued, a pre-enclosure poetics, which resists fixed perspective and static
pictorial or conceptual rendering.[3] As a profoundly post-enclosure poet,
Ashbery aims, not for Clare's innocence, but for a fluent sense of land-
scape within the open jar of timespace. Ashbery invents a landscape we
cannot stand in the middle of, that won't stay still within its frame, a
frame that keeps slipping. Time and the land are united, in a conspiracy
that sabotages all other yearnings for oneness, but opens up new dimen-
sions of the terrain.

"Haunted Landscape" (AWK, 80–81) illustrates this process well, so I
will close with a brief reading of that poem. In "Haunted Landscape"

frame and flux are most literally in tension, as the poem makes constant reference to corners and surfaces while creating a continuous movement in scene and sense that depends on evoking contexts without ever stabilizing them. Thinking here is not dwelling; the would-be settler is always just passing through. Our knowledge, as the title of the volume implies, is figurative, social, presumptuous, and temporal. A close reading of the poem is challenging because spatial references (here, ahead, behind), temporal references (then, now), and pronoun references (he, she, you) are all shifting and multiplying variables in this pseudo-journey without a subjective center or a linear path that stays in place as the scene keeps changing. Yet Ashbery achieves a serial continuity within this journey through competing ocular structures.

> Something brought them here. It was an outcropping of peace
> In the blurred afternoon slope on which so many picnickers
> Had left no trace. The hikers then always passed through
> And greeted you silently. And down in one corner
>
> Where the sweet william grew and a few other cheap plants
> The rhythm became strained, extenuated, as it petered out
> Among pots and watering cans and a trowel. There were no
> People now but everywhere signs of their recent audible passage.

In the mental landscape "the outcropping of peace" is, presumably, a pastoral respite from cognition, a promise of "presence" (thus an outcropping of what is otherwise submerged) in the "blurred afternoon slope" of vision's mountain. In short, this is Eden, the travelers are Adam and Eve, and their story is a compressed version of human history. The place is immediately haunted, though, as the complex perspective includes the past and then erases it: "so many picnickers had left no trace." There is no original Adam. The narrator's retrospective vision begins to merge with that of his subjects. By the end of the first stanza the haunted feeling has begun to transform the scene itself so that the "outcropping of peace" becomes a contrivance, a landscape designed to attract by its illusion of naturalness—a picnic ground. This is the logic in Ashbery's task of vision: the blurred slope of vision leads to a promise of transparence, which turns out to be haunted, an arrangement. The attention shifts from a central "here" which forgets the frame, to a margin "down in one corner," where the construction of the pastoral landscape becomes most apparent in the place where it dissolves, where "the rhythm became strained, extenuated, as it petered out / Among pots and watering cans and a trowel." But as the seekers approach the edge of the first landscape (as the present becomes the past), they begin constructing another on its site.

The third stanza in this sequence of four-line stanzas, then, seems less a development of the plot from the exposition than a new beginning.

> She had preferred to sidle through the cane and he
> To hoe the land in the hope that some day they would grow happy
> Contemplating the result: so much fruitfulness. A legend.
> He came now in the certainty of her braided greeting,
>
> Sunlight and shadow, and a great sense of what had been cast off
> Along the way, to arrive in this notch. Why were the insiders
> Secretly amused at their putting up handbills at night?
> By day hardly anyone came by and saw them.

The approach is now split; two perspectives (in addition to that of the narrator), two landscapes, open up. "She" (sensuous Eve) would "sidle through the cane"—move with a sideways motion, harvesting a "landscape" of existing thoughts, indulging in the pleasures with which she is presented. "He" (sententious Adam) aims at the production of new knowledge, a freshly cultivated landscape, through groundwork. His plan is a "legend," a dream of fruitfulness, and a key to knowledge. His ambitious dream includes an integration of harvesting and planting, a "braided greeting" (a marriage of intentions) achieved by "casting off" old dreams to get to the unifying truth, the "notch" in the mountain range of prospects where they can move through to view the fertile valley of ordered knowledge. This is a rather different point, of course, from the one we began in, "here" and "now" having together shifted without our noting it. And while "they" hand out handbills to announce their new insight, the insiders (the narrator's retrospective vision now enfolded into the scene) smirk because they know it too is haunted, already a cliché.

Stanzas 5 and 6 accelerate the rhythm of revision, moving, in Kubla Khan fashion, from the picturesque to the sublime, then to dwindling memory.

> They were thinking, too, that this was the right way to begin
> A farm that would later have to be uprooted to make way
> For the new plains and mountains that would follow after
> To be extinguished in turn as the ocean takes over
>
> Where the glacier leaves off and in the thundering of surf
> And rock, something, some note or other, gets lost,

And we have this to look back on, not much, but a sign
Of the petty ordering of our days as it was created and led us

By the nose through itself, and now it has happened
And we have it to look at, and have to look at it
For the good it now possesses which has shrunk from the
Outline surrounding it to a little heap or handful near the center.

This entire movement is registered within one sentence, projected onto one site, as if it were one thought, so that no perspective becomes fixed. In this metamorphic landscape Ashbery casts temporal knowledge in a geologist's spatial vision of history. We enter it expectantly as "they"— the seekers now gleefully embracing process over static purpose—project their landscapes out beyond themselves, farms yielding to plains and mountains, worn down by glaciers where the crumbling rocks meet the ocean's roar. There is certainly intensity here, suspended at the end of the stanza. This exuberant vision of process almost seems to take the place of the pastoral vision at the opening of the poem. But we come out the other side of the thought as a retrospective "we." Having reached the end of the line of the expansive sublime of process which projected broad horizons, we now look back to see the horizon "shrunk from the / Outline surrounding it to a little heap or handful near the center." This is our inevitable retrospective view of our ambitions, but it is not privileged.

Stanzas 8–10 recapitulate stanzas 5–7 in a milder, more sympathetic tone:

Others call this old age or stupidity, and we, living
In that commodity, know how only it can enchant the dear soul
Building up dreams through the night that are cast down
At the end with a graceful roar, like chimes swaying out over

The phantom village. It is our best chance of passing
Unnoticed into the dream and all that the outside said about it.
Carrying all that back to the source of so much that was precious.
At one of the later performances you asked why they called it a "miracle,"

Since nothing ever happened. That, of course, was the miracle
But you wanted to know why so much action took on so much life
And still managed to remain itself, aloof, smiling and courteous.
Is that the way life is supposed to happen? We'll probably never know

Until its cover turns into us: the eglantine for duress
And long relativity, until it becomes a touch of red under the bridge
At fixed night, and the cries of the wind are viewed as happy, salient.

The little heap or handful at the center, the very idea of a center, may look from the outside like a fetishistic commodity that will "lead us by the nose." Such an ironic perspective might well end another poet's meditation. But the ritual process of "building dreams . . . that are cast down . . . with a graceful roar" gets affirmed here, for all the sniveling or snickering of the retrospective view. The chimes swaying over the phantom village condense images from Wallace Stevens' "Mrs. Alfred Uruguay" (CPP, 225–226) in which the female pilgrim, ascending the mount of vision by the *via negativa,* passes the man of capable imagination on his way down, "poorly dressed, . . . lost in an integration of the martyr's bones" of creative sacrifice, to find "the ultimate elegance, the imagined land." Unlike "Mrs. Alfred Uruguay," "Haunted Landscape" refuses to stabilize the mountain landscape it begins with; it is more dispersed and temporal, much less dialectical. But the impulse to construct a "dream" in terms of landscape that can absorb the skepticism in "all that the outside said about it" remains Stevensian.

Having emerged from the series of landscapes into this retrospective posture, Ashbery does not end but establishes a new scene, like a Chinese box around the first. The trope of theater now makes the figures from the first part of the poem, including the insiders, characters in an endless series of performances, the journey and ascent to vision becoming a ritual gesture. In stanza 11 we seem to be even further from the dream, looking, now, at a painting, as life's cover turns into us, or we into it—a painting in which our anxieties themselves become a canvas of fixed night, our apocalyptic feelings decorative, "with a touch of red."

But Ashbery will never fix vision in this darkness, or aestheticize the void. The task of vision must continue. If the "duress and long relativity" which characterize dreaming in stanza 11 now seem fixed as in a frame with "knowledge" something like a book with a cover, the pun on "cover" makes the "eglantine of duress" also a ground cover, and we are back in landscape. The picture promptly falls off the wall, and we are returned to an uncertain dimension of living and knowing. A door is opened to let in an unidentified "man" and a new perspective, rearranging things once again and forcing our engagement through the irrational disturbance of plot.

Ashbery proves, once again, to be the Houdini of poetry who can escape any box he puts himself in, while still insisting on the necessity of the box. "Now time and the land are identical, / Linked forever." Time combined with space is the basis of this magic, as in the last stanza of the poem, in which moving and staying in place, past and future, time and the land become linked in a serial chain that even the poem will not undo.

Retrospective vision is, for Ashbery, even more tempting than prospective vision. We want to sum up, to gather history into space, to see the Ice-Storm (also I-Storm) which presses into the earth as a crystal text before it melts away. But the creative urge is by its nature more restless than imperial. The desire to end always competes, in Ashbery, with the desire to change. We may long to frame "A landscape stippled by frequent glacial interventions," historicized but finally firm. It "holds so well to its lunette one wants to keep it but we must / Go on despising it until that day when environment / Finally reads as a necessary but still vindictive opposition / To all caring, all explaining" (W, 77–78). That, of course, would not be a day for poetry.

8

Epilogue: "The Machine in the Garden"

The renovations in landscape I have been describing have often found their parallel, and even their model, in the visual arts. Frame and flux are central preoccupations of the painterly tradition in the twentieth century, as it dismantled illusionistic space. Like poets, painters wanted to capture the sense of mobility in modern life, and the multiple and shifting perspectives through which we apprehend reality. They created landscapes that foreground their creative process and the dynamic tension between world and image. The history of American landscape painting can therefore contribute summary images of the developments I have described, and can suggest concerns and directions in the continuing evolution of our relation to the natural scene.

In *The Machine in the Garden* Leo Marx describes the nineteenth century's effort to reconcile industrial progress with the pastoral ideals of the early Republic. One of his prime examples of this "middle landscape" is George Inness's "The Lackawanna Valley" (1856), which depicts the scene of the railroad's operations, amidst an otherwise rural space.

> Instead of causing disharmony, the train is a unifying device in the painting. The hills in the background and the trees of the middle distance gently envelop the industrial buildings and artifacts. No sharp lines set off the man-made from the natural terrain. Nor is the Lackawanna's smoke unpleasant. The cottony puffs that rise from the engine and the roundhouse are merely duplicates of a puff that rises from behind the church—an ingenious touch! Instead of cutting the space into sharp, rectilinear segments as railroad tracks often do, the right-of-way curves gracefully across the center of the canvas where it divides in two, forming the delicately touching ovals that dominate the

middle plane. It is noteworthy, too, that the animals in the pasture continue to graze or rest peacefully as the tidy, diminutive train approaches. Still, this is not a lament for Goldsmith's cherished lands; the stumps indicate that the pasture has just been hewn out of a wilderness. But, of course, it is the solitary figure reclining beneath the dominant vertical, the tree in the foreground, who finally establishes the quiet, relaxed mood. He holds no crook, but he contemplates the sight in the serene posture of the good shepherd looking out across Arcadia. (*The Machine in the Garden,* 221)

For Marx, then, the genre of landscape remains tied to pastoral myth, into which the machine is inserted. Inness preserves the Claudian values of the ideal landscape adapted by the antebellum Hudson River School. Illusionistic transparency—the erasure of the painter's part in the depiction—governs technique. According to Marx, the artist has tried to absorb the fact of modern mobility into an old idea of stable, tranquil agrarian life. For him this was a problematic gesture that denied the radical changes occurring in the structure of society, masking the suffering such changes were causing. Pastoral was being used to sustain an ideology that was no longer viable. But the art historian Barbara Novak has seen the picture somewhat differently (*Nature and Culture,* 171–174). For her, Inness's painting is unresolved. "Inness . . . was by instinct and

George Inness, "The Lackawanna Valley" (c. 1856). National Gallery of Art, Washington, D.C.

equipment a generation in the future." She agrees with Nicolai Cikovsky that the painting can be seen as a celebration of "the age of steam in its conquest of time and space" renouncing "the wilderness mystique." Still, she finds the stumps in the foreground disturbing, perhaps even ironic. "The picture's interpretation remains open, and it is impossible to read it 'correctly.'" To Novak, the painting offers more questions than answers about the imagination's relation to the changing landscape. Is Inness's painting a celebratory absorption of the present into the ideals of the past, a plunge into modernity, or is it an ambivalent reckoning with change? Either way, the painting puts the train near the middle of the landscape not only to establish the middle distance, but also to make it the object that defines the space. But the viewer remains separate from the train; he is a passive figure reclined under a tree on a hill, a mere witness to the transformation rather than a participant. The arrangement of space remains bound to the rules of traditional perspective, unified around a single vanishing point, and the beholder stands apart from the scene, mastering it even if his surrogate figure, under the tree, can only confront its contradictions.

The train is not a random figure of technology, of course. Marx selects it as the figure of accelerating change and mobility, the embodiment of the new timespace which technology engines. It affects not only the outer world, but even perception itself. Modern artists, Marx suggests, have focused on the ruin of an old system of beauty and meaning, exposing the "garden of ashes" (354) that technology has created. But the "new symbols of possibility" (365) he calls for were already forming, and not always away from the natural landscape. Modernity, such artists suggest, need not be a threat to nature; it can suggest a new vision of what nature is.

Arthur Dove's "Fields of Grain as Seen from Train" (1931) exemplifies the way landscape in art evolved to embody modernity's timespace. Rather than absorbing the machine into the pastoral model, Dove reimagined the natural landscape in the model of motion and change enhanced by the machine. Whereas Inness set a static, contemplative viewer, the artist's surrogate, opposite the approaching figure of the steam engine, Dove has fused them. Rejecting "nature's appearances" and the representational conventions of nineteenth-century landscape painting, in which a passive viewer remains detached from the static spectacle of nature, Dove developed an abstract expressionism which connected his subjectivity to the integrity of organic form. The artist/ viewer is on the train, which structures for him a new, dynamic connection to landscape. For Marx the machine separates man from nature, but

Arthur Dove, "Fields of Grain as Seen from Train" (1931). Albright-Knox Art
Gallery, Buffalo, New York.

this is not an inevitable fact in Dove's imagination. The sense of land-
scape as an agent of revelation of one's inner life did not preclude the
machine—in fact he painted telegraph poles, mill wheels, and giant
tanks, and used metal and wire as well as paint, integrating these ele-
ments with natural forms. Dove was no futurist ecstatic over technol-
ogy's conquest of earth. Unlike his contemporary Picabia, who celebrated
the displacement of nature by the machine, Dove retained important
connections to transcendentalism, as Cohn shows (*Arthur Dove*, 2–3).
But he is never nostalgic for an older relation to nature. "I would rather
have today than yesterday," he remarked. Dove's nature is informed not
only by modern transport, but also by modern technologies of percep-
tion and cognition—modern biology, physics, geometry, morphology,
microscopy. He captures the rhythm and speed of modern life without
relinquishing the scenic aspect of the rural landscape. In "Orange Grove
in California by Irving Berlin," for instance, nature is brought along with
the pace of contemporary life. "The music things were done," Dove said,
"to speed the line up to the pace at which we live today" (quoted in
Balken, 33). Dove's nature is a "dynamic, enigmatic mechanism" (21),
but also a site of intense connection to the life we actually live, not just
the one we dream of or long to recover.

In "Fields of Grain" mobility has become more than a pictorial subject of landscape; it is a way of seeing, and a quality of what is seen. Nature and technology are fused. The furrowed pasture is one with the track, the vanishing point of the field like a train tunnel. The shadows of the red hills suggest the smoke from the train. Nature joins in the dynamism of culture, sloughing off shape after shape, yet its ephemeral forms are drawn into a structural solidity through art. This solidity of the picture plane is not the same as the specular totality of traditional landscape's illusion. On the contrary, scope is evoked but eludes the viewer. The vanishing point runs off the canvas, turning the picture vertical rather than suggesting depth. The circular forms suggest circumscription, but they are only part of the picture, cut off from the forceful line of the furrowed field. The sense of scale is multiple, as the circles suggest at the same time windows through which the field is seen, the global world imaged in the curvilinear horizon, the image one might see through the lens of a microscope, and finally the geometric elements of compositional structure itself. The circle also suggests the portal of an ocean liner, the landscape thus becoming fluid, the mountains and fields of grain suggesting the waves that lie on the two coasts united by the train. The sexual symbolism of line and circle bring the body into the painting without painting the body. "His immersion in nature became so complete that little separation or distance was perceived between the fecundity of the landscape and the creativity of the artist" (Cohn, *Arthur Dove*, 28).

In closing with the work of Arthur Dove I might seem to be defining a modernist moment, now past—the end of the line of landscape. It is true that some recent landscape painting, like some recent landscape poetry, deals less with our immersion in nature than with our separation from it, the condition of living in the dimension of our simulations. Roy Lichtenstein's benday dot series, in which spare, iconographic landscape images are rendered in the medium of the pixel matrix, suggest that our window onto the world has become a screen. Stevens might dream of "The Poem that Took the Place of a Mountain," but Ammons' *Garbage* anguishes that we have built the ziggurat of Babel: "all these words . . . will replace our mountains with trash" (75). Yet if, as Fredric Jameson has claimed, the door back to modernism is closed forever, there may be many other landscape possibilities ahead. We might take our image for the future from Robert Smithson, whose "earthworks" were radically engaged with changing and fracturing the frame of the landscape tradition, not abandoning the tradition altogether.[1] He sought to replace the idea of landscape as "the garden of history" with his "sites of time." The artist's work, he thought, was not to create the illusion of a space beyond entropy, but rather to engage with entropic forces in creating "ruins in reverse." "A bleached and fractured world surrounds the artist. To organize this mess of corrosion into patterns, grids and subdivisions is an esthetic process that has scarcely been touched" (*Writings of Robert Smithson,* 82). We might take as our icon for the possibilities of landscape Smithson's "Spiral Jetty," which extends fifteen hundred feet into the Great Salt Lake, in which it is now, through erosion, submerged. Its spiral (existing in films, designs, maps, and texts as well as under water) draws us compellingly toward that substance which Marianne Moore tells us we cannot stand in the middle of. But we never quite arrive, and thus we spiral back again and again, into ourselves and into the shifting of our human gaze.

Notes

1. Introduction: Frame and Flux

1. See, for instance, Oelschlaeger, Cronon, Spirn, and Botkin for four very different approaches to this paradox.

2. Many critics—Raymond Williams, John Barrell, David Wyatt, Christopher Fitter, and others—have emphasized the historical context of landscape as a genre, associating it with man's modern liberation from nature, a distance that allowed for aesthetic response. Landscape came about, it is said, when Petrarch climbed a mountain for the mere pleasure of taking a view. It came more or less to an end, so the same argument goes, with modernism and the ascendancy of the city. But it has also been argued—by Jay Appleton, John Barrow, Simon Schama, and others—that man's imaginative relation to the forms of the land is primeval and evolutionary, and that the modern design we more narrowly associate with the art-historical term "landscape" draws on ancient patterns and associations.

3. Conscious of this textual relation to the land, two recent books, one on the visual arts (*The Languages of Landscape* by Mark Roskill) and the other on the physical environment (*The Language of Landscape* by Anne Whiston Spirn), play freely between the sense that our landscape designs are encoded like texts, and the sense that nature can be "read" to reveal both the organic and its social history and meaning of places. Spirn writes: "Humans are not the sole authors of landscape" (17). Language may or may not be the proper term for this "natural" meaning (Spirn is surprisingly indifferent to semiotic theory, and never addresses the objections to the term "language" which she quotes as epigraphs); nevertheless, we can see that such meaning arises in the context of human attention and becomes, within the "second nature" in which we live and perceive, textually structured.

2. Frost's Crossings

1. See Merleau-Ponty, "The Intertwining: The Chiasm," in *The Visible and the Invisible*.
2. Frost finally published "To a Moth Seen in Winter," an early composition, in his late volume *A Witness Tree* (1941). Why did he retrieve the poem? The volume as a whole is retrospective, and the poem, with its evocation of an "old incurable untimeliness," suits the "Time Out" theme of the section he placed it in. But it may be, too, that the poem contained some unfinished business. Frost's exposure of the rhetorical basis of correspondence came early. But the question that he asks, throughout, is what to make of a diminished thing.
3. Robert Faggen also notes Frost's use of chiasmus here: "The juxtaposition of pronouns and chiastic structure of the line . . . underscore the interpenetration of perception and consciousness" (75).
4. These connections have been made by many critics, but most thoroughly by Robert Faggen. Guy Rotella has also recently connected Frost to the modern physics of Heisenberg and Bohr.
5. Richard Poirier's chapter "Time and the Keeping of Poetry" in *Robert Frost: The Work of Knowing* attempts to reconcile Frost's sense of entropy and flux with his sense of poetry's retentive structures. I am adding to that early discussion by moving it beyond the thematic level, to a closer examination of the formal construction of lyric time. Poirier shows how Frost aligns himself with the sexual and regenerative forces of nature. But he fails to recognize a tension between the representation of these forces within a pastoral construction of time and an evolutionary construction of time.
6. Elder's *Reading the Mountains of Home* offers a more nuanced analysis of the poem.

3. Stevens' Eccentricity

1. See, for instance, readings of "The Gift Outright" by Myra Jehlen, Jerome McGann, and, most recently, James Fenton.
2. Frank Lentricchia in "Patriarchy Against Itself" (*Ariel and the Police*) historicizes Stevens in the tone of an exposé. Even Alan Filreis in *Wallace Stevens and the Actual World,* who presents a poet deeply engaged in the politics of World War II and the Cold War era, tends to emphasize Stevens' antihistoricism as an evasion of pressing historical matters. In a more personal arena, Mark Halliday in *Stevens and the Interpersonal* presents an ethical critique of a poet who suppresses, but inevitably feels, the force of human relations. Other recent critics have been more willing to recognize Stevens' self-conscious involvement in the life around him. James Longenbach argues in *Wallace Stevens: The Plain Sense of Things* that the poet's creativity is directly related to his engagement with the historical and social realities of his time; Margaret Dickie in *Lyric Contingencies* describes a poet aware of contingencies in the act of writing itself, a poet involved with speaker, audience, and language as he constructs the world of the poem.
3. Harold Bloom, *Wallace Stevens: The Poems of Our Climate,* p. 23. Bloom's position is continued by Joseph Carroll in *Wallace Stevens' Supreme Fiction.*

4. Rob Wilson locates Stevens' "fragrance of vegetal" in "Last Looks at the Lilacs" in a shaving lather (*Wallace Stevens Journal,* vol. 16, no. 2 [Fall 1992], p. 182). Helen Vendler has recently mentioned to me that "*pax* across the window pane" ("Puella Parvula") may refer to Memorial Church in Harvard Yard.

5. My thinking is influenced here by Stanley Cavell, *In Quest of the Ordinary: Lines of Skepticism and Romanticism.*

6. Since the 1993 publication of the original version of this chapter, Voros' *Notations of the Wild* (1997) has made a similar point about Stevens' grounding of his poems in the physical world.

7. For a full discussion of Stevens' relationship to the visual arts, see Glen G. MacLeod, *Wallace Stevens and Modern Art.*

8. For a discussion of Stevens' early transcendentalism and his evolving poetics of nature, see Guy Rotella, *Reading and Writing Nature,* pp. 95–140.

9. Margaret Dickie quotes this poem to initiate her argument about lyric contingency.

10. Louis Martz's "'From the Journal of Crispin': An Early Version of 'The Comedian as the Letter C,'" pp. 3–30, argued persuasively that Crispin's quest for a new aesthetic paralleled the quest of American visual artists (mostly, I note, landscape artists) described by his contemporary Paul Rosenfeld.

11. See Rob Wilson, *American Sublime,* pp. 169–196.

12. My reading here is informed by James Longenbach's discussion of the poem in *Wallace Stevens: The Plain Sense of Things,* pp. 303–304.

13. Theorists from Joseph Frank (throughout *The Widening Gyre*) to Fredric Jameson (154–180) and David Harvey (10–35) have agreed about this tendency of modernism to spatialize time. Modernism concerned itself with the ephemeral and fleeting only to conceive the eternal in mythic and aesthetic terms, where Romanticism had insisted on its continuity with nature. Stevens, I am arguing, articulates a tragic gap between the aspiration for spatial apotheosis, and the experience of space as a maelstrom of flux and change. His turn toward the maelstrom, his imbuing of space with the same vital, dialectical force associated with time, constitutes a heroic ethos in the poem.

14. Bergson, like William James with his "stream of consciousness," allowed for creative, intuitional identification with the unity of time as flow. See Stephen Kern, *The Culture of Time and Space: 1880–1918.* But Stevens' auroras display their plurality against the yearning to master the maze with absolute knowledge.

15. Many critics connect Stevens and Heidegger. See, for instance, Kermode, "Dwelling Poetically in Connecticut," and Bove's *Destructive Poetics.* The fullest exploration of this idea of nature as home can be found in Voros, *Notations of the Wild.*

16. See especially chapter 8.

17. Martin Price long ago, in *To the Palace of Wisdom,* discussed eighteenth-century landscape poetry as providing a "theater of the mind" where the poet might work out the drama of his desire outside of the burdened frame of human relations.

4. Moore's America

1. Elisa New begins her important book *The Line's Eye* by putting aside this Emerson essay and attending, instead, to his "Experience." But Moore, a great admirer of Emerson, did not distinguish these phases of his work. Many of the precepts that Emerson enumerates in "Nature" are central to Moore's emblematic poetry, and it is the advent of modernism and her own originality, rather than a shift in Emerson, that accounts for her differences from "Nature." Furthermore, as Sharon Cameron has pointed out, even "Experience" retains much of the old imperial Emerson; his "impersonal" is easily identified with the transcendental, empowered self. Moore's impersonal functions very differently, toward the effect of humility, not transcendence.
2. For a thoughtful reconciliation of the aesthetic of the sublime with environmental values, see Christopher Hitt's "Toward an Ecological Sublime" in *Ecocriticism,* a special issue of *New Literary History.*

5. Amy Clampitt: Nomad Exquisite

1. I have followed Clampitt's own pervasive use of the term "nomad" here. She draws her metaphor from specific human practices and applies it broadly to a view of nature and art. The term has gained prominence from the work of Gilles Deleuze, who applies it to Nietzsche's style and ideology, and develops it as a model for decentered cognition. Deleuze's concept of the rhizome as an alternative to the vertical tree as a model of cognitive structure also resonates with Clampitt, who throughout her poems finds pattern in the plants that "have no taproot." Landscape is, to use Deleuze's concept, the visual expression of a territorialized site. In these terms the poets in my study actively deterritorialize, not to disclose some truth behind prior arrangements, but to keep culture's process of arrangement and rearrangement fluent. While this theoretical and ideological use of the term "nomad" has rich implications for poetry in the postmodern era, it is not my emphasis here.

6. A. R. Ammons: Pilgrim, Sage, Ordinary Man

1. See especially Harold Bloom's "Emerson and Ammons: A Coda" and his chapter on Ammons in *The Ringers in the Tower,* pp. 257–291.
2. For an interesting critique of Emerson that relates to Ammons' revisions of him, see Sharon Cameron, "The Way of Life by Abandonment: Emerson's Impersonal," *Critical Inquiry* 25 (Autumn 1998).
3. For a full reading of *Garbage,* see my essay "What to Make of a Diminished Thing: Modern Nature and Poetic Response."
4. Cavell's *In Quest of the Ordinary* provides an interesting philosophical investigation of this Romantic sense of home.
5. Ammons' constant analogizing between natural processes and social organizations (economic, political, poetic, corporate) anticipates recent work by Félix Guattari in "The Three Ecologies." The ecocritical readings of Ammons are at

once too literal and too open-ended. The word "ecology" does enter the poet's work early on, and his imagery often consists of organisms in relation to their environment. Hence Donald Reiman has noted Ammons' "ecological natural-ism," and Frederick Buell has praised his "ecocentric decentering of the self." He promotes a sustainable environment through a "homological" rather than an "analogical" connection to the physical world, according to Leonard Scigaj, who ignores the constant references to analogical structure in Ammons' poetry. The poet of motion, of "tentative, provisional attitudes" (SM, 5), cannot be pigeon-holed into an environmentalist platform.

6. This is Stanley Cavell's variation on the Cartesian axiom, as he applies it to Ro-manticism in *In Quest of the Ordinary.*

7. Justus Lawler has argued in *Celestial Pantomime* that this movement from one to many to an enlarged oneness is the pattern of all lyric and the meaning of its form, despite whatever discursive subject matter a work may entertain. Harold Bloom makes a similar argument in *The Breaking of the Vessels,* where he ex-plains the logic of visionary poetry as following three dictums: it must not be broken, it will be broken, it must seem not to have been broken.

8. See Helen Vendler's "Dwelling in the Flow of Shapes" in *Critical Essays on A. R. Ammons* and Miriam Clark's "Dwelling on 'the Ridge Farm': Action, Motion, and A. R. Ammons' Moral Landscape" in *Complexities of Motion.*

9. Robert Harrison provides a thoughtful reading of this poem in his book *Forests,* in which he connects Ammons' lines to Stanley Cavell's reading of Thoreau's *Walden,* and inevitably also to Heidegger's idea of "dwelling." In exploring the connection of logos to nature, a connection of longing, Ammons recognizes that oneness with nature is not the condition of human dwelling. Later the poet would prefer a vocabulary from cognitive science or evolutionary linguistics. We are, as Terrance Deacon has suggested, a "symbolic species," and for humans, Ammons suggests, "home is where the doodle is."

10. Ammons announced the arrival of the future when he drew on the vocabulary of science to widen the sphere of the lyric subject. He celebrates this expansion in the introduction to his special issue of *Poetry.* He quotes Wordsworth's "Pref-ace to *Lyrical Ballads,* 1802": "If the time should ever come when what is now called Science, thus familiarized to men, shall be ready to put on, as it were, a form of flesh and blood, the Poet will lend his divine spirit to aid the transfigu-ration, and will welcome the Being thus produced, as a dear and genuine inmate of the household of men" (quoted in SM, 11).

11. "*Sphere* finally was the place where I was able to deal with the problem of the One and the Many to my satisfaction. It was a time when we were first beginning to see an image of the earth from outer space on the television screen, at a time when it was inevitable to think about that as the central image of our lives—that sphere. With *Sphere* I had particularized and unified what I knew about things as well as I could." SM, 65.

12. My representation of Thoreau is indebted especially to Laura Dassow Walls' *Thoreau on Science: A Material Faith.*

7. John Ashbery: Landscapeople

1. Ashbery explained to Sue Gangel in 1977: "I don't know what my life is, what I want to be escaping *from*. I want to move to some other *space*, I guess, when I write, which perhaps was where I had been but without being fully conscious of it." Joe David Bellamy, ed., *American Poetry Observed: Poets on Their Work.*
2. Gilles Deleuze and Félix Guattari, *A Thousand Plateaus: Capitalism and Schizophrenia.*
3. See John Barrell, *The Idea of Landscape and the Sense of Place.*

8. Epilogue: "The Machine in the Garden"

1. My remarks on Robert Smithson are indebted to Gary Shapiro's *Earthwards: Robert Smithson and Art After Babel.*

Works Cited

Alpers, Paul. *What Is Pastoral?* Chicago: University of Chicago Press, 1996.

Ammons, A. R. *Brink Road.* New York: Norton, 1996.

———— *A Coast of Trees.* New York: Norton, 1981.

———— *Collected Poems, 1951–1971.* New York: Norton, 1972.

———— *Garbage.* New York: Norton, 1993.

———— *Glare.* New York: Norton, 1996.

———— *The Selected Poems: Expanded Edition.* New York: Norton, 1986.

———— *Set in Motion: Essays, Interviews, and Dialogues,* ed. Zofia Burr. Ann Arbor: University of Michigan Press, 1996.

———— *The Snow Poems.* New York: Norton, 1977.

———— *Sphere: The Form of a Motion.* New York: Norton, 1974.

———— *Sumerian Vistas: Poems.* New York: Norton, 1987.

———— *Tape for the Turn of the Year.* New York: Norton, 1993.

Ashbery, John. *April Galleons: Poems.* New York: Viking, 1987.

———— *As We Know: Poems.* New York: Viking, 1979.

———— *The Double Dream of Spring.* New York: Dutton, 1970.

———— *Flow Chart.* New York: Knopf, 1991.

———— *Hotel Lautréamont.* New York: Knopf (distributed by Random House), 1992.

———— *Houseboat Days: Poems.* New York: Viking, 1977.

———— *Reported Sightings: Art Chronicles, 1957–1987,* ed. David Bergman. New York: Knopf, 1989.

———— *Rivers and Mountains.* New York: Holt, Rinehart and Winston, 1966.

———— *Some Trees* (1956). New York: Corinth Books, 1970.

———— *A Wave: Poems.* New York: Viking, 1984.

Auden, W. H. *Selected Poems,* ed. Edward Mendelson. New York: Vintage Books, 1979.

Bagby, George F. *Frost and the Book of Nature.* Knoxville: University of Tennessee Press, 1993.

Bahti, Timothy. *Ends of the Lyric: Direction and Consequence in Western Poetry.* Baltimore: Johns Hopkins University Press, 1996.

Balken, Debra Bricker. "Continuities and Digression in the Work of Arthur Dove from 1907 to 1933." *Arthur Dove: A Retrospective.* Andover, Mass.: Addison Gallery of American Art; Cambridge, Mass.: MIT Press, 1997.

Barrell, John. *The Idea of Landscape and the Sense of Place, 1730–1840: An Approach to John Clare.* Cambridge: Cambridge University Press, 1972.

Barrow, John D. *The Artful Universe.* Oxford: Clarendon, 1995.

Bate, Jonathan. "Culture and Environment: From Austen to Hardy." *New Literary History: Ecocriticism* 30.3 (1999): 541–560.

——— *Romantic Ecology: Wordsworth and the Environmental Tradition.* New York: Routledge, 1991.

Baudrillard, Jean. *Simulacra and Simulations,* trans. Sheila Faria Glaser. Ann Arbor: University of Michigan Press, 1994.

Bellamy, Joe David. *American Poetry Observed: Poets on Their Work.* Urbana: University of Illinois Press, 1984.

Beowulf, trans. Seamus Heaney. New York: Farrar, Straus and Giroux, 2000.

Berger, John. *Selected Essays and Articles: The Look of Things,* ed. Nikos Strangos. New York: Viking, 1974.

Bergson, Henri. *Introduction to Metaphysics,* trans. T. F. Hulme. New York and London: G. P. Putnam's Sons, 1912.

Berry, Wendell. *Collected Poems.* San Francisco: North Point, 1984.

Bishop, Elizabeth. *The Complete Poems, 1927–1979.* New York: Farrar, Straus and Giroux, 1979.

Bloom, Harold. *The Breaking of the Vessels.* Chicago: University of Chicago Press, 1982.

——— *The Figures of Capable Imagination.* New York: Seabury, 1976.

——— *The Ringers in the Tower: Studies in the Romantic Tradition.* Chicago: University of Chicago Press, 1971.

——— *Wallace Stevens: The Poems of Our Climate.* Ithaca: Cornell University Press, 1976.

Bly, Robert. *Silence in the Snowy Fields.* Middletown, Conn.: Wesleyan University Press, 1962.

——— *Selected Poems.* New York: Harper, 1986.

Bogan, Louise. *Achievement in American Poetry.* Chicago: H. Regeny, 1951.

Boorstin, Daniel. *The Image; or, What Happened to the American Dream.* New York: Atheneum, 1962.

Botkin, Daniel. *Our Natural History: The Lessons of Lewis and Clark.* Baltimore: Johns Hopkins University Press, 1992.

Bove, Paul A. *Destructive Poetics: Heidegger and Modern American Poetry.* New York: Columbia University Press, 1980.

Brower, Reuben. *The Poetry of Robert Frost: Constellations of Intention.* New York: Oxford University Press, 1963.

Bryant, William Cullen. *The Poetical Works of William Cullen Bryant,* ed. Parke Godwin, vol. 1. New York: Russell and Russell, 1883.

Buell, Frederick. "Ammons' Peripheral Vision: *Tape for the Turn of the Year* and *Garbage.*" *Complexities of Motion: New Essays on A. R. Ammons's Long Poems,* ed. Steven P. Schneider. Madison: Fairleigh Dickinson University Press, 1999.

Buell, Lawrence. *The Environmental Imagination: Thoreau, Nature Writing, and the Formation of American Culture.* Cambridge, Mass.: Harvard University Press, 1995.

Cameron, Sharon. *Lyric Time: Dickinson and the Limits of Genre.* Baltimore: Johns Hopkins University Press, 1979.

——— "The Way of Life by Abandonment: Emerson's Impersonal." *Critical Inquiry* 25.1 (1998): 1–31.

——— *Writing Nature: Henry Thoreau's Journal.* New York: Oxford University Press, 1985.

Carroll, Joseph. *Wallace Stevens' Supreme Fiction: A New Romanticism.* Baton Rouge: Louisiana State University Press, 1987.

Cavell, Stanley. *In Quest of the Ordinary: Lines of Skepticism and Romanticism.* Chicago: University of Chicago Press, 1988.

——— *The Senses of Walden.* New York: Viking, 1972.

——— *This New Yet Unapproachable America: Lectures after Emerson after Wittgenstein.* Albuquerque: Living Batch Press, 1989.

Clampitt, Amy. *The Collected Poems of Amy Clampitt.* New York: Knopf, 1997.

——— *Predecessors, Et Cetera: Essays.* Ann Arbor: University of Michigan Press, 1991.

Clark, Miriam. "Dwelling on 'The Ridge Farm': Action, Motion and A. R. Ammons's Moral Landscape." *Complexities of Motion: New Essays on A.R. Ammons's Long Poems,* ed. Steven P. Schneider. Madison: Fairleigh Dickinson University Press, 1999.

Cohn, Sherrye. *Arthur Dove: Nature as Symbol.* Ann Arbor: University of Michigan Research Press, 1985.

Coleridge, Samuel Taylor. *The Complete Poetical Works of Samuel Taylor Coleridge,* ed. Ernest Hartley Coleridge (1912). Oxford: Clarendon Press, 1962.

Cooper, J. Fenimore. *The Last of the Mohicans.* New York: Random House, 2001.

Costello, Bonnie. "The Soil and Man's Intelligence: Three Contemporary Landscape Poets." *Contemporary Literature* 30.3 (1989): 412–433.

——— "What to Make of a Diminished Thing: Modern Nature and Poetic Response." *American Literary History* 10.4 (1998): 569–605.

Crary, Jonathan. *Techniques of the Observer.* Cambridge, Mass.: MIT Press, 1990.

Cronon, William. *Nature's Metropolis: Chicago and the Great West.* New York: Norton, 1991.

——— "The Trouble with Wilderness." *Uncommon Ground: Toward Reinventing Nature,* ed. William Cronon. New York: Norton, 1995.

Culler, Jonathan. *The Pursuit of Signs: Semiotics, Literature, Deconstruction.* Ithaca: Cornell University Press, 1981.

Deacon, Terrence. *The Symbolic Species: The Co-Evolution of Language and the Brain.* New York: Norton, 1997.

Deleuze, Gilles, and Guattari, Félix. *Anti-Oedipus: Capitalism and Schizophrenia,* trans. Robert Hudey et al. New York: Viking, 1977.

——— *A Thousand Plateaus: Capitalism and Schizophrenia,* trans. Brian Massumi. Minneapolis: University of Minnesota Press, 1987.

De Man, Paul. *Allegories of Reading: Figural Language in Rousseau, Nietzsche, Rilke, and Proust.* New Haven: Yale University Press, 1979.

Dickie, Margaret. *Lyric Contingencies: Emily Dickinson and Wallace Stevens.* Philadelphia: University of Pennsylvania Press, 1991.

Elder, John. *Imagining the Earth: Poetry and the Vision of Nature.* Urbana: University of Illinois Press, 1985.

——— "Nature's Refrain in American Poetry." *The Columbia History of American Poetry,* ed. Jay Parini. New York: Columbia University Press, 1993.

——— *Reading the Mountains of Home.* Cambridge, Mass.: Harvard University Press, 1998.

Eliot, T. S. *Collected Poems, 1909–1962.* New York: Harcourt Brace Jovanovich, 1963.

Emerson, Ralph Waldo. *Collected Poems and Translations,* ed. Harold Bloom and Paul Kane. New York: Library of America, 1994.

——— "The Poet." *Essays: Second Series.* Boston: Houghton Mifflin, 1903.

——— *Nature, Addresses, and Lectures.* Boston: Houghton Mifflin, 1903; New York: AMS, 1968.

Empson, William. *Some Versions of Pastoral.* London: Chatto and Windus, 1935.

——— *The Structure of Complex Words.* Ann Arbor: University of Michigan Press, 1967.

Evernden, Neil. *The Social Creation of Nature.* Baltimore: Johns Hopkins University Press, 1992.

Faggen, Robert. *Robert Frost and the Challenge of Darwin.* Ann Arbor: University of Michigan Press, 1997.

Filreis, Alan. *Wallace Stevens and the Actual World.* Princeton: Princeton University Press, 1991.

Fitter, Chris. *Poetry, Space, Landscape: Toward a New Theory.* New York: Cambridge University Press, 1995.

Frank, Joseph. *The Widening Gyre: Crisis and Mastery in Modern Literature.* Bloomington: Indiana University Press, 1968.

Friedman, Martin. "As Far as the Eye Can See." *Visions of America: Landscape as Metaphor in the Late Twentieth Century,* ed. Martin Friedman. Denver: Denver Art Museum, 1994.

Frost, Robert. *Robert Frost: Collected Poems, Prose, & Plays.* New York: Library of America, 1995.

——— *Selected Letters,* ed. Lawrance Thompson. New York: Holt, Rinehart, and Winston, 1964.

Gilbert, Roger. *Walks in the World: Representation and Experience in Modern American Poetry.* Princeton: Princeton University Press, 1991.

Glotfelty, Cheryll, and Fromm, Harold, eds. *The Ecocriticism Reader: Landmarks in Literary Ecology.* Athens: University Press of Georgia, 1996.

Graham, Jorie. *The Dream of the Unified Field: Selected Poems, 1974–1994.* Hopewell, N.J.: Ecco Press, 1995.

Guattari, Félix. "The Three Ecologies," trans. Chris Turner. *New Formations* 8 (1989).

Halliday, Mark. *Stevens and the Interpersonal.* Princeton: Princeton University Press, 1991.

Hardy, Thomas. *Selected Poems,* ed. Andrew Motion. London: Everyman, 1994.

Harrison, Robert. *Forests: The Shadow of Civilization.* Chicago: University of Chicago Press, 1992.

Harvey, David. *The Condition of Postmodernity: An Inquiry into the Origins of Cultural Change.* New York: Blackwell, 1989.

Heidegger, Martin. "Building, Dwelling, Thinking." *Basic Writings,* ed. David Krell. New York: Harper & Row, 1977.

Hitt, Christopher. "Toward an Ecological Sublime." *New Literary History* 30.3 (1999): 603–623.

Jameson, Fredric. *Postmodernism; or, the Cultural Logic of Late Capitalism.* Durham: Duke University Press, 1991.

Jarrell, Randall. *Poetry and the Age.* New York: Knopf, 1953.

Jay, Martin. *Downcast Eyes: The Denigration of Vision in Twentieth-Century French Thought.* Berkeley: University of California Press, 1993.

Jehlen, Myra. *American Incarnation: The Individual, the Nation, and the Continent.* Cambridge, Mass.: Harvard University Press, 1986.

Kermode, Frank. "Dwelling Poetically in Connecticut." *Wallace Stevens: A Celebration,* ed. Frank Doggett and Robert Buttel. Princeton: Princeton University Press, 1980.

Kern, Stephen. *The Culture of Time and Space: 1880–1918.* Cambridge, Mass.: Harvard University Press, 1983.

Kirschten, Robert. *Critical Essays on A. R. Ammons.* New York: G. K. Hall, 1997.

Kolodny, Annette. *The Land Before Her: Fantasy and Experience of the American Frontiers, 1630–1860.* Chapel Hill: University of North Carolina Press, 1984.

———— *The Lay of the Land.* Chapel Hill: University of North Carolina Press, 1975.

Lakoff, George. *Metaphors We Live By.* Chicago: University of Chicago Press, 1980.

Lawler, Justus. *Celestial Pantomime.* New Haven: Yale University Press, 1974.

Lentricchia, Frank. *Ariel and the Police: Michel Foucault, William James, Wallace Stevens.* Madison: University of Wisconsin Press, 1988.

Liu, Alan. *Wordsworth, the Sense of History.* Stanford: Stanford University Press, 1989.

Longenbach, James. *Wallace Stevens: The Plain Sense of Things.* New York: Oxford University Press, 1991.

Lyotard, Jean François. *The Post-modern Condition: A Report on Knowledge,* trans. Geoff Bennington and Brian Massumi. Minneapolis: University of Minnesota Press, 1984.

MacLeod, Glen. *Wallace Stevens and Modern Art: From the Armory Show to Abstract Expressionism.* New Haven: Yale University Press, 1993.

Martz, Louis. " 'From the Journal of Crispin': An Early Version of 'The Comedian as the Letter C.' " *Wallace Stevens: A Celebration,* ed. Frank Doggett and Robert Buttel. Princeton: Princeton University Press, 1980.

Marx, Karl, and Engels, Friedrich. *The Communist Manifesto.* New York: Russell and Russell, 1963.

Marx, Leo. The *Machine in the Garden: Technology and the Pastoral Ideal in America.* New York: Oxford University Press, 1964.

McGann, Jerome. *Black Riders: The Visible Language of Modernism.* Princeton: Princeton University Press, 1993.

Mencken, H. L. *The American Language; an Inquiry into the Development of English in the United States.* New York: Knopf, 1923.

Merleau-Ponty, Maurice. *The Visible and the Invisible,* trans. Alphonso Lingis, ed. Claude Lefort. Evanston, Ill.: Northwestern University Press, 1968.

Miller, Angela. *The Empire of the Eye: Landscape Representation and American Cultural Politics, 1825–1875.* Ithaca: Cornell University Press, 1993.

Miller, Cristanne. *Marianne Moore: Questions of Authority.* Cambridge, Mass.: Harvard University Press, 1995.

Miller, David, ed. *American Iconology: New Approaches to Nineteenth-Century Art and Literature.* New Haven: Yale University Press, 1993.

Mitchell, W. J. T., ed. *Landscape and Power.* Chicago: University of Chicago Press, 1994.

Moore, Marianne. *The Complete Poems of Marianne Moore.* New York: Macmillan, 1967.

——— *The Complete Prose of Marianne Moore,* ed. Patricia C. Willis. New York: Viking, 1986.

Murphy, Patrick D. *Farther Afield in the Study of Nature-Oriented Literature.* Charlottesville: University Press of Virginia, 2000.

New, Elisa. *The Line's Eye: Poetic Experience, American Sight.* Cambridge, Mass.: Harvard University Press, 1998.

Nietzsche, Friedrich. *The Birth of Tragedy, and The Case of Wagner,* trans. Walter Kaufmann. New York: Vintage Books, 1967.

Novak, Barbara. *Nature and Culture: American Landscape and Painting, 1825–1875.* New York: Oxford University Press, 1980.

Oelschlaeger, Max. *The Idea of Wilderness: From Prehistory to the Age of Ecology.* New Haven: Yale University Press, 1991.

Panofsky, Erwin. *Perspective as Symbolic Form* (1927). New York: Zone Books, 1991.

Patke, Rajeev S. *The Long Poems of Wallace Stevens: An Interpretive Study.* Cambridge and New York: Cambridge University Press, 1985.

Peck, H. Daniel. *Thoreau's Morning Work: Memory and Perception in A Week on the Concord and Merrimack Rivers, the Journal, and Walden.* New Haven: Yale University Press, 1990.

Perloff, Marjorie. *Poetic License: Essays on Modernist and Post-modern Lyric.* Evanston: Northwestern University Press, 1990.

Poirier, Richard. *Poetry and Pragmatism.* Cambridge, Mass.: Harvard University Press, 1992.

——— *Robert Frost: The Work of Knowing.* New York: Oxford University Press, 1977.

Porter, Carolyn. *Seeing and Being: The Plight of the Participant-Observer in Emerson, James, Adams, Faulkner.* Middletown, Conn.: Wesleyan University Press; Irvington, N.Y.: distributed by Columbia University Press, 1981.

Postrel, Virginia. *The Future and Its Enemies: The Growing Conflict over Creativity, Enterprise, and Progress.* New York: Free Press, 1998.

Price, Martin. *To the Palace of Wisdom: Studies in Order and Energy from Dryden to Blake.* Carbondale: Southern Illinois University Press, 1970.

Reiman, Donald. "A. R. Ammons: Ecological Naturalism and the Romantic Tradition." *Critical Essays on A. R. Ammons,* ed. Robert Kirschten. New York: G. K. Hall, 1997.

Roskill, Mark. *The Languages of Landscape.* University Park: Pennsylvania State University Press, 1997.

Ross, Andrew. *The Failure of Modernism: Symptoms of American Poetry.* New York: Columbia University Press, 1986.

Rotella, Guy. *Reading and Writing Nature: The Poetry of Robert Frost, Wallace Stevens, Marianne Moore, and Elizabeth Bishop.* Boston: Northeastern University Press, 1991.

Salmond, Anne. "Theoretical Landscapes: On Cross-Cultural Conception of Knowledge." *Semantic Anthropology,* ed. David Parkin. London: Academic Press, 1982.

Schama, Simon, *Landscape and Memory.* New York: Knopf, 1995.

Scheese, Don. *Nature Writing: The Pastoral Impulse in America.* New York: Twayne, 1996.

Schneider, Steven P., ed. *Complexities of Motion: New Essays on A. R. Ammons' Long Poems.* Madison: Fairleigh Dickinson University Press, 1999.

Scigaj, Leonard M. *Sustainable Poetry: Four American Ecopoets.* Louisville: University of Kentucky Press, 1999.

Shakespeare, William. *Hamlet.* New York: Signet, 1987.

Shapiro, Gary. *Earthwards: Robert Smithson and Art after Babel.* Berkeley: University of California Press, 1995.

Slatin, John. *The Savage's Romance.* Philadelphia: University of Pennsylvania Press, 1986.

Slotkin, Richard. *The Fatal Environment: The Myth of the Frontier in the Age of Industrialization.* New York: Atheneum, 1985.

Smith, Henry Nash. *Virgin Land: The American West as Symbol and Myth.* New York: Vintage Books, 1950.

Smithson, Robert. *The Writings of Robert Smithson: Essays with Illustrations,* ed. Nancy Holt. New York: New York University Press, 1979.

Snyder, Gary. *No Nature: New and Selected Poems.* New York: Pantheon, 1992.

—— *The Practice of the Wild: Essays.* San Francisco: North Point Press, 1990.

—— *The Real Work: Interviews and Talks: 1964–1979.* New York: New Directions, 1980.

—— *Regarding Wave.* New York: New Directions, 1970.

—— *Turtle Island.* New York: New Directions, 1974.

Spirn, Anne Whiston. *The Language of Landscape.* New Haven: Yale University Press, 2000.

Stein, Gertrude. *The Geographical History of America.* New York: Random House, 1936.

Steinman, Lisa. *Made in America: Science, Technology, and American Modernist Poets.* New Haven: Yale University Press, 1987.

Stevens, Wallace. *Collected Poetry & Prose.* New York: Library of America, 1997.

—— *Letters.* Selected and edited by Holly Stevens. New York: Knopf, 1966.

Stewart, Susan. *On Longing: Narratives of the Miniature, the Gigantic, the Souvenir, the Collection.* Baltimore: Johns Hopkins University Press, 1984.

Stoppard, Tom. *Arcadia.* London: Faber and Faber, 1993.

Varela, et. al. *The Embodied Mind: Cognitive Science and Human Experience.* Cambridge: MIT Press, 1991.

Vendler, Helen Hennessy. *On Extended Wings.* Cambridge, Mass.: Harvard University Press, 1969.

—— "A. R. Ammons: Dwelling in the Flow of Shapes." *Critical Essays on A. R. Ammons,* ed. Robert Kirschten. New York: G. K. Hall, 1997.

Voros, Gyorgyi. *Notations of the Wild: Ecology in the Poetry of Wallace Stevens.* Iowa City: Iowa University Press, 1997.

Walls, Laura Dassow. *Thoreau on Science: A Material Faith.* Boston: Houghton Mifflin, 1999.

Whitman, Walt. *Leaves of Grass,* ed. Jerome Loving. Oxford and New York: Oxford University Press, 1990.

Williams, Raymond. *The Country and the City.* New York: Oxford University Press, 1975.

Williams, William Carlos. *Imaginations,* ed. Webster Schott. New York: New Directions, 1970.

———— *Selected Essays.* New York: Random House, 1954.

Wilson, Rob. *American Sublime: The Genealogy of a Poetic Genre.* Madison: University of Wisconsin Press, 1991.

Worcester, David. *The Wealth of Nature.* New York: Oxford University Press, 1993.

Wordsworth, William. *The Poetical Works of William Wordsworth,* ed. Paul D. Sheats. Boston: Houghton Mifflin, 1982.

Wright, Charles. *Quarter Notes: Improvisations and Interviews.* Ann Arbor: University of Michigan Press, 1995.

———— *The World of the Ten Thousand Things: Poems 1980–1990.* New York: Noonday Press, 1990.

Wyatt, David. *The Fall into Eden: Landscape and Imagination in California.* Cambridge and New York: Cambridge University Press, 1991.

Yeats, William Butler. *The Collected Poems of W. B. Yeats,* ed. Richard J. Finneran. New York: Collier, 1989.

Acknowledgments

"Vacant Lot with Pokeweed" by Amy Clampitt, from *The Collected Poems of Amy Clampitt,* copyright © 1997 by the Estate of Amy Clampitt, is reprinted by permission of Alfred A. Knopf, a division of Random House, Inc. "Fascicle" and "The Sense of Now," from *Brink Road* by A. R. Ammons, copyright © 1996 by A. R. Ammons, are reprinted by permission of W. W. Norton & Company, Inc.

The Lackawanna Valley by George Inness (c. 1856; oil on canvas, 33⅞ × 50³⁄₁₆ inches; gift of Mrs. Huttleston Rogers; photograph © 2002 Board of Trustees, National Gallery of Art) is reproduced courtesy of the National Gallery of Art, Washington, D.C. *Fields of Grain as Seen from Train* by Arthur G. Dove (1931; oil on canvas, 24 × 34⅛ inches; gift of Seymour H. Knox, Jr., 1958) is reproduced courtesy of the Albright-Knox Art Gallery, Buffalo, New York.

A version of the first section of Chapter 3 was published as "Wallace Stevens: The Adequacy of Landscape" in *The Wallace Stevens Journal,* 17, no. 1 (Fall 1993). A version of Chapter 6 was published in *Raritan,* XXI:3 (Winter 2002). An earlier version of Chapter 7 was published in *The Tribe of John: Ashbery and Contemporary Poetry,* ed. Susan M. Schultz (Tuscaloosa: University of Alabama Press, 1995).

I would like to thank my student assistants, Reena Sastri and Nichole Gleisner, for help with the book.

Index